STAR WARS®
DARK TIMES

VOLUME SEVEN

A SPARK REMAINS

THE RISE OF THE EMPIRE

From 1,000 to 0 years before the events in Star Wars: *Episode IV*—A New Hope

After the seeming final defeat of the Sith, the Republic enters a state of complacency.
In the waning years of the Republic, the Senate rife with corruption, the ambitious
Senator Palpatine causes himself to be elected Supreme Chancellor.
This is the era of the prequel trilogy.

The events in this story take place a few months after the
events in *Star Wars:* Episode III—*Revenge of the Sith.*

STAR WARS®
DARK TIMES

VOLUME SEVEN

A SPARK REMAINS

Script
RANDY STRADLEY

Art
DOUGLAS WHEATLEY

Colors
DAN JACKSON

Letters
MICHAEL HEISLER

Cover Art
BENJAMIN CARRÉ

DARK HORSE BOOKS

LUCAS BOOKS

President and Publisher
MIKE RICHARDSON

Collection Designer
JIMMY PRESLER

Editor
DAVE MARSHALL

Assistant Editor
FREDDYE LINS

Neil Hankerson **Executive Vice President** • Tom Weddle **Chief Financial Officer** • Randy Stradley **Vice President of Publishing** • Michael Martens **Vice President of Book Trade Sales** • Scott Allie **Editor in Chief** • Matt Parkinson **Vice President of Marketing** • David Scroggy **Vice President of Product Development** • Dale LaFountain **Vice President of Information Technology** • Darlene Vogel **Senior Director of Print, Design, and Production** • Ken Lizzi **General Counsel** • Davey Estrada **Editorial Director** • Chris Warner **Senior Books Editor** • Diana Schutz **Executive Editor** • Cary Grazzini **Director of Print and Development** • Lia Ribacchi **Art Director** • Cara Niece **Director of Scheduling** • Tim Wiesch **Director of International Licensing** • Mark Bernardi **Director of Digital Publishing**

Special thanks to Jennifer Heddle, Leland Chee, Troy Alders, Carol Roeder, Jann Moorhead, and David Anderman at Lucas Licensing.

STAR WARS: DARK TIMES Volume Seven—A Spark Remains

This volume collects issues one through five of the Dark Horse comic-book series
Star Wars: Dark Times—A Spark Remains.

Published by Dark Horse Books, a division of Dark Horse Comics, Inc.
10956 SE Main Street, Milwaukie, OR 97222

DarkHorse.com | StarWars.com

International Licensing: 503-905-2377
To find a comics shop in your area, call the Comic Shop Locator Service
toll-free at 1-888-266-4226

First printing: April 2014
ISBN 978-1-61655-262-6

1 3 5 7 9 10 8 6 4 2
Printed in China

AFTER NARROWLY ESCAPING CAPTURE by bounty hunter Falco Sang *and* Darth Vader, Jedi Master Dass Jennir has become of great interest to the Dark Lord. Vader holds Sang in captivity, training him to serve the Empire, while the hunt for Jennir and other Jedi continues.

Jennir has finally been reunited with the crew of the *Uhumele*—and much has changed in all their lives since their last encounter.

The crew has tragically lost several members at the hand of the Empire, and they have gained one member, another Jedi, Beyghor Sahdett. Jennir, on the other hand, has found love, with Ember Chankeli, and a renewed reason to live . . .

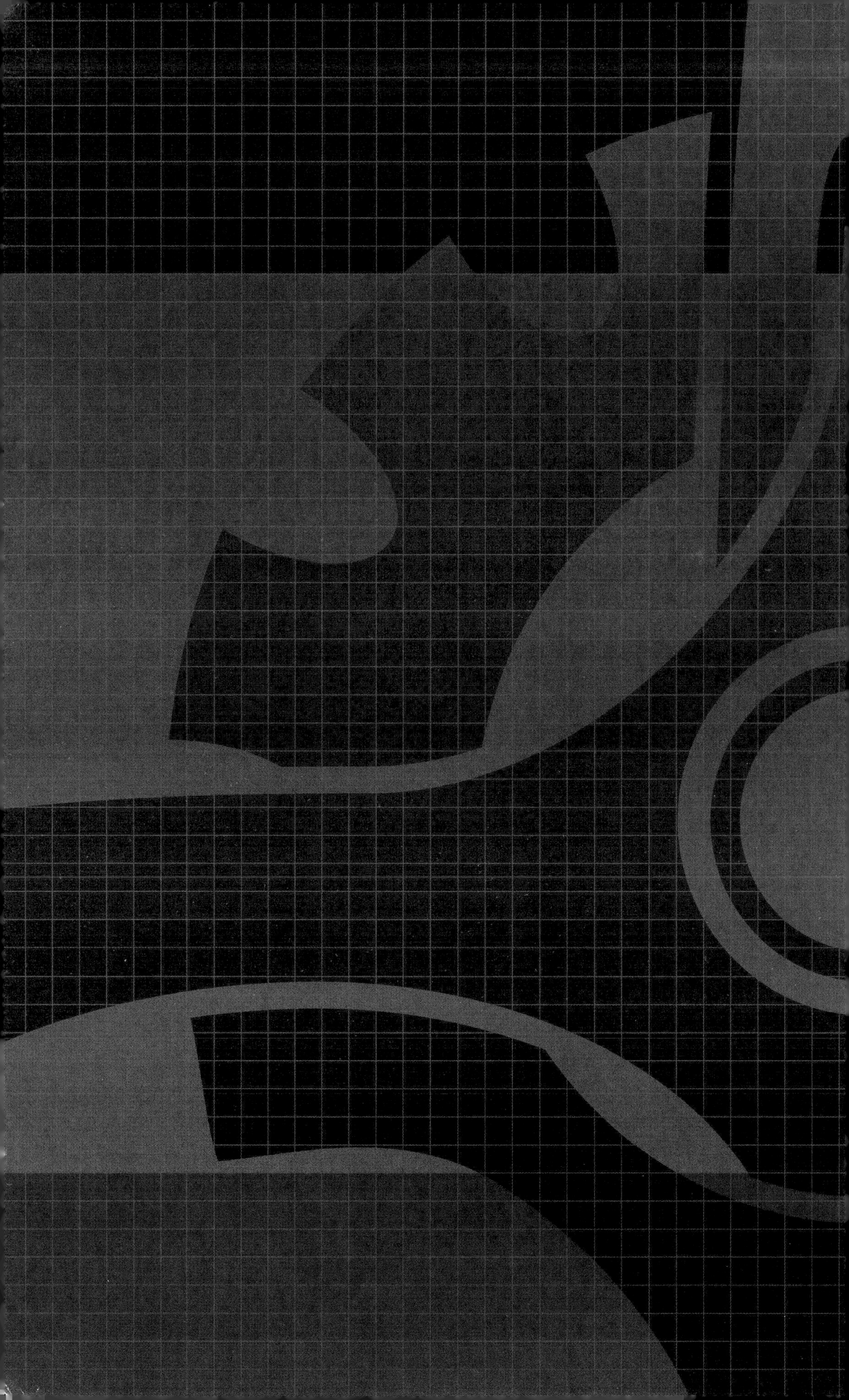

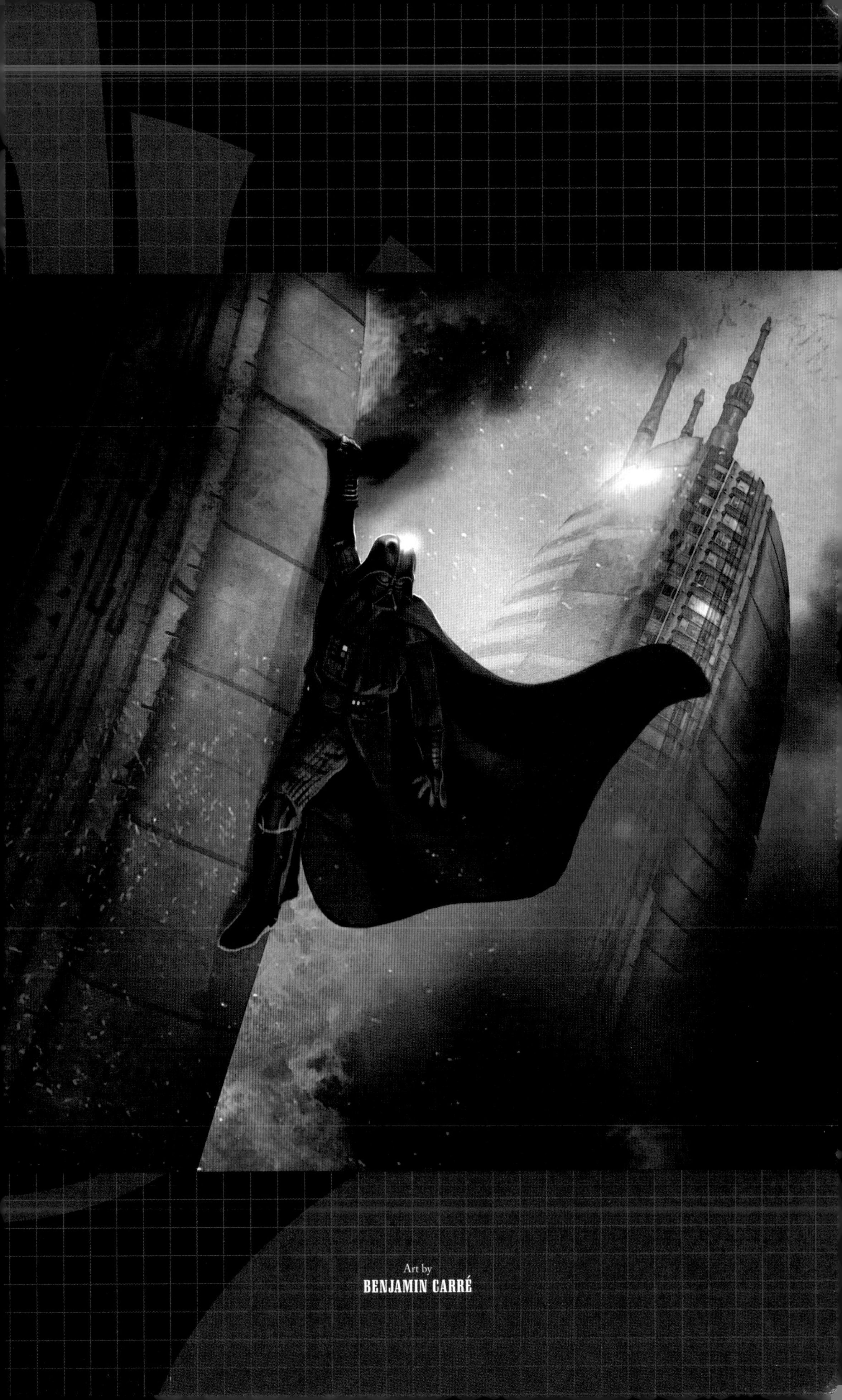

Art by
BENJAMIN CARRÉ

KESTAVEL -- NEAR BORLEIAS, IN THE COLONIES REGION.

THEY'RE APPROACHING THE SECOND ARCH!

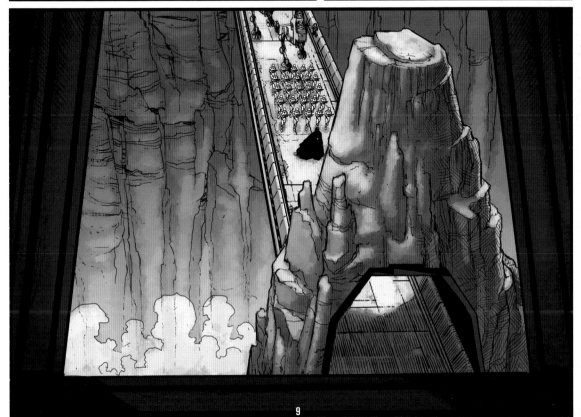

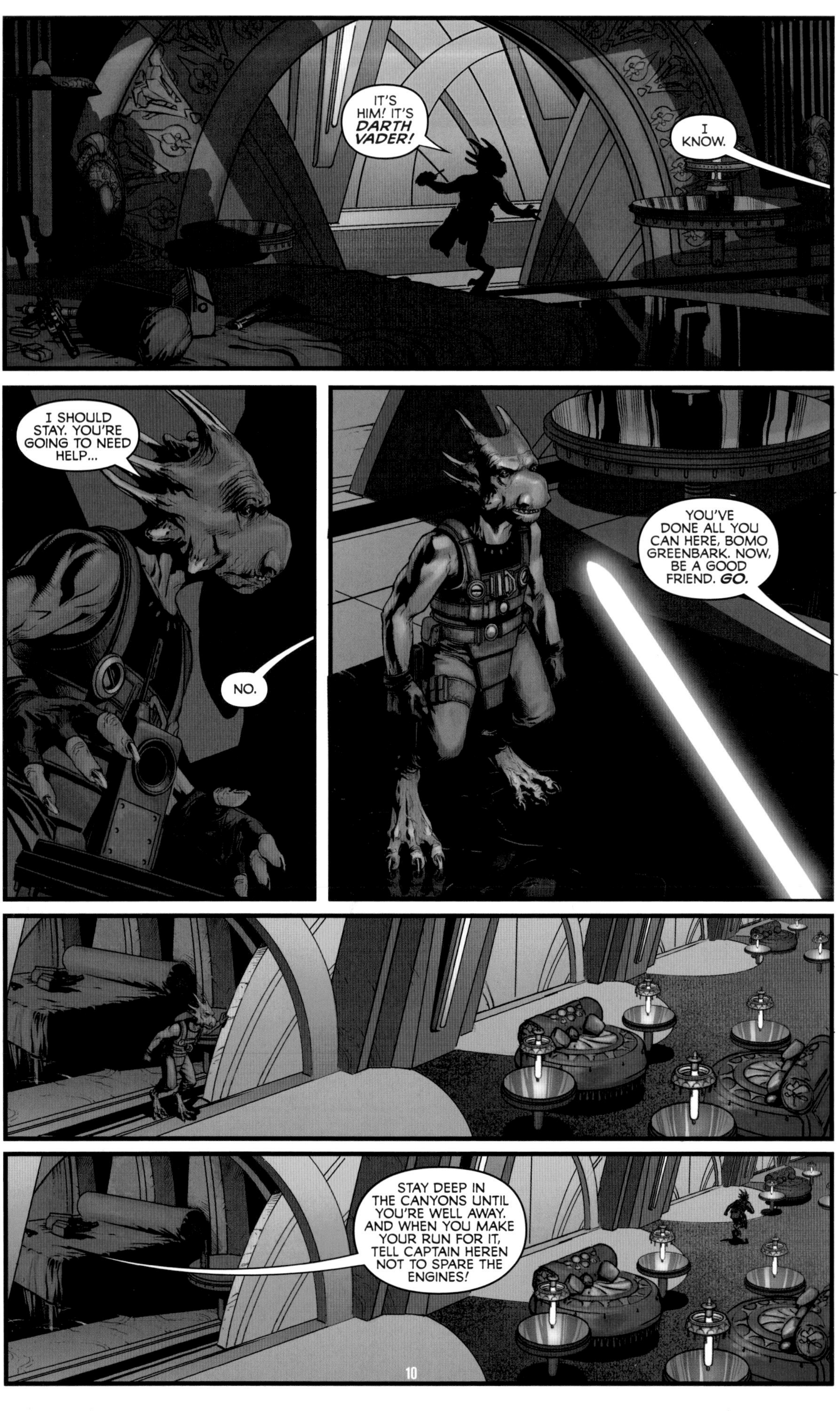

IT'S HIM! IT'S *DARTH VADER!*
I KNOW.
I SHOULD STAY. YOU'RE GOING TO NEED HELP...
NO.
YOU'VE DONE ALL YOU CAN HERE, BOMO GREENBARK. NOW, BE A GOOD FRIEND. *GO.*
STAY DEEP IN THE CANYONS UNTIL YOU'RE WELL AWAY. AND WHEN YOU MAKE YOUR RUN FOR IT, TELL CAPTAIN HEREN NOT TO SPARE THE ENGINES!

FORWARD!

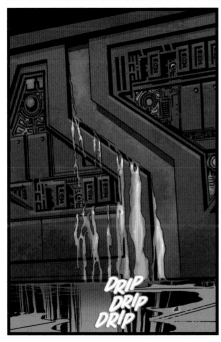

DRIP
DRIP
DRIP

FOOSH!

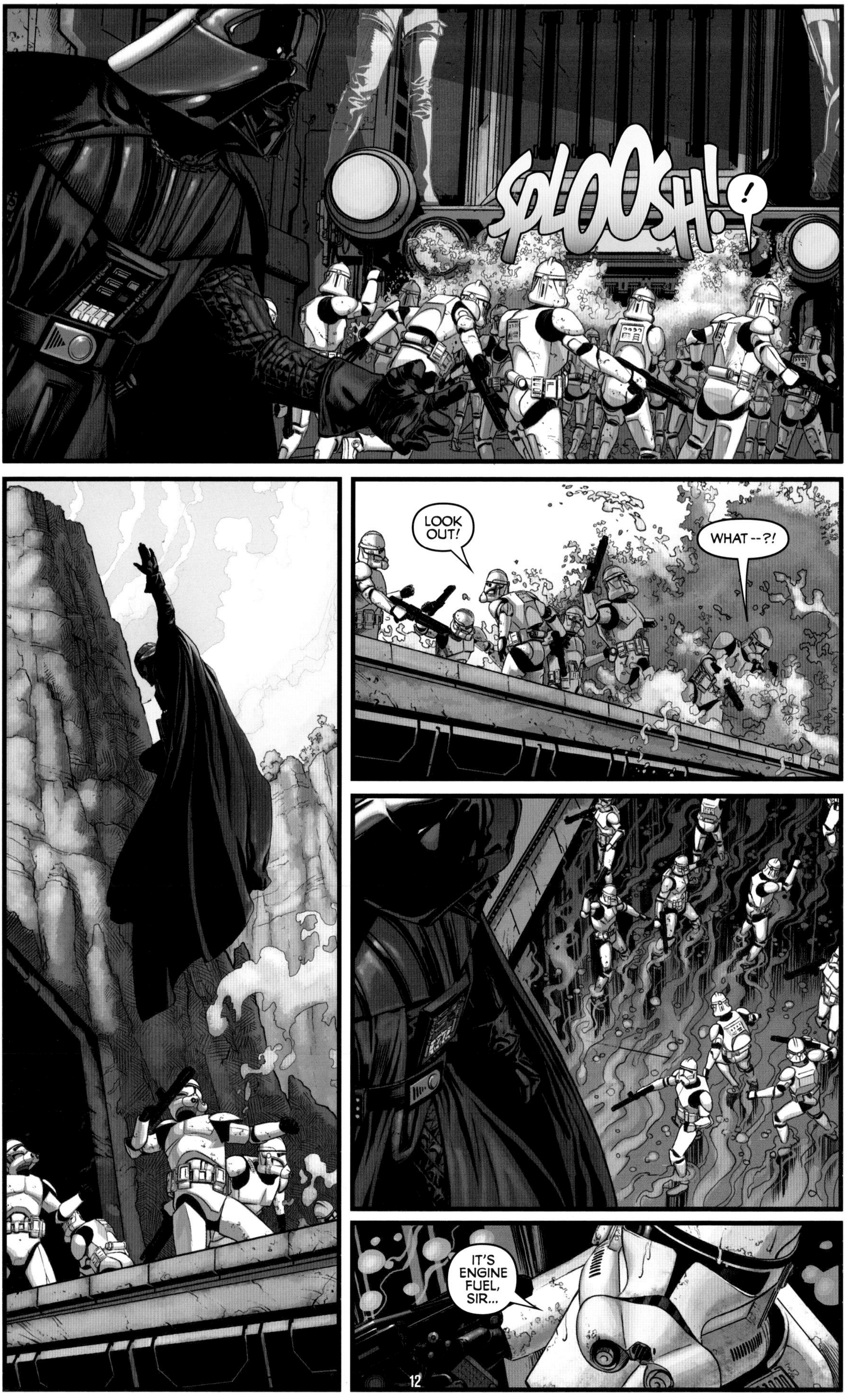
SPLOOSH!
!
LOOK OUT!
WHAT --?!
IT'S ENGINE FUEL, SIR...

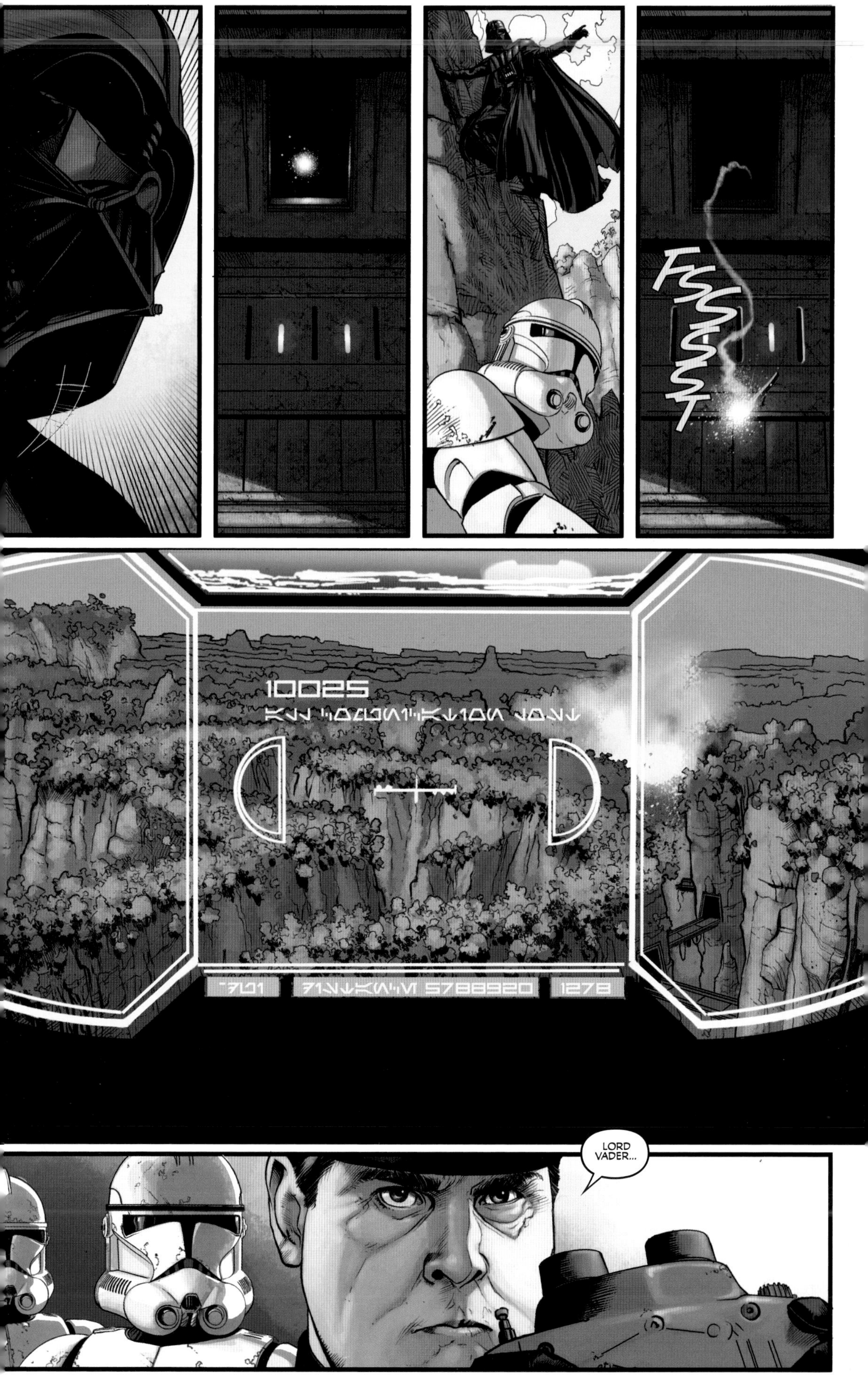
FSSSST
10025
5788920
1278
LORD VADER...

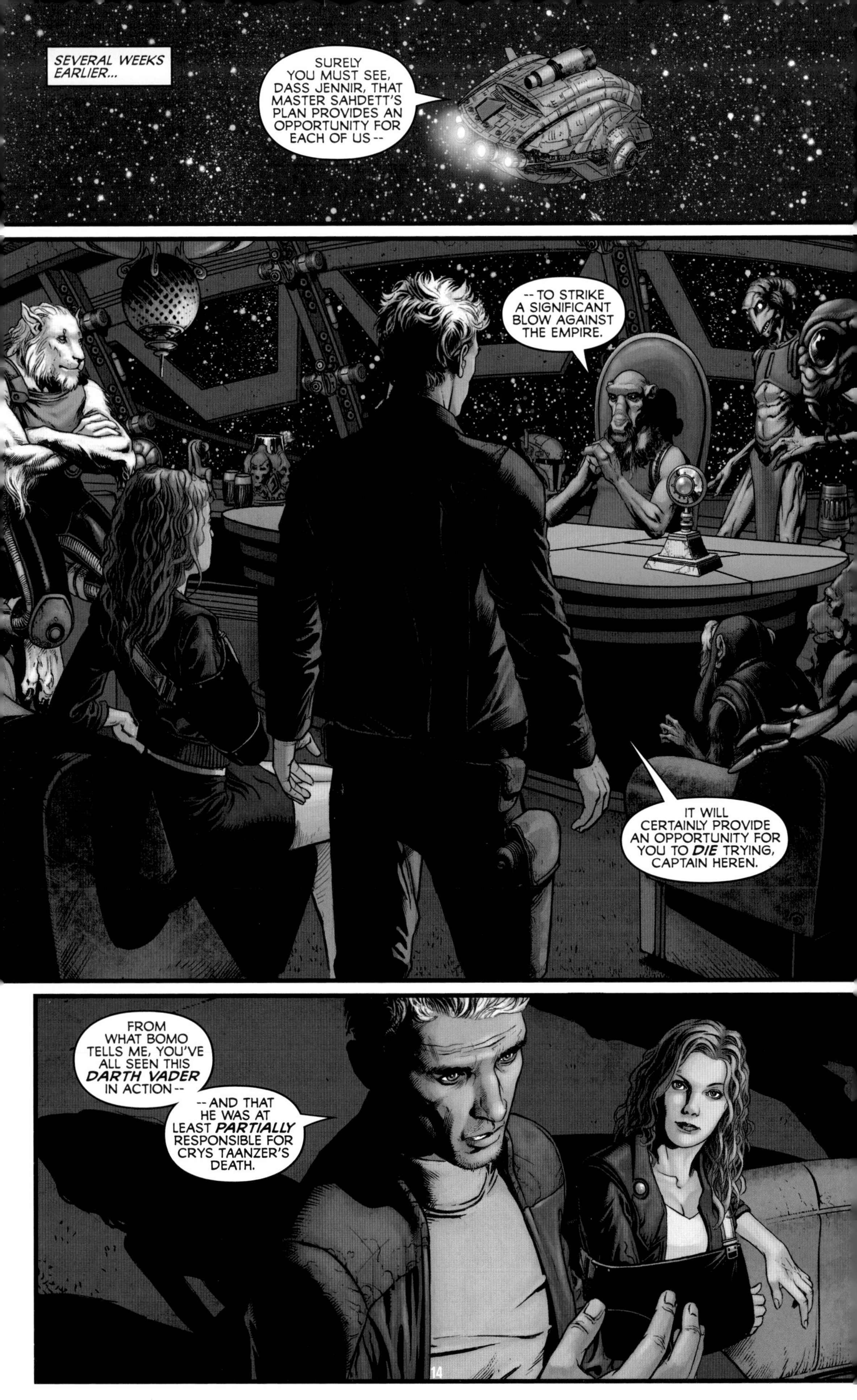
SEVERAL WEEKS EARLIER...
SURELY YOU MUST SEE, DASS JENNIR, THAT MASTER SAHDETT'S PLAN PROVIDES AN OPPORTUNITY FOR EACH OF US --
-- TO STRIKE A SIGNIFICANT BLOW AGAINST THE EMPIRE.
IT WILL CERTAINLY PROVIDE AN OPPORTUNITY FOR YOU TO *DIE* TRYING, CAPTAIN HEREN.
FROM WHAT BOMO TELLS ME, YOU'VE ALL SEEN THIS *DARTH VADER* IN ACTION --
-- AND THAT HE WAS AT LEAST *PARTIALLY* RESPONSIBLE FOR CRYS TAANZER'S DEATH.

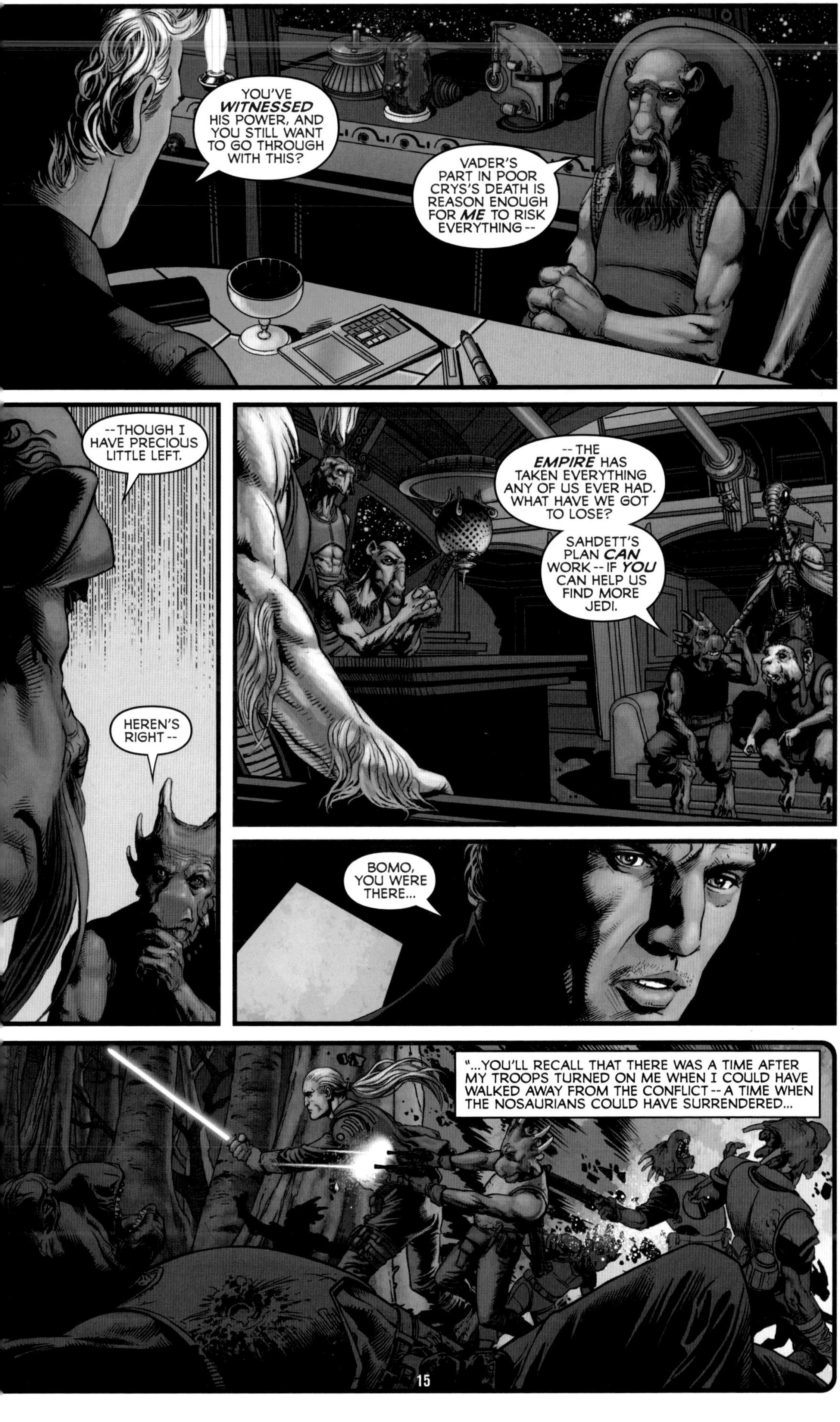

YOU'VE WITNESSED HIS POWER, AND YOU STILL WANT TO GO THROUGH WITH THIS?
VADER'S PART IN POOR CRYS'S DEATH IS REASON ENOUGH FOR ME TO RISK EVERYTHING --
--THOUGH I HAVE PRECIOUS LITTLE LEFT.
HEREN'S RIGHT --
-- THE EMPIRE HAS TAKEN EVERYTHING ANY OF US EVER HAD. WHAT HAVE WE GOT TO LOSE?
SAHDETT'S PLAN CAN WORK -- IF YOU CAN HELP US FIND MORE JEDI.
BOMO, YOU WERE THERE...
"...YOU'LL RECALL THAT THERE WAS A TIME AFTER MY TROOPS TURNED ON ME WHEN I COULD HAVE WALKED AWAY FROM THE CONFLICT -- A TIME WHEN THE NOSAURIANS COULD HAVE SURRENDERED...

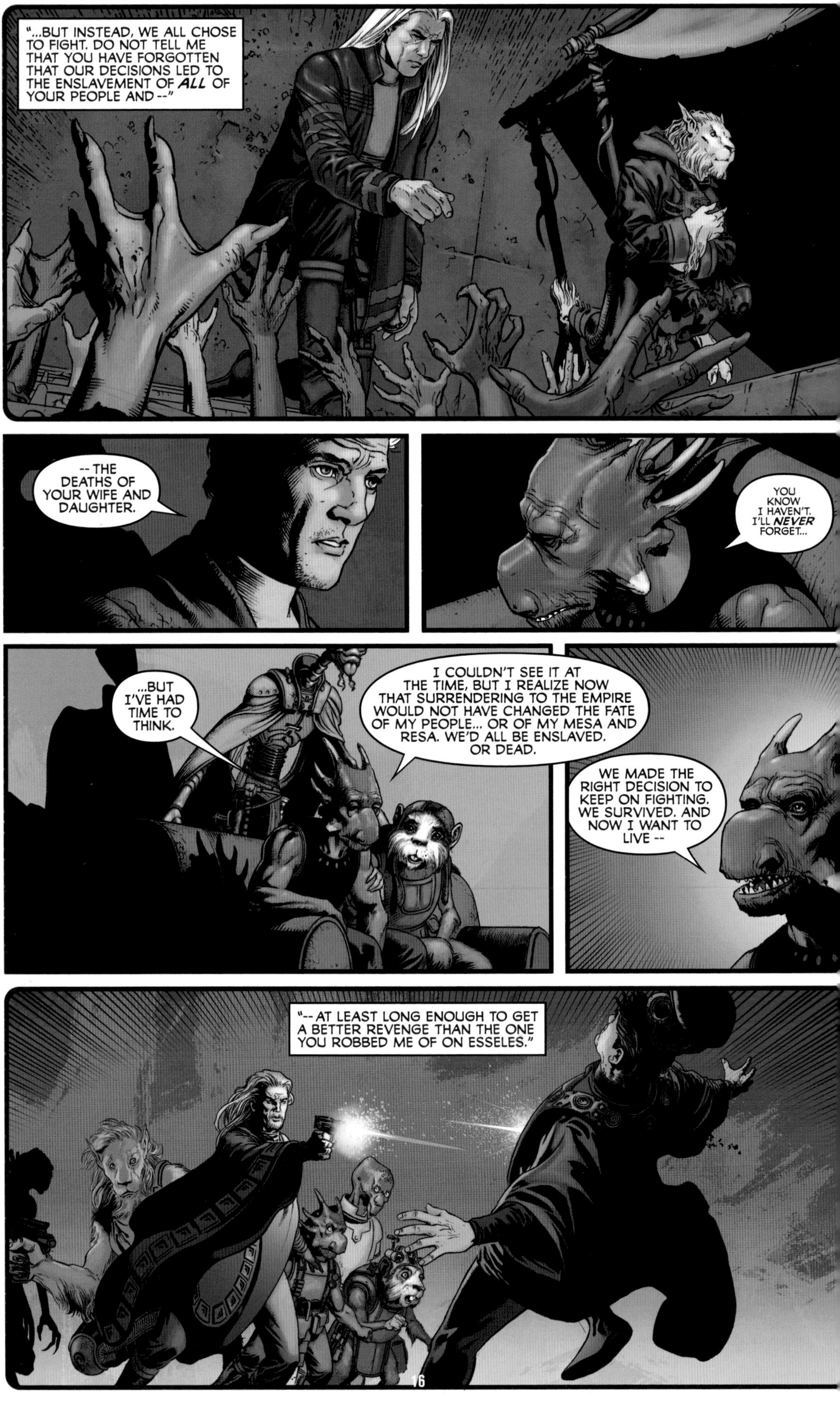
"...BUT INSTEAD, WE ALL CHOSE TO FIGHT. DO NOT TELL ME THAT YOU HAVE FORGOTTEN THAT OUR DECISIONS LED TO THE ENSLAVEMENT OF ALL OF YOUR PEOPLE AND --"
-- THE DEATHS OF YOUR WIFE AND DAUGHTER.
YOU KNOW I HAVEN'T. I'LL NEVER FORGET...
...BUT I'VE HAD TIME TO THINK.
I COULDN'T SEE IT AT THE TIME, BUT I REALIZE NOW THAT SURRENDERING TO THE EMPIRE WOULD NOT HAVE CHANGED THE FATE OF MY PEOPLE... OR OF MY MESA AND RESA. WE'D ALL BE ENSLAVED. OR DEAD.
WE MADE THE RIGHT DECISION TO KEEP ON FIGHTING. WE SURVIVED. AND NOW I WANT TO LIVE --
"-- AT LEAST LONG ENOUGH TO GET A BETTER REVENGE THAN THE ONE YOU ROBBED ME OF ON ESSELES."

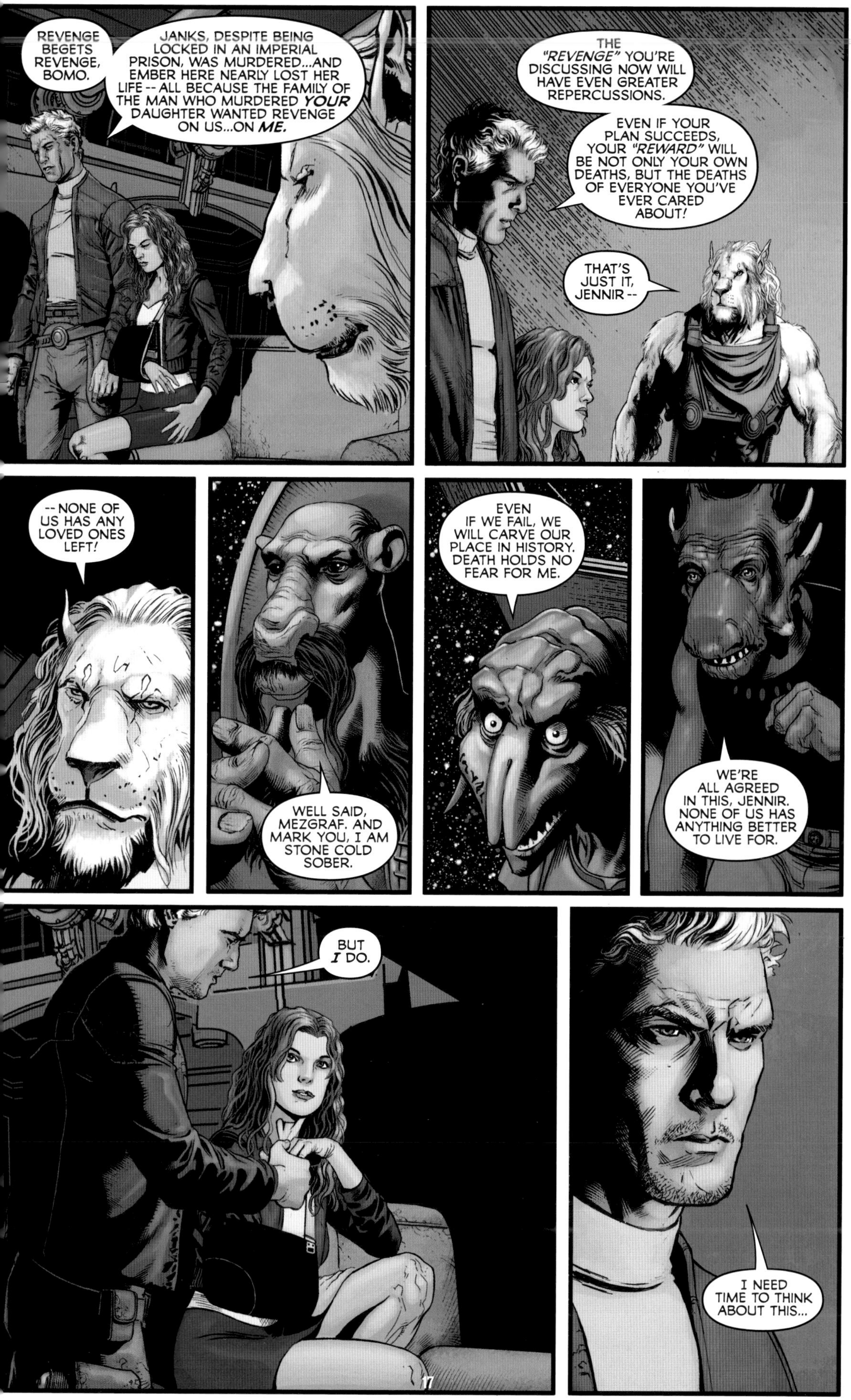

REVENGE BEGETS REVENGE, BOMO.
JANKS, DESPITE BEING LOCKED IN AN IMPERIAL PRISON, WAS MURDERED...AND EMBER HERE NEARLY LOST HER LIFE -- ALL BECAUSE THE FAMILY OF THE MAN WHO MURDERED *YOUR* DAUGHTER WANTED REVENGE ON US...ON *ME.*
THE *"REVENGE"* YOU'RE DISCUSSING NOW WILL HAVE EVEN GREATER REPERCUSSIONS.
EVEN IF YOUR PLAN SUCCEEDS, YOUR *"REWARD"* WILL BE NOT ONLY YOUR OWN DEATHS, BUT THE DEATHS OF EVERYONE YOU'VE EVER CARED ABOUT!
THAT'S JUST IT, JENNIR --
-- NONE OF US HAS ANY LOVED ONES LEFT!
WELL SAID, MEZGRAF. AND MARK YOU, I AM STONE COLD SOBER.
EVEN IF WE FAIL, WE WILL CARVE OUR PLACE IN HISTORY. DEATH HOLDS NO FEAR FOR ME.
WE'RE ALL AGREED IN THIS, JENNIR. NONE OF US HAS ANYTHING BETTER TO LIVE FOR.
BUT *I* DO.
I NEED TIME TO THINK ABOUT THIS...

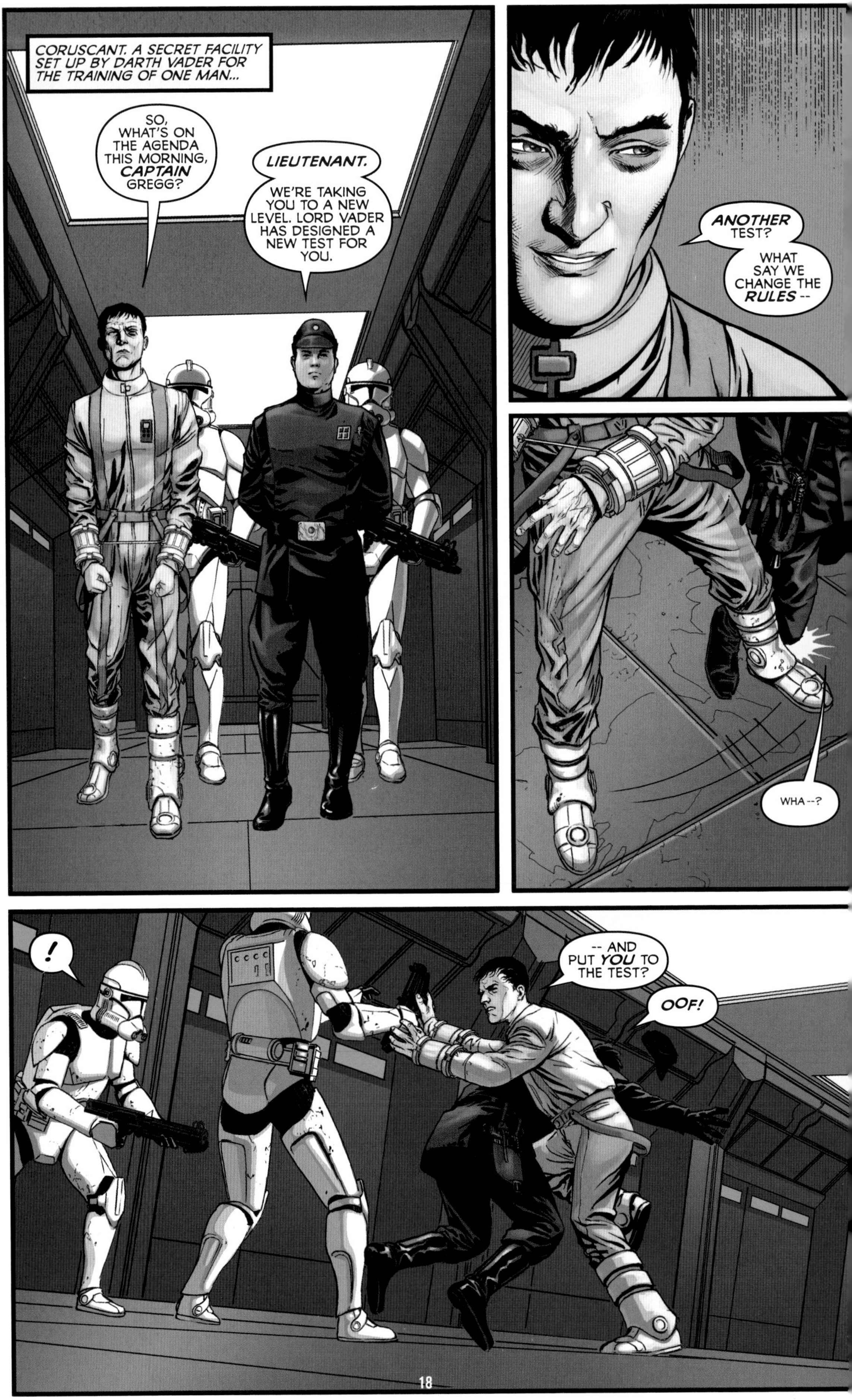
CORUSCANT. A SECRET FACILITY SET UP BY DARTH VADER FOR THE TRAINING OF ONE MAN...
SO, WHAT'S ON THE AGENDA THIS MORNING, CAPTAIN GREGG?
LIEUTENANT.
WE'RE TAKING YOU TO A NEW LEVEL. LORD VADER HAS DESIGNED A NEW TEST FOR YOU.
ANOTHER TEST?
WHAT SAY WE CHANGE THE RULES --
WHA --?
!
-- AND PUT YOU TO THE TEST?
OOF!

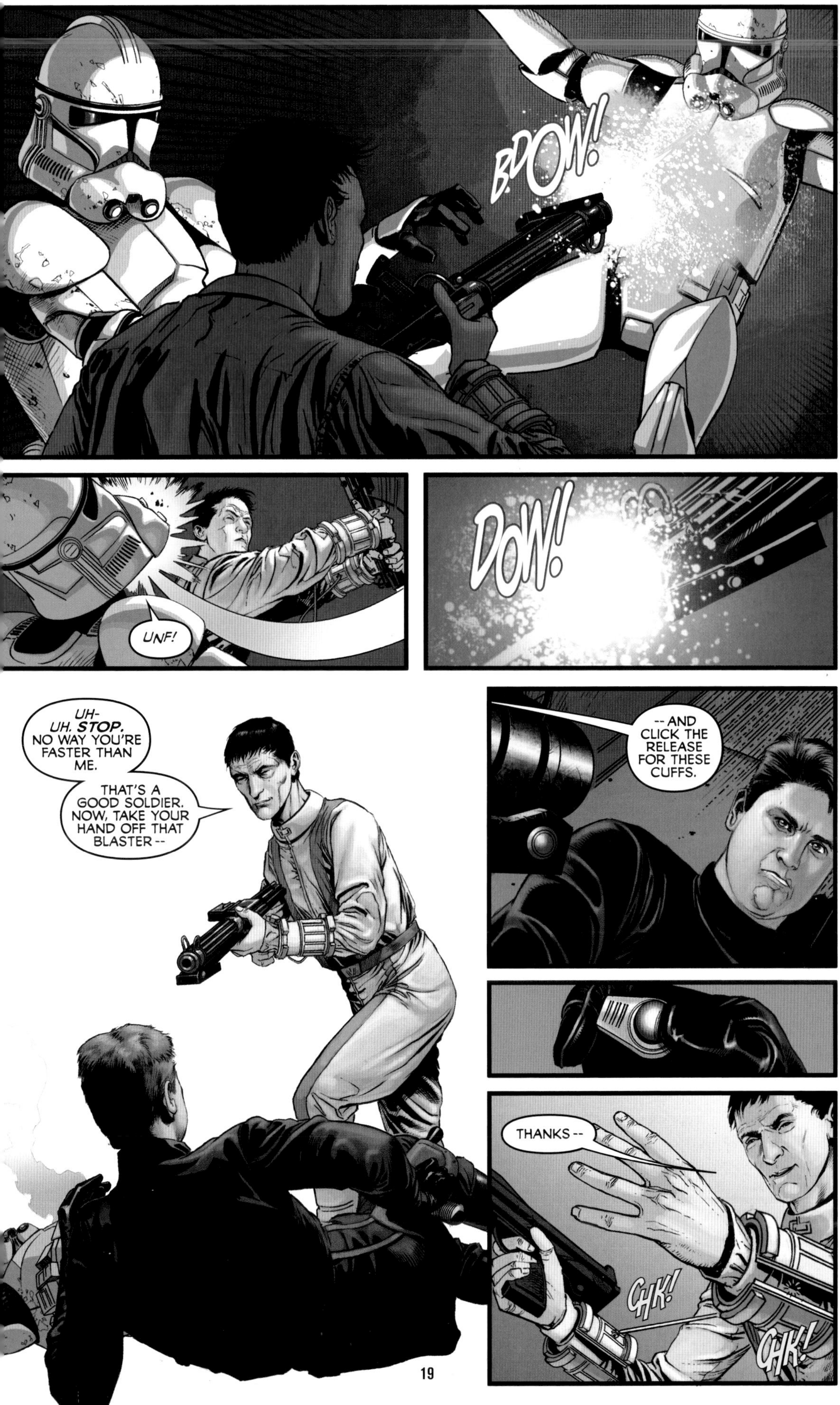
BDOW!
UNF!
DOW!
UH-
UH. STOP.
NO WAY YOU'RE FASTER THAN ME.
THAT'S A GOOD SOLDIER. NOW, TAKE YOUR HAND OFF THAT BLASTER --
-- AND CLICK THE RELEASE FOR THESE CUFFS.
THANKS --
CHK!
CHK!

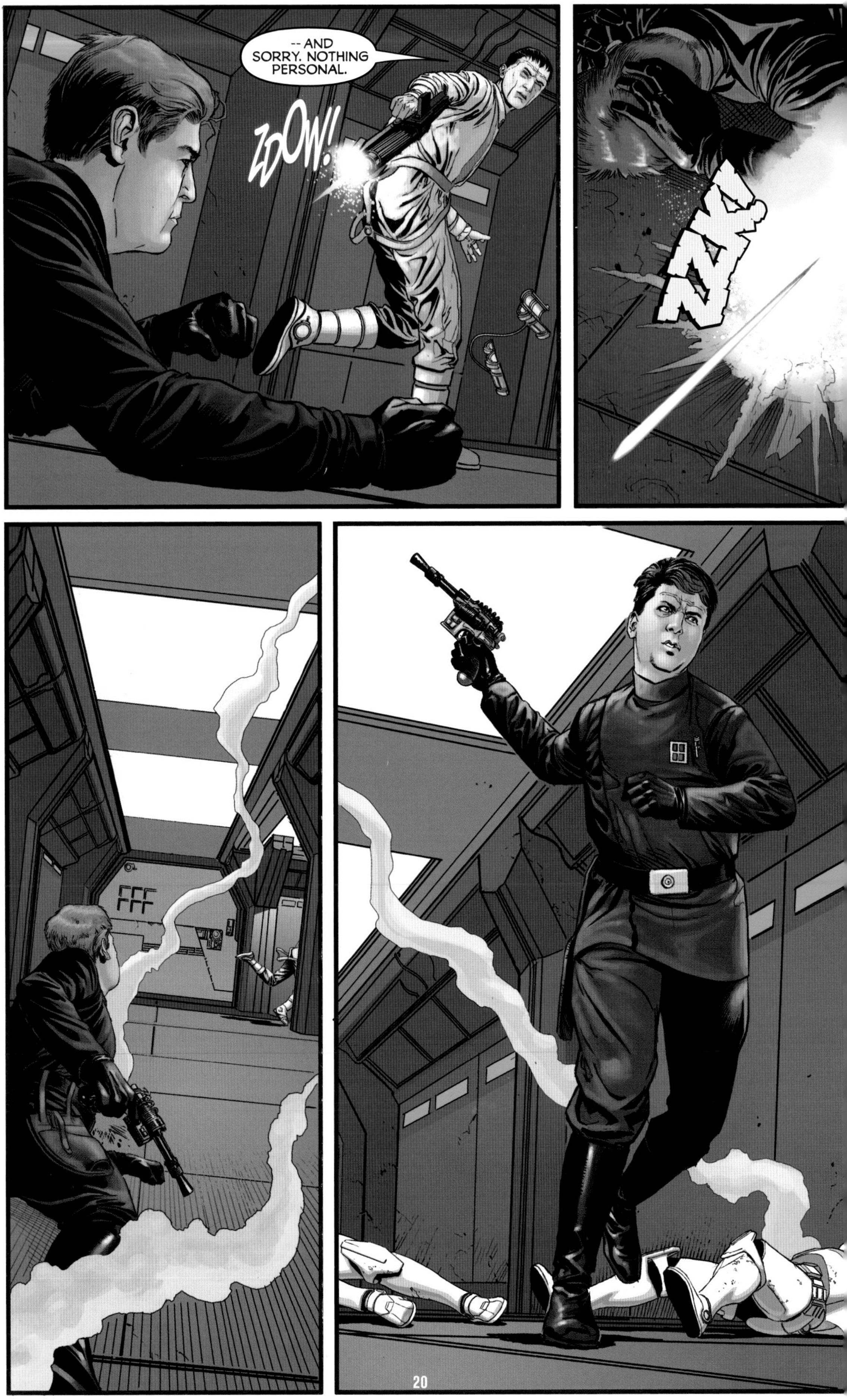
-- AND SORRY. NOTHING PERSONAL.
ZDOW!!
ZZAK!

HEY!

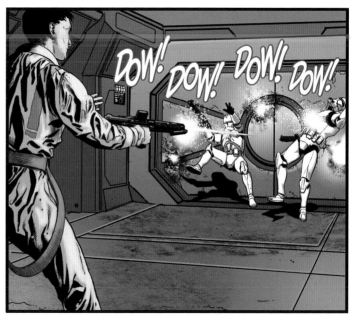

DOW! DOW! DOW! DOW!

SHHHHHH

DEET! DOOT! CLICK! CLICK!

BDOW!

HA! I'M FREE!

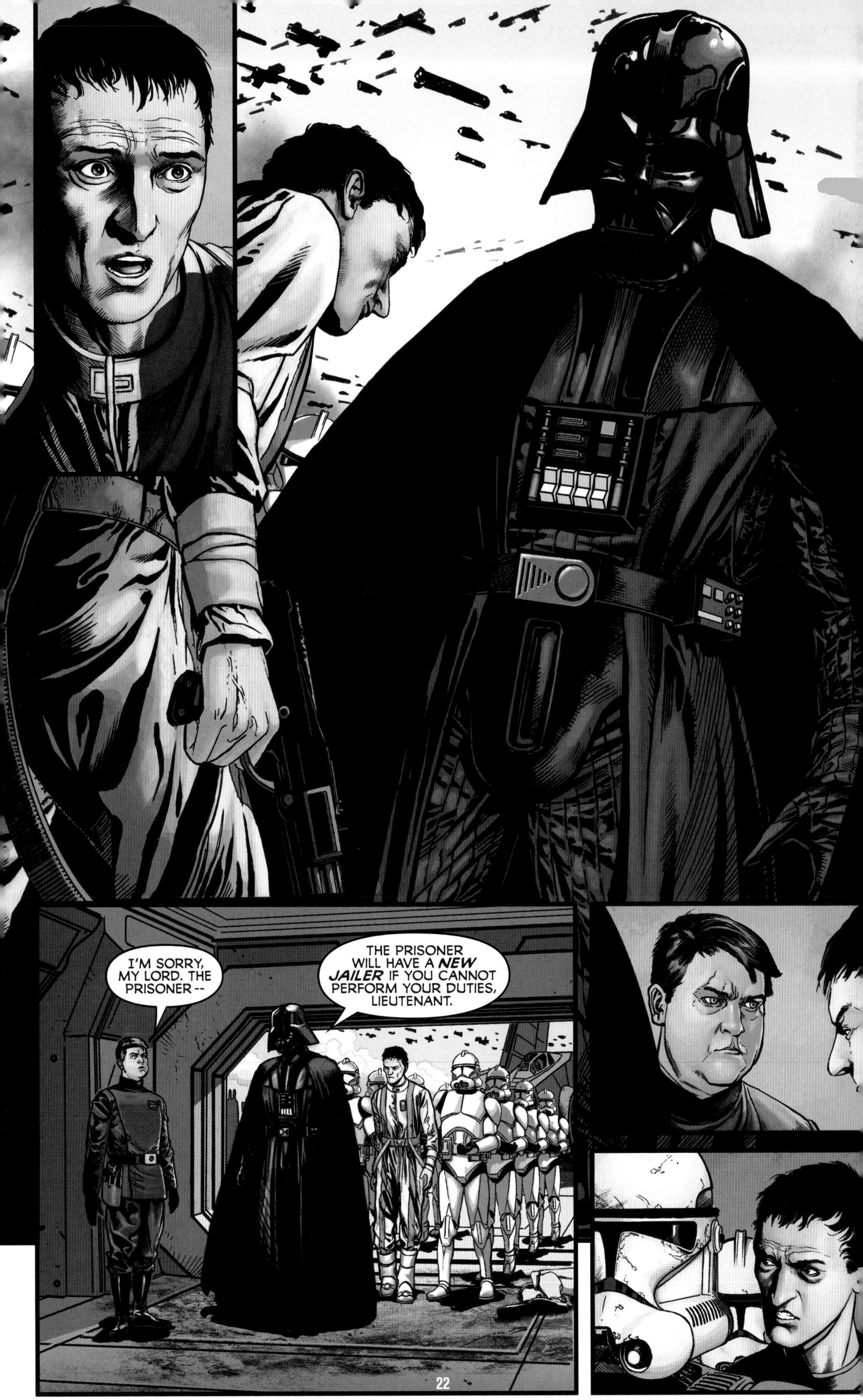
I'M SORRY, MY LORD. THE PRISONER --
THE PRISONER WILL HAVE A *NEW JAILER* IF YOU CANNOT PERFORM YOUR DUTIES, LIEUTENANT.

JENNIR?

YOU'RE UP. WHAT'S THE MATTER?

I'M SORRY, EMBER. GO BACK TO SLEEP. THIS IS MY PROBLEM.

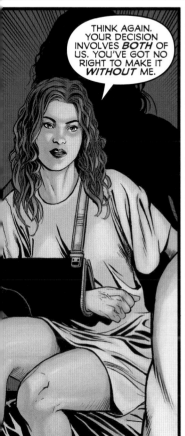

THINK AGAIN. YOUR DECISION INVOLVES *BOTH* OF US. YOU'VE GOT NO RIGHT TO MAKE IT *WITHOUT* ME.

YOU THINK I DON'T KNOW THE RISKS? THAT I DON'T KNOW WHAT BOMO AND THE OTHERS ARE TALKING ABOUT? I'M *WITH* YOU, *WHATEVER* YOU DECIDE --

-- BUT I DON'T WANT YOU TO MAKE A DECISION YOU DON'T LIKE BECAUSE YOU'RE WORRIED ABOUT ME.

THERE'S MORE TO THIS THAN YOU CAN KNOW --

ARE YOU SAYING I'M STUPID?!

NO! THAT'S NOT IT AT ALL. BUT...

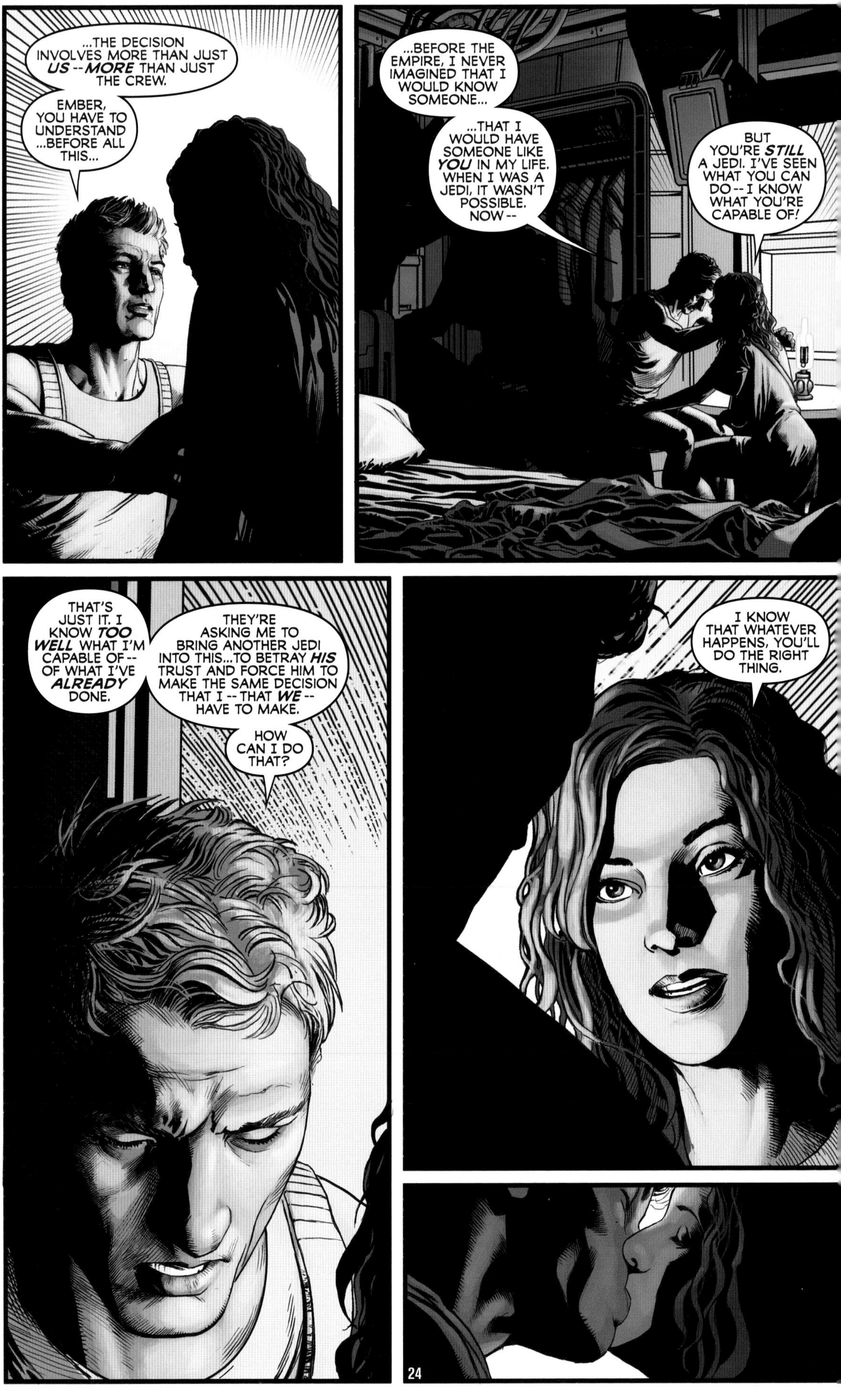
...THE DECISION INVOLVES MORE THAN JUST US -- MORE THAN JUST THE CREW.
EMBER, YOU HAVE TO UNDERSTAND ...BEFORE ALL THIS...
...BEFORE THE EMPIRE, I NEVER IMAGINED THAT I WOULD KNOW SOMEONE...
...THAT I WOULD HAVE SOMEONE LIKE YOU IN MY LIFE. WHEN I WAS A JEDI, IT WASN'T POSSIBLE. NOW --
BUT YOU'RE STILL A JEDI. I'VE SEEN WHAT YOU CAN DO -- I KNOW WHAT YOU'RE CAPABLE OF!
THAT'S JUST IT. I KNOW TOO WELL WHAT I'M CAPABLE OF -- OF WHAT I'VE ALREADY DONE.
THEY'RE ASKING ME TO BRING ANOTHER JEDI INTO THIS...TO BETRAY HIS TRUST AND FORCE HIM TO MAKE THE SAME DECISION THAT I -- THAT WE -- HAVE TO MAKE.
HOW CAN I DO THAT?
I KNOW THAT WHATEVER HAPPENS, YOU'LL DO THE RIGHT THING.

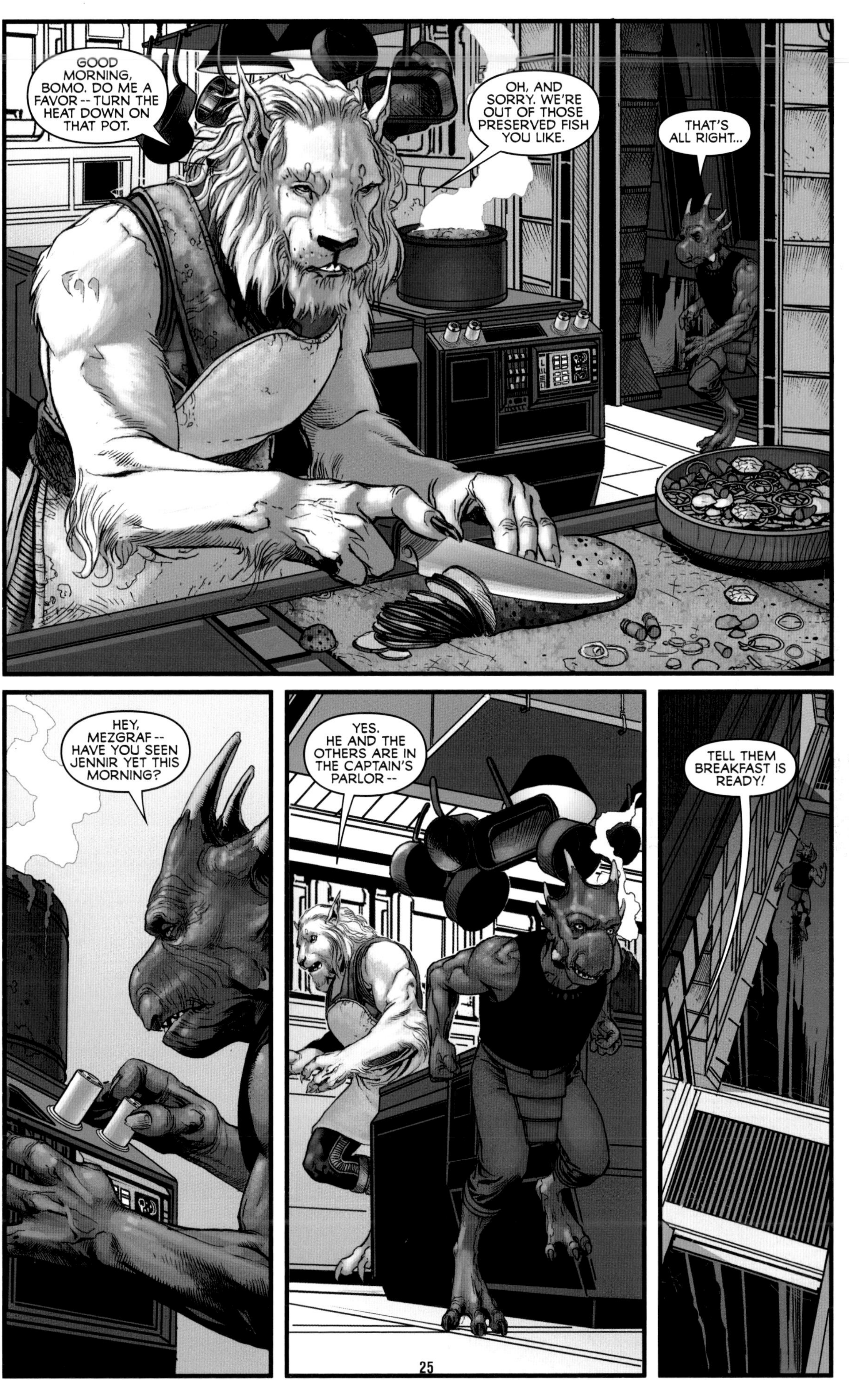
GOOD MORNING, BOMO. DO ME A FAVOR -- TURN THE HEAT DOWN ON THAT POT.
OH, AND SORRY. WE'RE OUT OF THOSE PRESERVED FISH YOU LIKE.
THAT'S ALL RIGHT...
HEY, MEZGRAF -- HAVE YOU SEEN JENNIR YET THIS MORNING?
YES. HE AND THE OTHERS ARE IN THE CAPTAIN'S PARLOR --
TELL THEM BREAKFAST IS READY!

OUR EMPIRE MAY YET BE YOUNG, BUT IT IS STRONG!

WHILE EMPEROR PALPATINE RULES FROM CORUSCANT, OUR VALIANT CLONE ARMY CONTINUES TO KEEP US SAFE FROM THE GALAXY'S MANY THREATS!

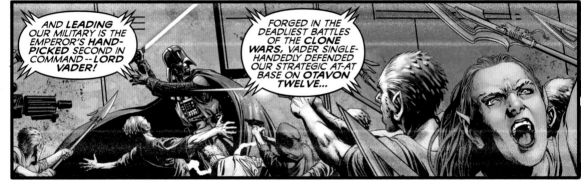

AND LEADING OUR MILITARY IS THE EMPEROR'S HAND-PICKED SECOND IN COMMAND--LORD VADER!

FORGED IN THE DEADLIEST BATTLES OF THE CLONE WARS, VADER SINGLE-HANDEDLY DEFENDED OUR STRATEGIC AT-AT BASE ON OTAVON TWELVE...

...QUELLED THE UPRISING OF THE MIGHTY WOOKIEE WARRIORS OF KASHYYYK...

...AND THWARTED THE MURDEROUS PLOT OF GENERAL GENTIS THAT LEFT THOUSANDS DEAD ON GALACTIC CENTER!

FROM BANDOMEER TO THE GHOST NEBULA, WHEREVER A THREAT ARISES, LORD VADER IS THERE TO MEET IT...

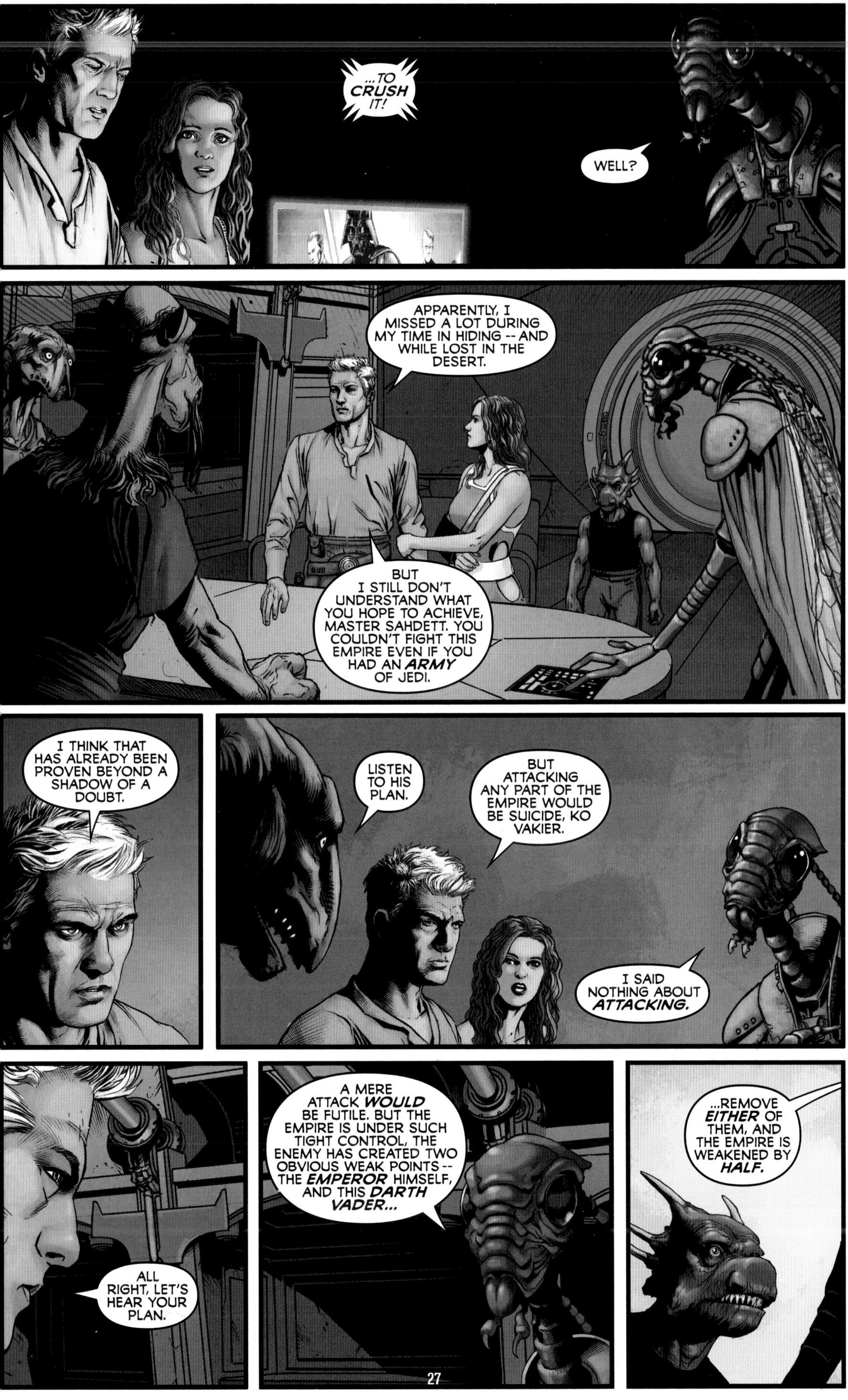
...TO CRUSH IT!
WELL?
APPARENTLY, I MISSED A LOT DURING MY TIME IN HIDING -- AND WHILE LOST IN THE DESERT.
BUT I STILL DON'T UNDERSTAND WHAT YOU HOPE TO ACHIEVE, MASTER SAHDETT. YOU COULDN'T FIGHT THIS EMPIRE EVEN IF YOU HAD AN ARMY OF JEDI.
I THINK THAT HAS ALREADY BEEN PROVEN BEYOND A SHADOW OF A DOUBT.
LISTEN TO HIS PLAN.
BUT ATTACKING ANY PART OF THE EMPIRE WOULD BE SUICIDE, KO VAKIER.
I SAID NOTHING ABOUT ATTACKING.
ALL RIGHT, LET'S HEAR YOUR PLAN.
A MERE ATTACK WOULD BE FUTILE. BUT THE EMPIRE IS UNDER SUCH TIGHT CONTROL, THE ENEMY HAS CREATED TWO OBVIOUS WEAK POINTS -- THE EMPEROR HIMSELF, AND THIS DARTH VADER...
...REMOVE EITHER OF THEM, AND THE EMPIRE IS WEAKENED BY HALF.

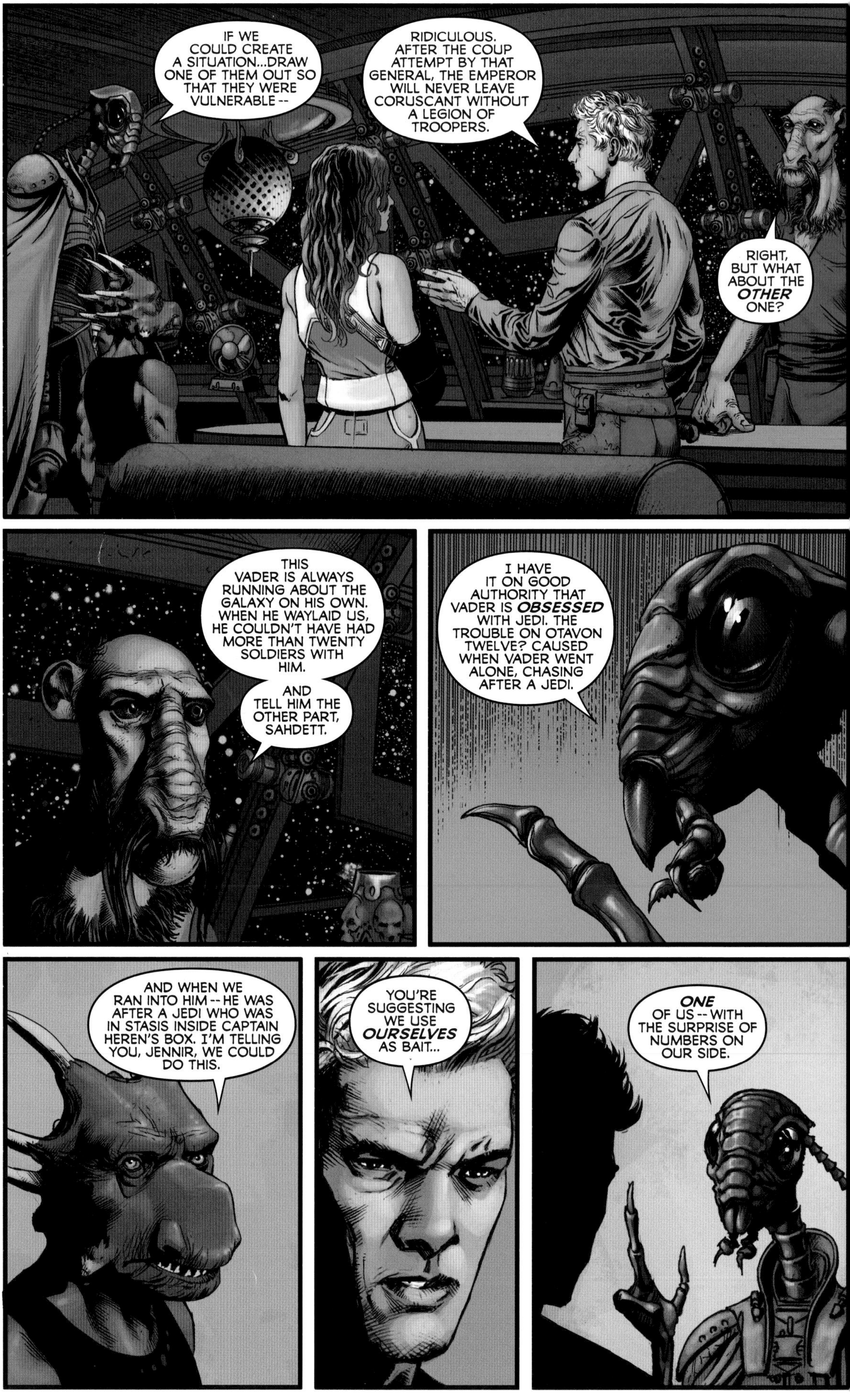
IF WE COULD CREATE A SITUATION...DRAW ONE OF THEM OUT SO THAT THEY WERE VULNERABLE--
RIDICULOUS. AFTER THE COUP ATTEMPT BY THAT GENERAL, THE EMPEROR WILL NEVER LEAVE CORUSCANT WITHOUT A LEGION OF TROOPERS.
RIGHT, BUT WHAT ABOUT THE *OTHER* ONE?
THIS VADER IS ALWAYS RUNNING ABOUT THE GALAXY ON HIS OWN. WHEN HE WAYLAID US, HE COULDN'T HAVE HAD MORE THAN TWENTY SOLDIERS WITH HIM.
AND TELL HIM THE OTHER PART, SAHDETT.
I HAVE IT ON GOOD AUTHORITY THAT VADER IS *OBSESSED* WITH JEDI. THE TROUBLE ON OTAVON TWELVE? CAUSED WHEN VADER WENT ALONE, CHASING AFTER A JEDI.
AND WHEN WE RAN INTO HIM--HE WAS AFTER A JEDI WHO WAS IN STASIS INSIDE CAPTAIN HEREN'S BOX. I'M TELLING YOU, JENNIR, WE COULD DO THIS.
YOU'RE SUGGESTING WE USE *OURSELVES* AS BAIT...
ONE OF US--WITH THE SURPRISE OF NUMBERS ON OUR SIDE.

YOU'VE BEEN GIVING THIS SOME THOUGHT, HAVEN'T YOU?

ALL RIGHT, I'M IN--

EXCELLENT.

YEAH!

GOOD FELLOW!

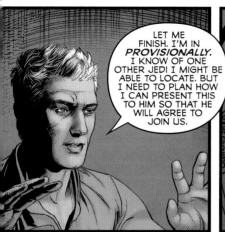

LET ME FINISH. I'M IN *PROVISIONALLY.* I KNOW OF ONE OTHER JEDI I MIGHT BE ABLE TO LOCATE. BUT I NEED TO PLAN HOW I CAN PRESENT THIS TO HIM SO THAT HE WILL AGREE TO JOIN US.

I NEED MORE TIME TO THINK.

ARE YOU *SURE* ABOUT THIS?

ALMOST. I JUST NEED TO DISCUSS SOME DETAILS...

"...WITH RATTY."

PLEASE, COME IN! I DON'T BELIEVE I'VE HAD THE HONOR OF A VISIT BY YOU TO MY QUARTERS.

I THOUGHT IT TIME. HOW IS H2?

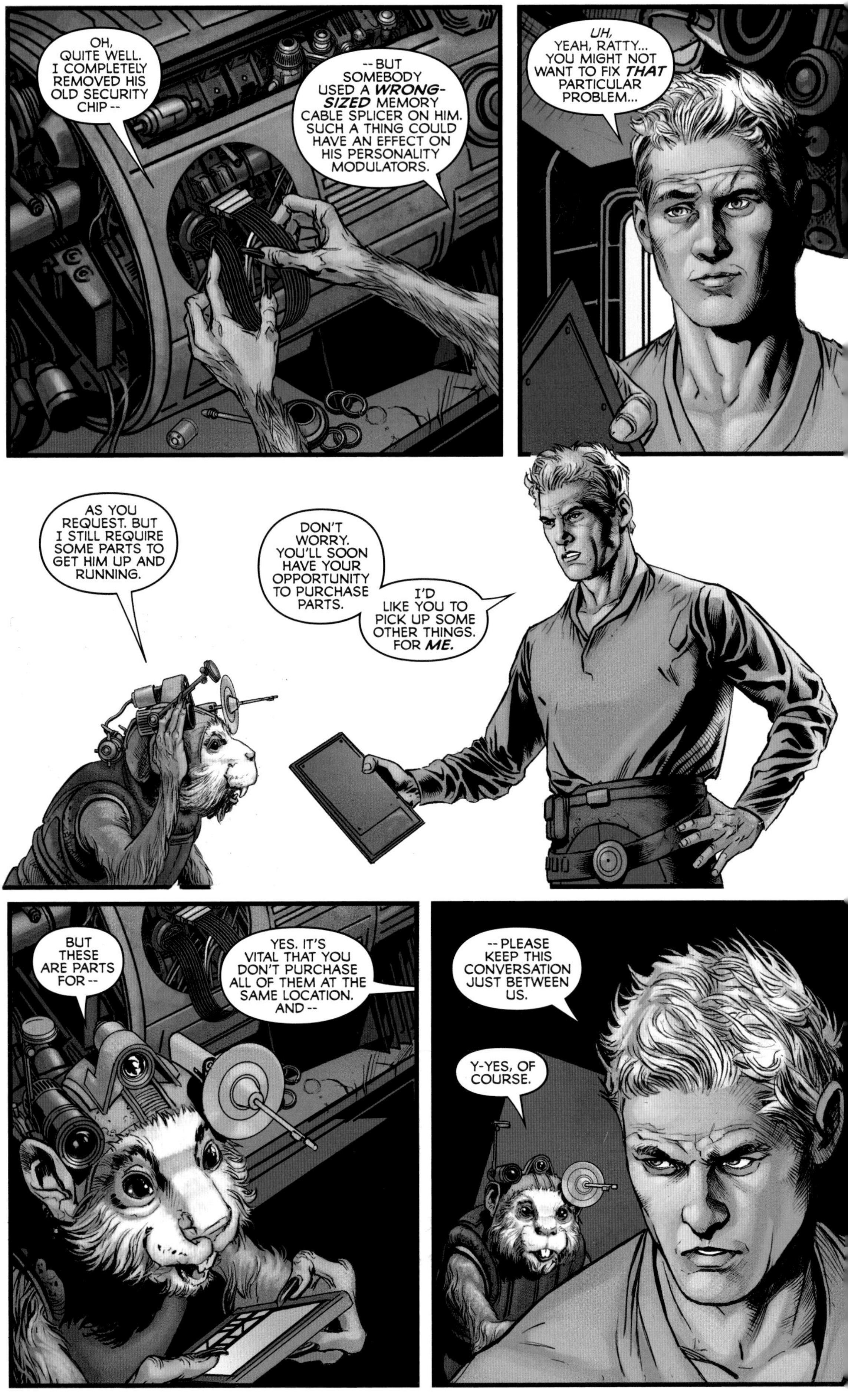
OH, QUITE WELL. I COMPLETELY REMOVED HIS OLD SECURITY CHIP --
-- BUT SOMEBODY USED A WRONG-SIZED MEMORY CABLE SPLICER ON HIM. SUCH A THING COULD HAVE AN EFFECT ON HIS PERSONALITY MODULATORS.
UH, YEAH, RATTY... YOU MIGHT NOT WANT TO FIX THAT PARTICULAR PROBLEM...
AS YOU REQUEST. BUT I STILL REQUIRE SOME PARTS TO GET HIM UP AND RUNNING.
DON'T WORRY. YOU'LL SOON HAVE YOUR OPPORTUNITY TO PURCHASE PARTS.
I'D LIKE YOU TO PICK UP SOME OTHER THINGS. FOR ME.
BUT THESE ARE PARTS FOR --
YES. IT'S VITAL THAT YOU DON'T PURCHASE ALL OF THEM AT THE SAME LOCATION. AND --
-- PLEASE KEEP THIS CONVERSATION JUST BETWEEN US.
Y-YES, OF COURSE.

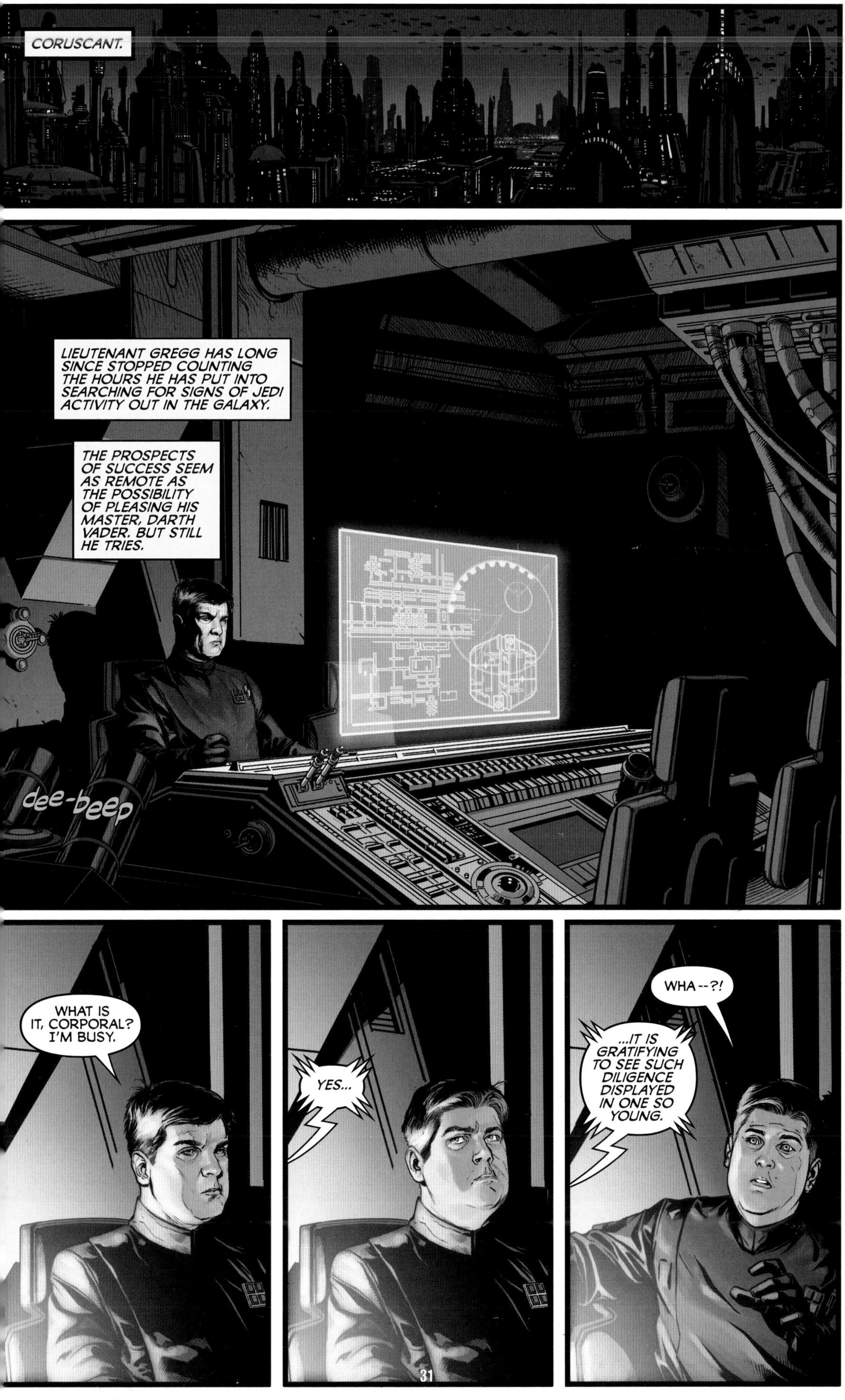

CORUSCANT.
LIEUTENANT GREGG HAS LONG SINCE STOPPED COUNTING THE HOURS HE HAS PUT INTO SEARCHING FOR SIGNS OF JEDI ACTIVITY OUT IN THE GALAXY.
THE PROSPECTS OF SUCCESS SEEM AS REMOTE AS THE POSSIBILITY OF PLEASING HIS MASTER, DARTH VADER. BUT STILL HE TRIES.
dee-beep
WHAT IS IT, CORPORAL? I'M BUSY.
YES...
...IT IS GRATIFYING TO SEE SUCH DILIGENCE DISPLAYED IN ONE SO YOUNG.
WHA--?!

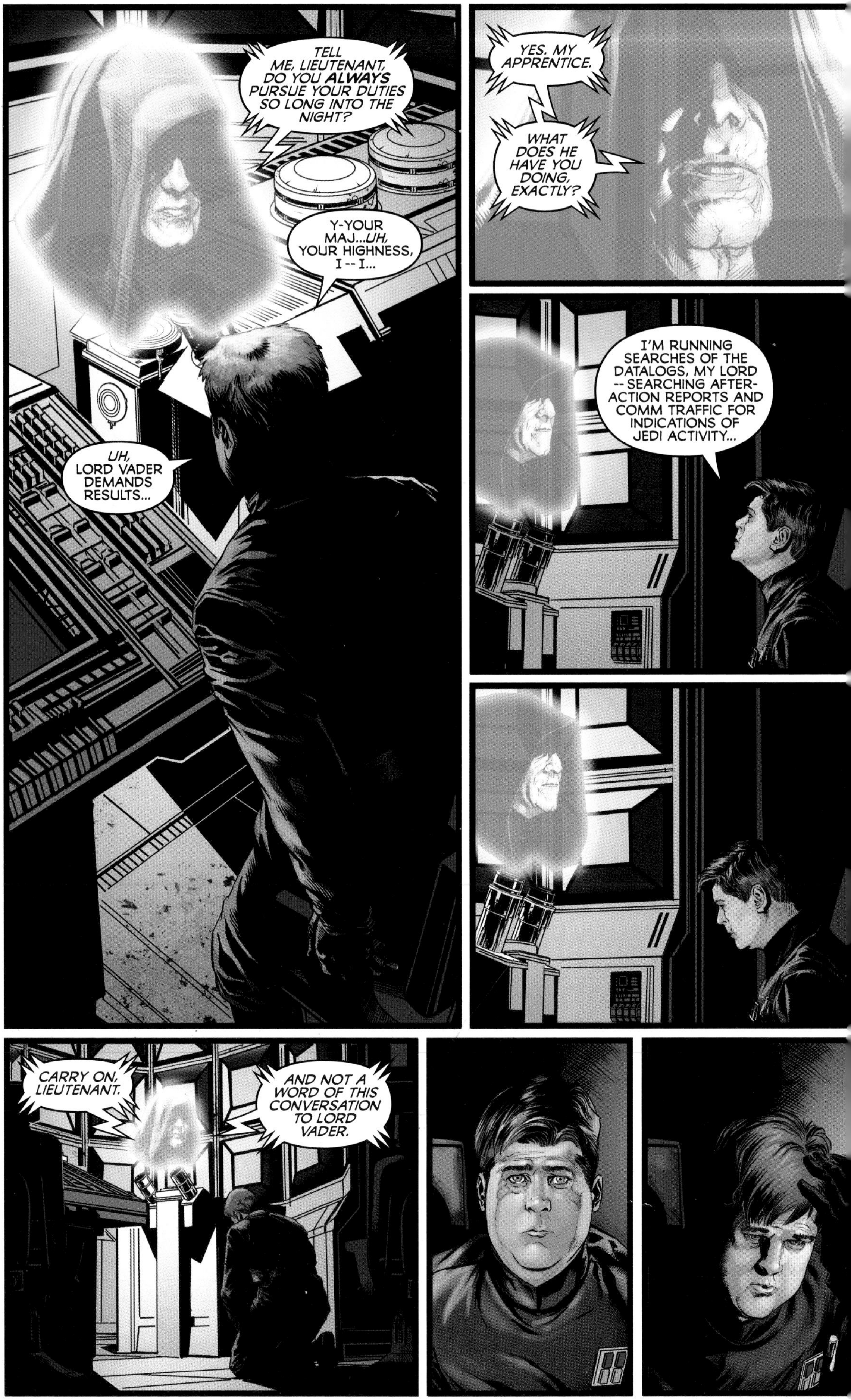
TELL ME, LIEUTENANT, DO YOU **ALWAYS** PURSUE YOUR DUTIES SO LONG INTO THE NIGHT?
Y-YOUR MAJ...*UH,* YOUR HIGHNESS, I -- I...
UH, LORD VADER DEMANDS RESULTS...
YES. MY APPRENTICE.
WHAT DOES HE HAVE YOU DOING, EXACTLY?
I'M RUNNING SEARCHES OF THE DATALOGS, MY LORD -- SEARCHING AFTER-ACTION REPORTS AND COMM TRAFFIC FOR INDICATIONS OF JEDI ACTIVITY...
CARRY ON, LIEUTENANT.
AND NOT A WORD OF THIS CONVERSATION TO LORD VADER.

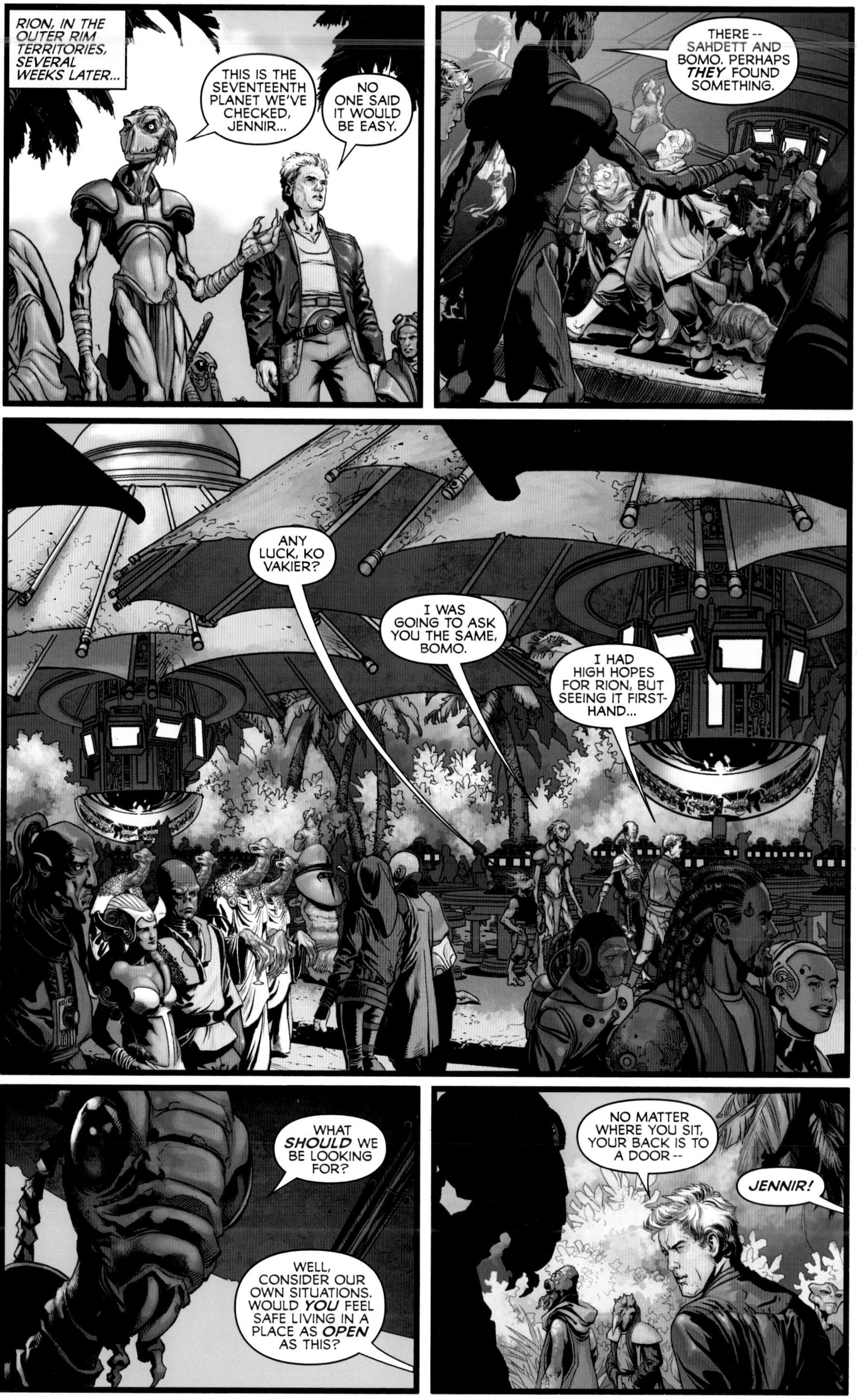
RION, IN THE OUTER RIM TERRITORIES, SEVERAL WEEKS LATER...
THIS IS THE SEVENTEENTH PLANET WE'VE CHECKED, JENNIR...
NO ONE SAID IT WOULD BE EASY.
THERE -- SAHDETT AND BOMO. PERHAPS *THEY* FOUND SOMETHING.
ANY LUCK, KO VAKIER?
I WAS GOING TO ASK YOU THE SAME, BOMO.
I HAD HIGH HOPES FOR RION, BUT SEEING IT FIRST-HAND...
WHAT *SHOULD* WE BE LOOKING FOR?
WELL, CONSIDER OUR OWN SITUATIONS. WOULD *YOU* FEEL SAFE LIVING IN A PLACE AS *OPEN* AS THIS?
NO MATTER WHERE YOU SIT, YOUR BACK IS TO A DOOR --
JENNIR!

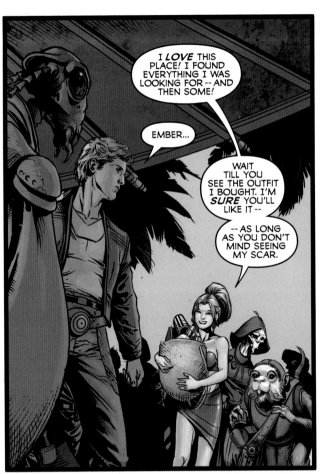

I *LOVE* THIS PLACE! I FOUND EVERYTHING I WAS LOOKING FOR -- AND THEN SOME!

EMBER...

WAIT TILL YOU SEE THE OUTFIT I BOUGHT. I'M *SURE* YOU'LL LIKE IT --

-- AS LONG AS YOU DON'T MIND SEEING MY SCAR.

EMBER, PLEASE. YOU MUST BE CAREFUL. SHOUTING MY NAME IN A PUBLIC PLACE COULD BE DANGEROUS!

I'M SORRY. IT WON'T HAPPEN AGAIN.

BUT LOOK WHAT ELSE WE DID! DOESN'T H2 LOOK BETTER WITHOUT ALL OF THE BLASTER HOLES AND SCORCH MARKS?

LOOK AT ME, MASTER! I'M MAGNIFICENT!

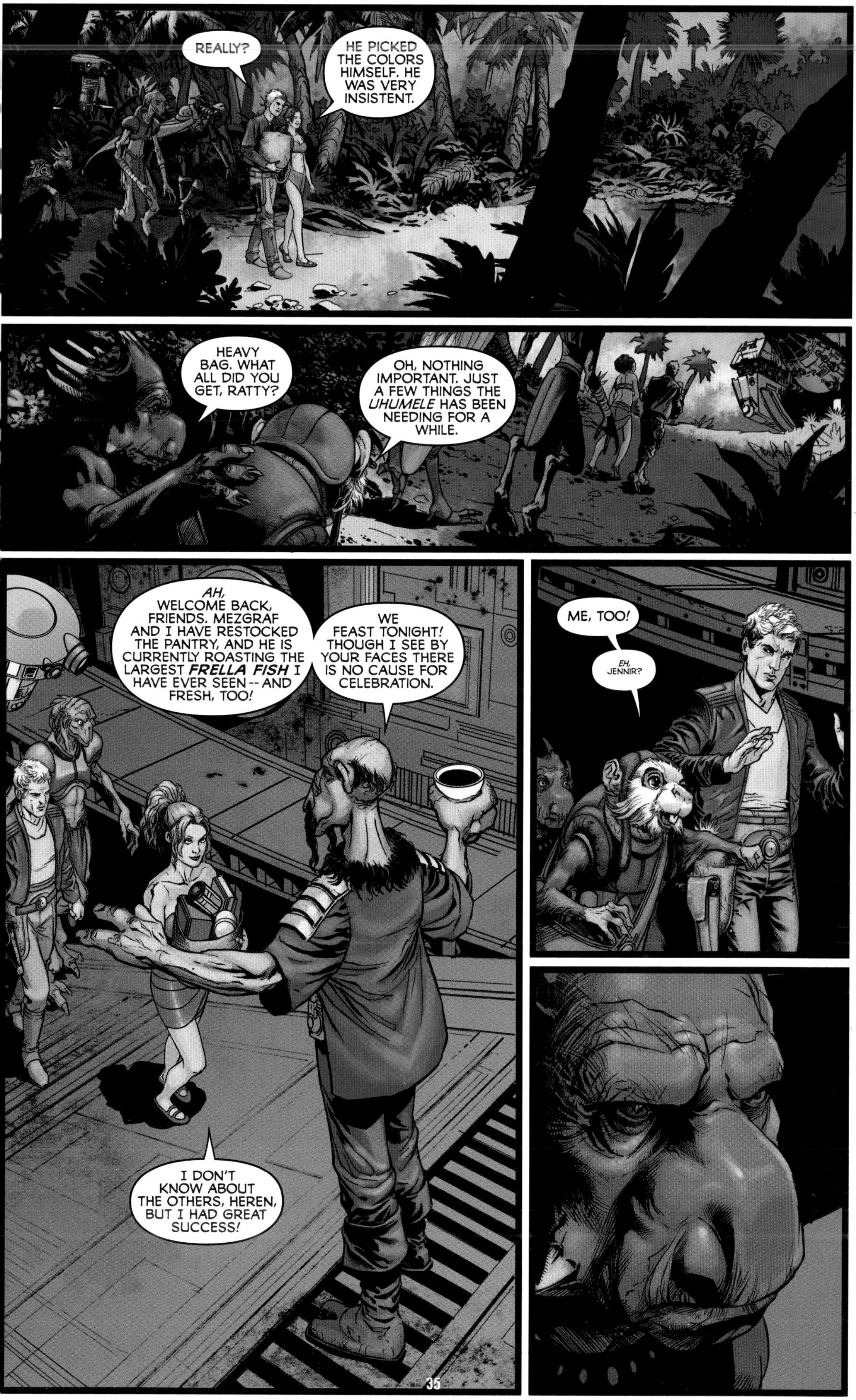
REALLY?
HE PICKED THE COLORS HIMSELF. HE WAS VERY INSISTENT.
HEAVY BAG. WHAT ALL DID YOU GET, RATTY?
OH, NOTHING IMPORTANT. JUST A FEW THINGS THE *UHUMELE* HAS BEEN NEEDING FOR A WHILE.
AH, WELCOME BACK, FRIENDS. MEZGRAF AND I HAVE RESTOCKED THE PANTRY, AND HE IS CURRENTLY ROASTING THE LARGEST ***FRELLA FISH*** I HAVE EVER SEEN-- AND FRESH, TOO!
WE FEAST TONIGHT! THOUGH I SEE BY YOUR FACES THERE IS NO CAUSE FOR CELEBRATION.
I DON'T KNOW ABOUT THE OTHERS, HEREN, BUT I HAD GREAT SUCCESS!
ME, TOO!
EH, JENNIR?

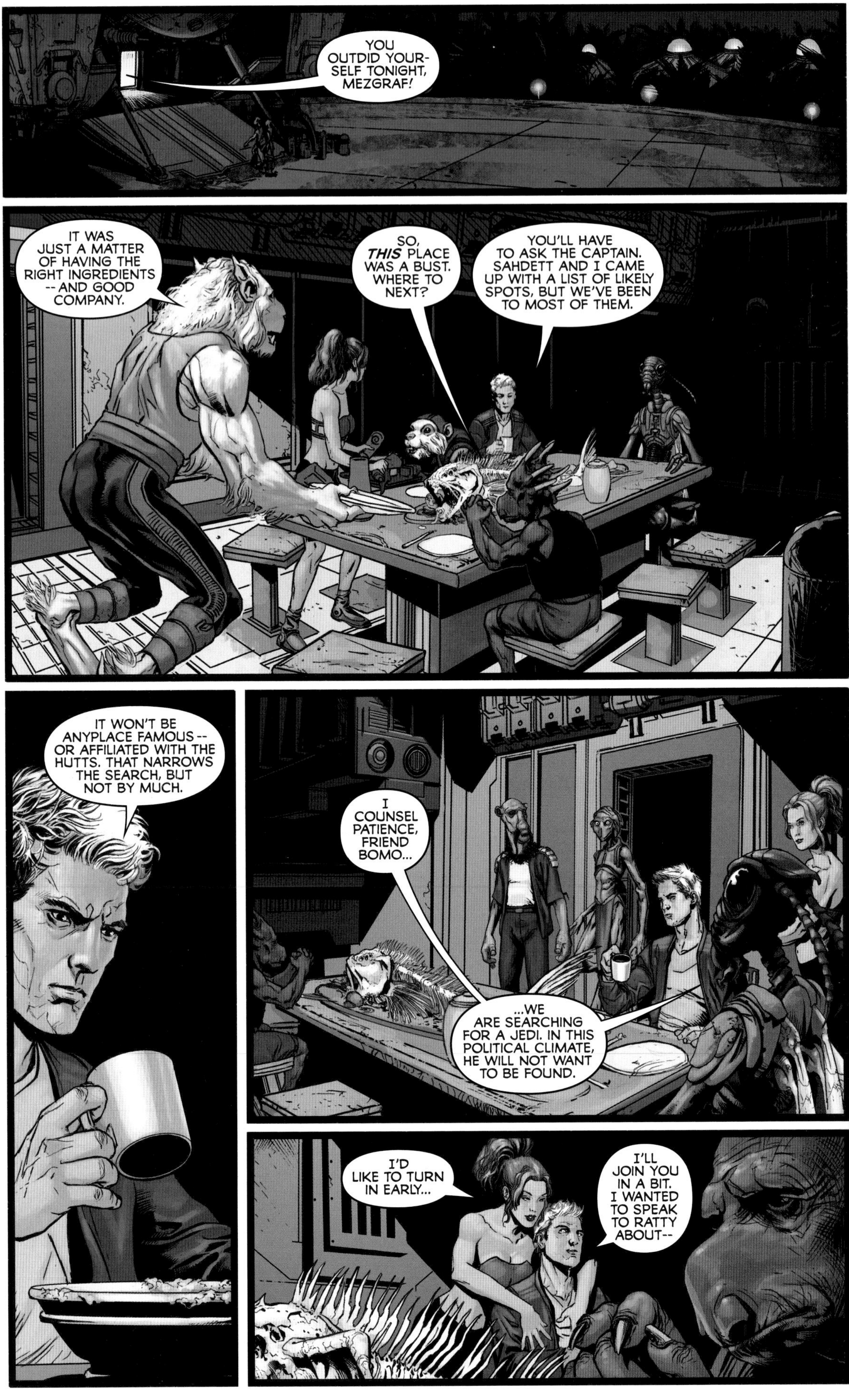
YOU OUTDID YOUR-SELF TONIGHT, MEZGRAF!
IT WAS JUST A MATTER OF HAVING THE RIGHT INGREDIENTS --AND GOOD COMPANY.
SO, *THIS* PLACE WAS A BUST. WHERE TO NEXT?
YOU'LL HAVE TO ASK THE CAPTAIN. SAHDETT AND I CAME UP WITH A LIST OF LIKELY SPOTS, BUT WE'VE BEEN TO MOST OF THEM.
IT WON'T BE ANYPLACE FAMOUS-- OR AFFILIATED WITH THE HUTTS. THAT NARROWS THE SEARCH, BUT NOT BY MUCH.
I COUNSEL PATIENCE, FRIEND BOMO...
...WE ARE SEARCHING FOR A JEDI. IN THIS POLITICAL CLIMATE, HE WILL NOT WANT TO BE FOUND.
I'D LIKE TO TURN IN EARLY...
I'LL JOIN YOU IN A BIT. I WANTED TO SPEAK TO RATTY ABOUT--

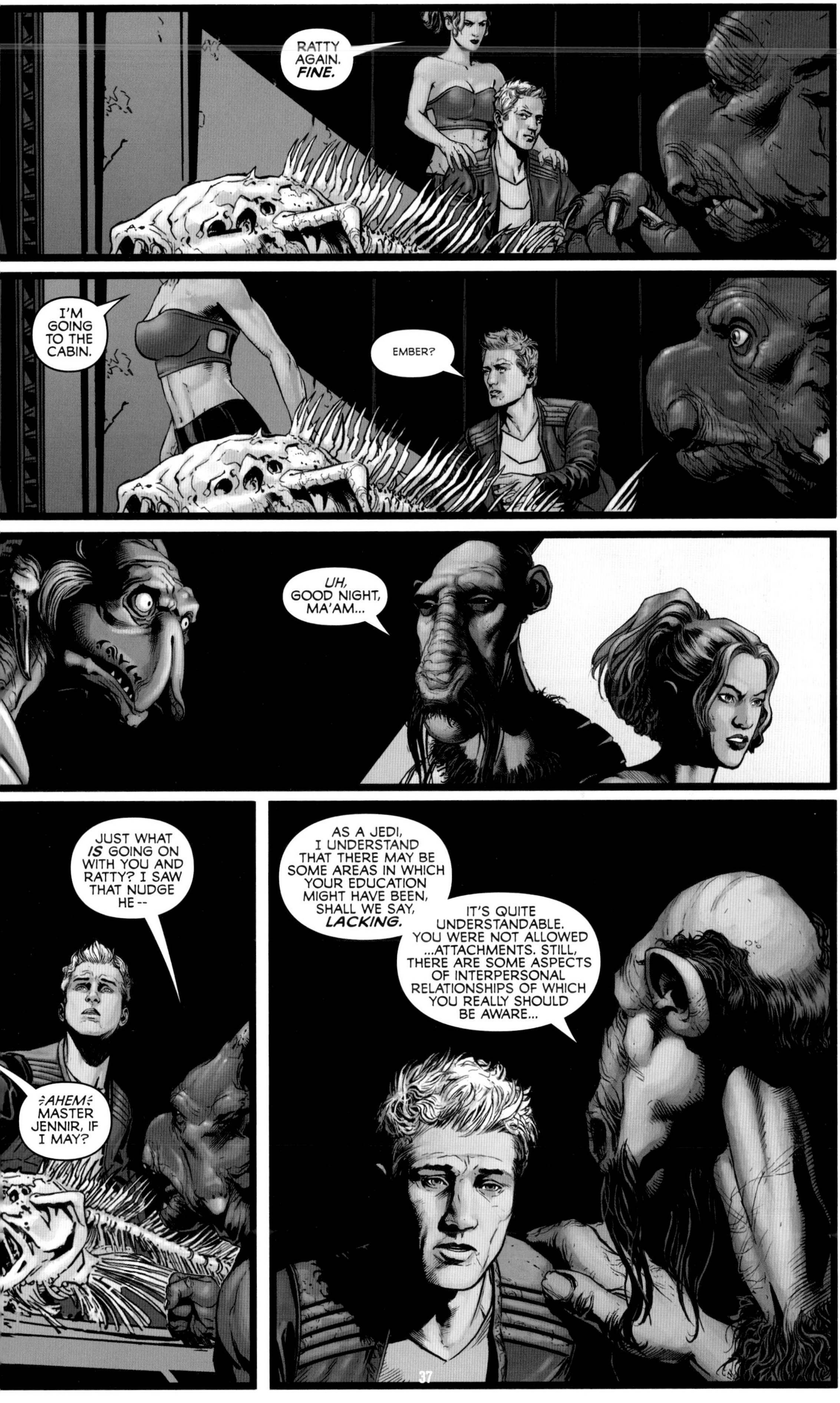
RATTY AGAIN. *FINE.*
I'M GOING TO THE CABIN.
EMBER?
UH, GOOD NIGHT, MA'AM...
JUST WHAT *IS* GOING ON WITH YOU AND RATTY? I SAW THAT NUDGE HE --
AHEM MASTER JENNIR, IF I MAY?
AS A JEDI, I UNDERSTAND THAT THERE MAY BE SOME AREAS IN WHICH YOUR EDUCATION MIGHT HAVE BEEN, SHALL WE SAY, *LACKING.*
IT'S QUITE UNDERSTANDABLE. YOU WERE NOT ALLOWED ...ATTACHMENTS. STILL, THERE ARE SOME ASPECTS OF INTERPERSONAL RELATIONSHIPS OF WHICH YOU REALLY SHOULD BE AWARE...

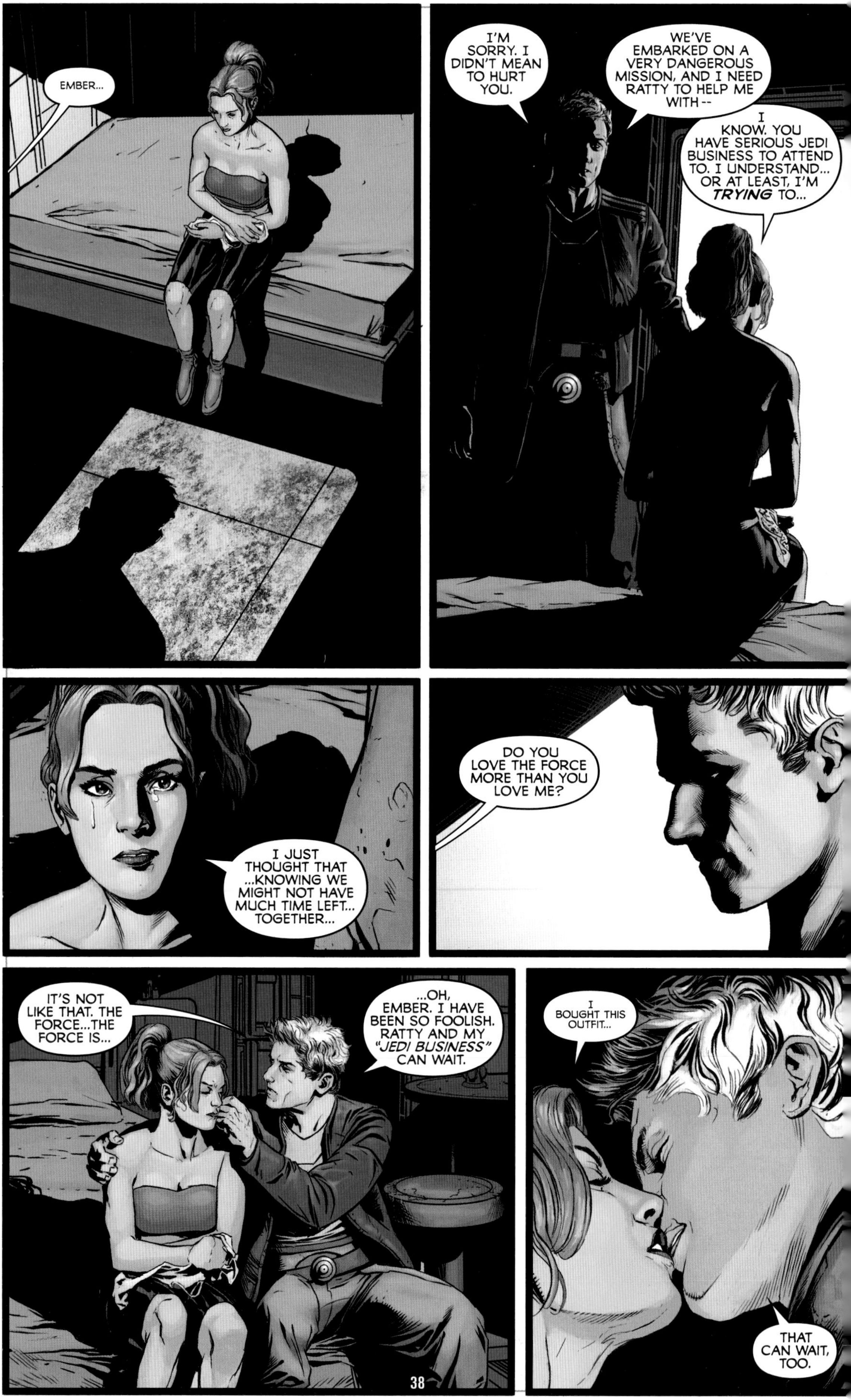
EMBER...
I'M SORRY. I DIDN'T MEAN TO HURT YOU.
WE'VE EMBARKED ON A VERY DANGEROUS MISSION, AND I NEED RATTY TO HELP ME WITH --
I KNOW. YOU HAVE SERIOUS JEDI BUSINESS TO ATTEND TO. I UNDERSTAND... OR AT LEAST, I'M *TRYING* TO...
I JUST THOUGHT THAT ...KNOWING WE MIGHT NOT HAVE MUCH TIME LEFT... TOGETHER...
DO YOU LOVE THE FORCE MORE THAN YOU LOVE ME?
IT'S NOT LIKE THAT. THE FORCE...THE FORCE IS...
...OH, EMBER. I HAVE BEEN SO FOOLISH. RATTY AND MY *"JEDI BUSINESS"* CAN WAIT.
I BOUGHT THIS OUTFIT...
THAT CAN WAIT, TOO.

WHAT'S GOING ON? NO CUFFS ON ME? NO GUN IN YOUR HAND?

TRYING SOMETHING NEW. I CAME UP WITH IT AFTER YOUR LAST ATTEMPT TO ESCAPE. ALL OF THE DOORS ARE VOICE CODED AND DEAD-LOCKED.

YOU COULD KILL ME, BUT THEN YOU'D BE LOCKED IN HERE ALONE...WITH *HIM*...

VADER.

I DON'T KNOW WHY YOU ALWAYS HAVE TO ANTAGONIZE HIM -- WHY YOU *INSIST* ON TREATING THIS LIKE A PRISON SENTENCE. YOU SHOULD FEEL HONORED.

"HONORED"?!

CLEARLY VADER SAW *SOMETHING* IN YOU WORTH PRESERVING -- OTHERWISE YOU'D STILL BE ON PRINE. AS ASHES.

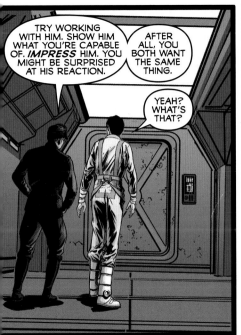

TRY WORKING WITH HIM. SHOW HIM WHAT YOU'RE CAPABLE OF. *IMPRESS* HIM. YOU MIGHT BE SURPRISED AT HIS REACTION.

AFTER ALL, YOU BOTH WANT THE SAME THING.

YEAH? WHAT'S THAT?

DASS JENNIR'S HEAD.

FORGET IT! I'M NOT SHARING MY BOUNTY!

DON'T WORRY. HE DOESN'T WANT THE BOUNTY -- JUST YOUR HELP.

THAT'S WHY HE HAD *THIS* BROUGHT HERE.

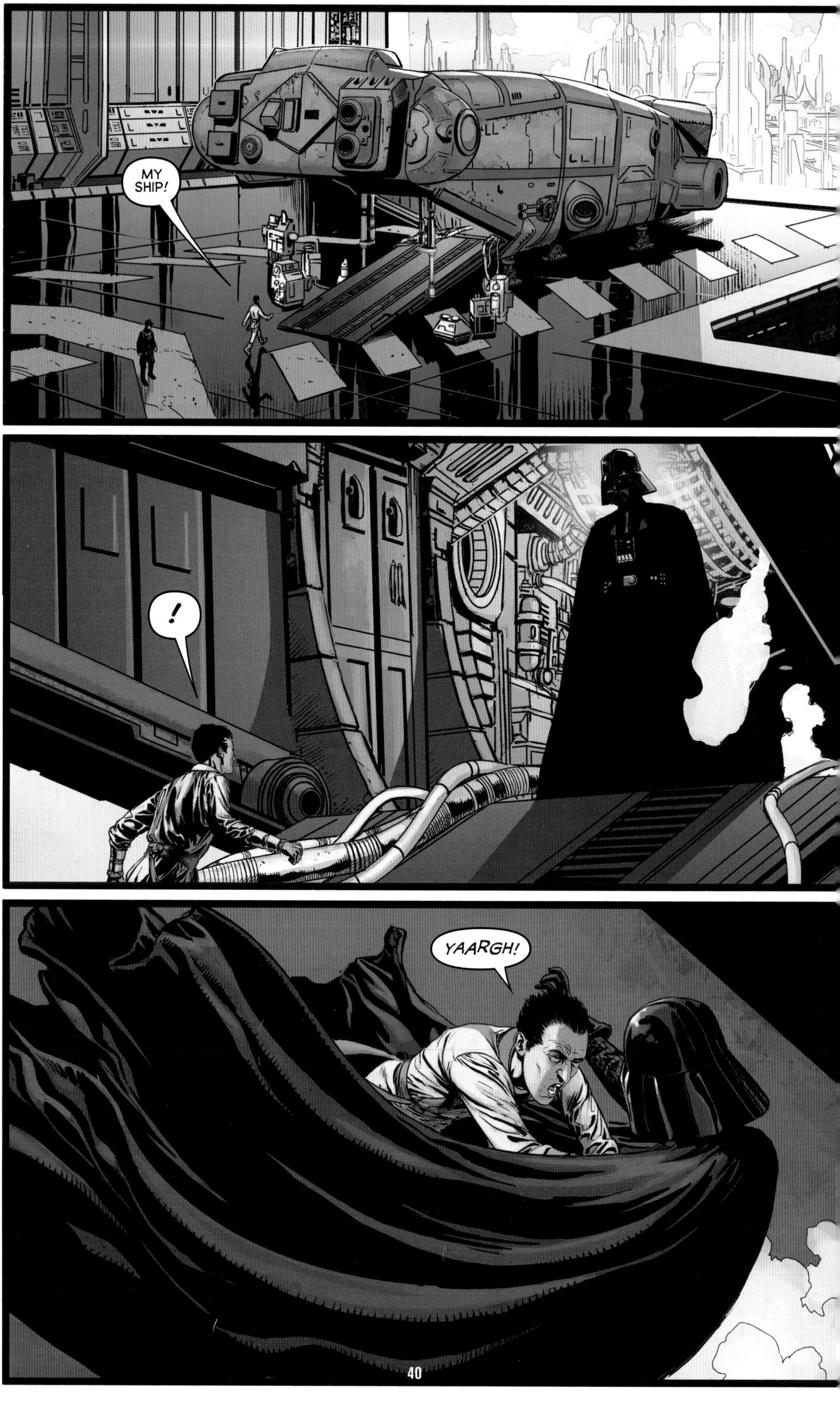
MY SHIP!
!
YAARGH!

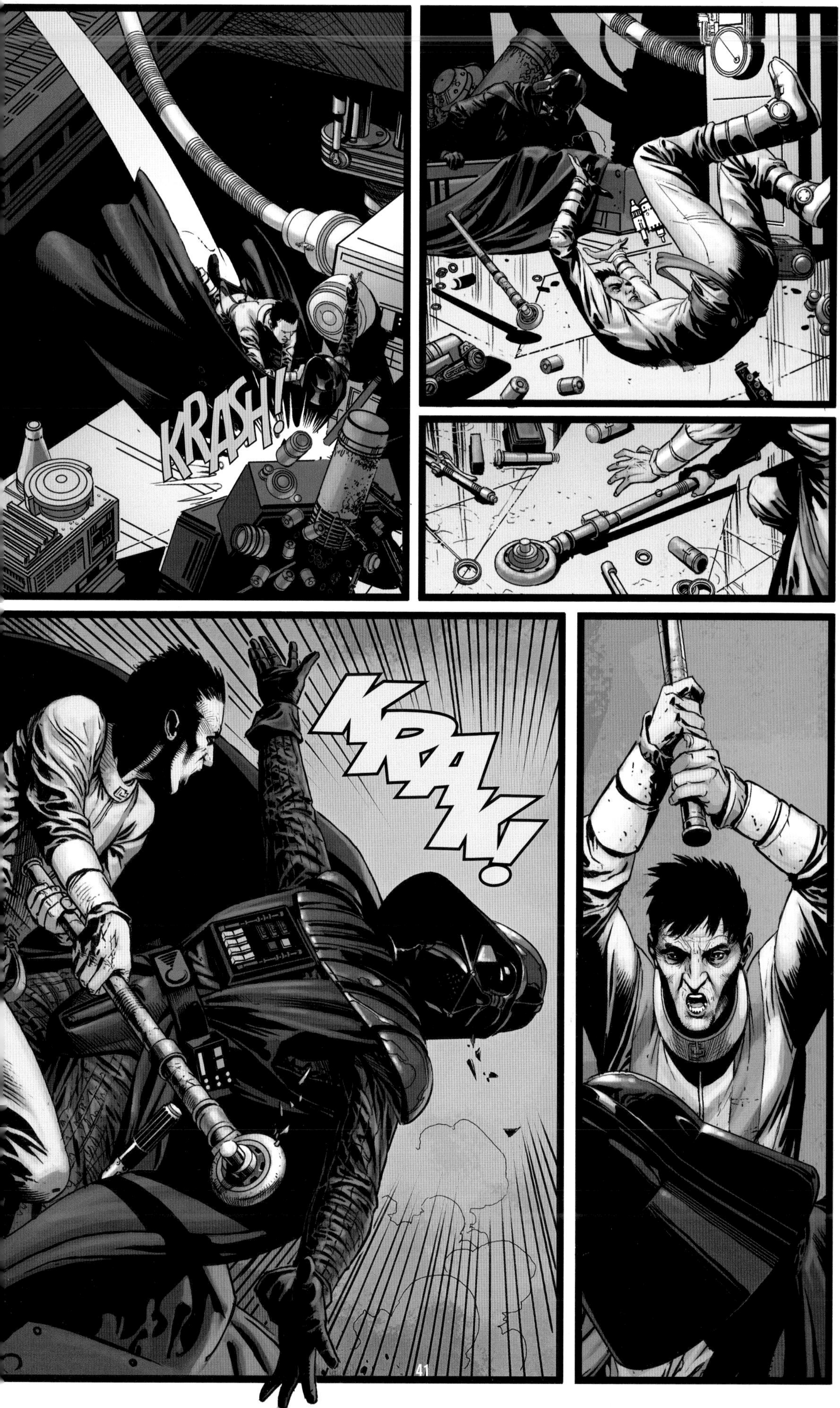
KRASH!
KRAK!

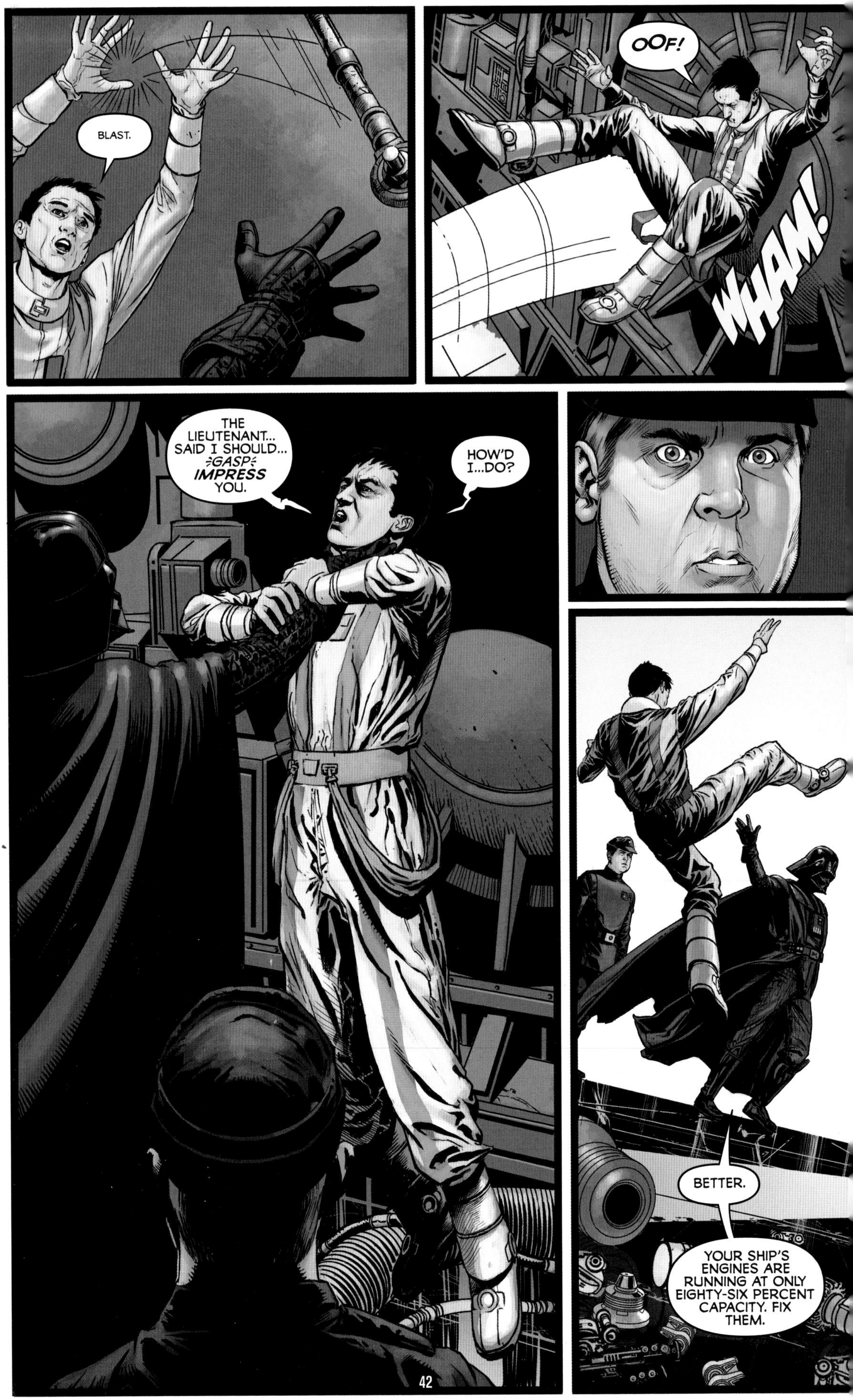

BLAST.
OOF!
WHAM!
THE LIEUTENANT... SAID I SHOULD... ⁼GASP⁼ IMPRESS YOU.
HOW'D I...DO?
BETTER.
YOUR SHIP'S ENGINES ARE RUNNING AT ONLY EIGHTY-SIX PERCENT CAPACITY. FIX THEM.

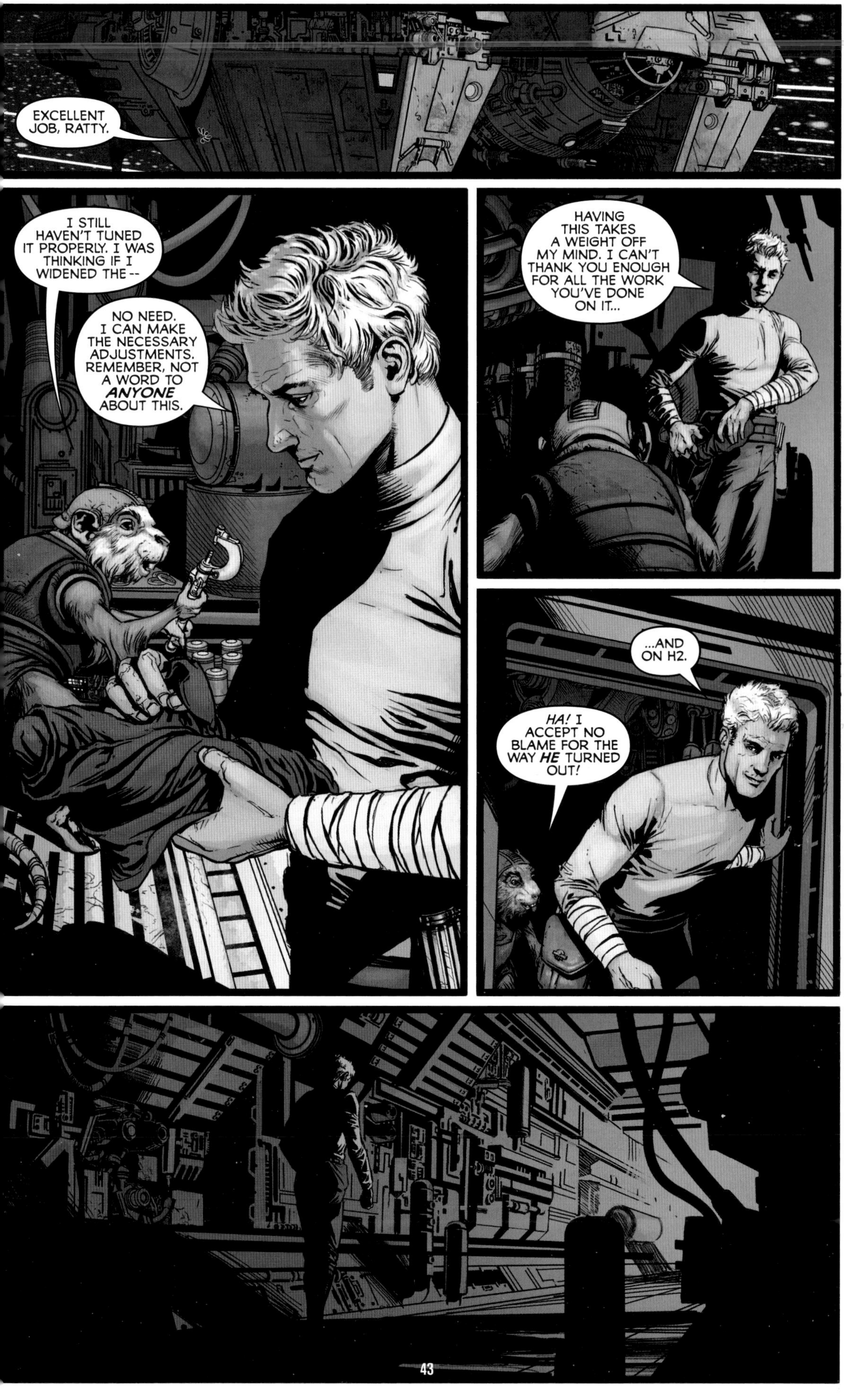
EXCELLENT JOB, RATTY.
I STILL HAVEN'T TUNED IT PROPERLY. I WAS THINKING IF I WIDENED THE--
NO NEED. I CAN MAKE THE NECESSARY ADJUSTMENTS. REMEMBER, NOT A WORD TO ANYONE ABOUT THIS.
HAVING THIS TAKES A WEIGHT OFF MY MIND. I CAN'T THANK YOU ENOUGH FOR ALL THE WORK YOU'VE DONE ON IT...
...AND ON H2.
HA! I ACCEPT NO BLAME FOR THE WAY HE TURNED OUT!

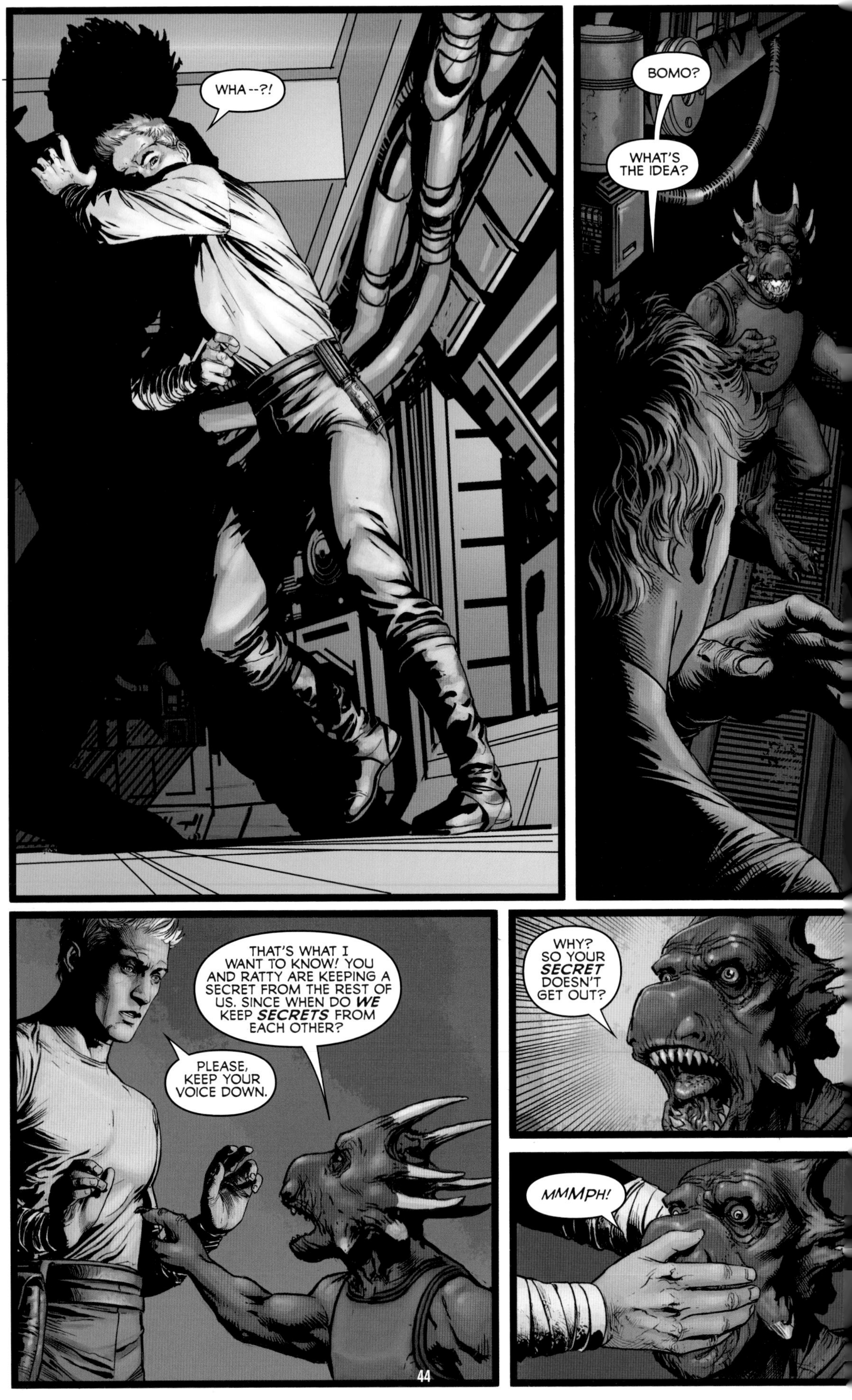
WHA--?!
BOMO?
WHAT'S THE IDEA?
THAT'S WHAT I WANT TO KNOW! YOU AND RATTY ARE KEEPING A SECRET FROM THE REST OF US. SINCE WHEN DO *WE* KEEP *SECRETS* FROM EACH OTHER?
PLEASE, KEEP YOUR VOICE DOWN.
WHY? SO YOUR *SECRET* DOESN'T GET OUT?
MMMPH!

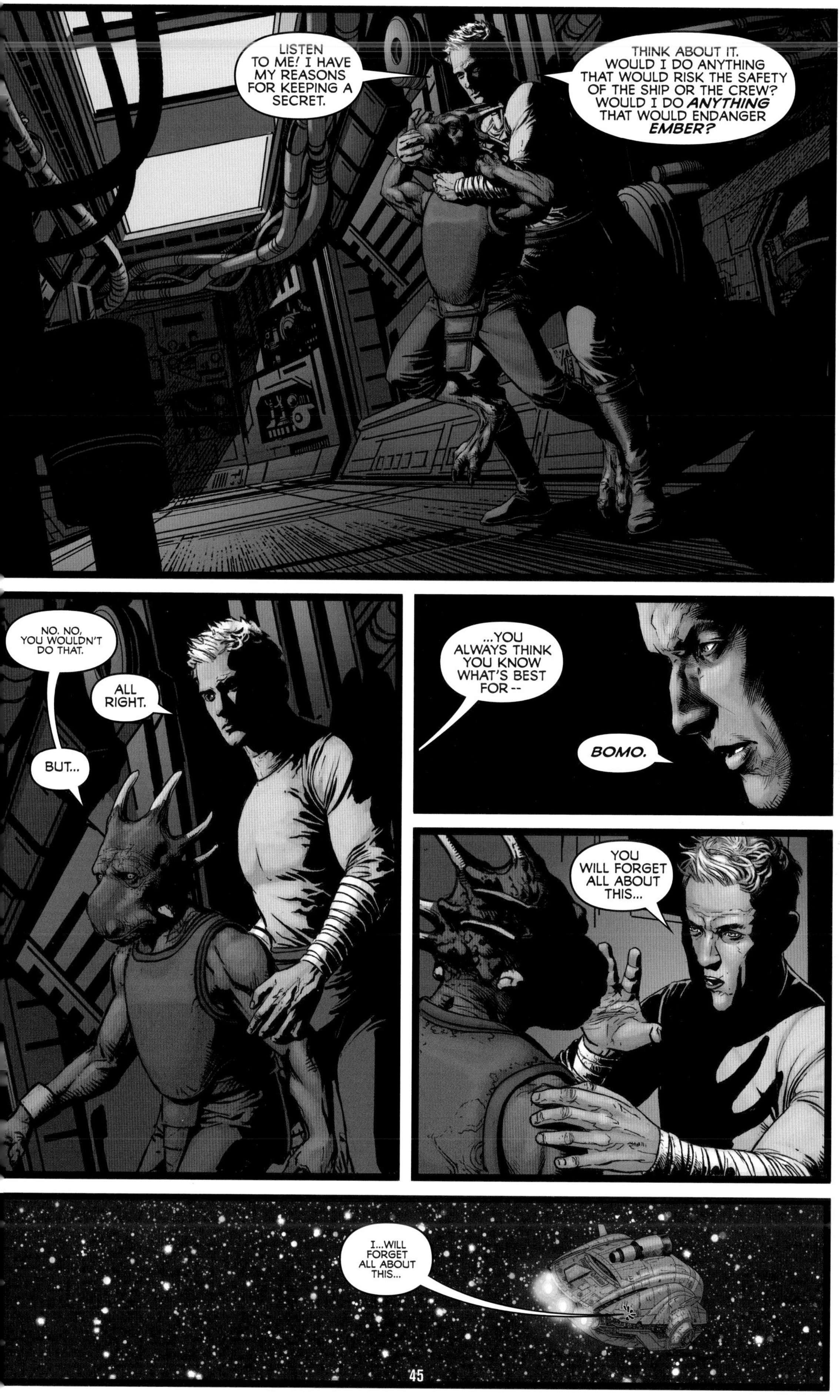

LISTEN TO ME! I HAVE MY REASONS FOR KEEPING A SECRET.
THINK ABOUT IT. WOULD I DO ANYTHING THAT WOULD RISK THE SAFETY OF THE SHIP OR THE CREW? WOULD I DO *ANYTHING* THAT WOULD ENDANGER *EMBER?*
NO. NO, YOU WOULDN'T DO THAT.
ALL RIGHT.
BUT...
...YOU ALWAYS THINK YOU KNOW WHAT'S BEST FOR --
BOMO.
YOU WILL FORGET ALL ABOUT THIS...
I...WILL FORGET ALL ABOUT THIS...

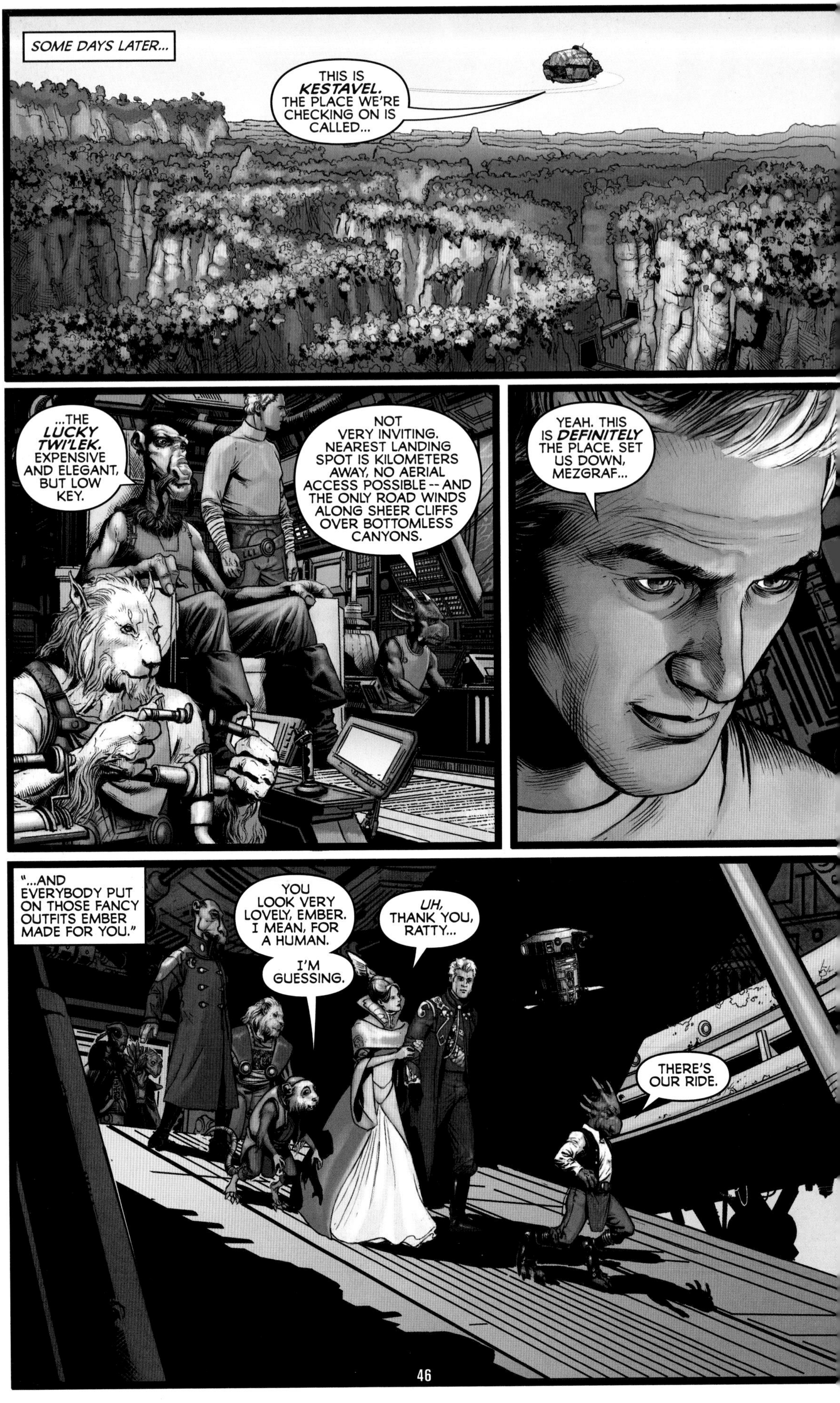
SOME DAYS LATER...
THIS IS KESTAVEL. THE PLACE WE'RE CHECKING ON IS CALLED...
...THE LUCKY TWI'LEK. EXPENSIVE AND ELEGANT, BUT LOW KEY.
NOT VERY INVITING. NEAREST LANDING SPOT IS KILOMETERS AWAY, NO AERIAL ACCESS POSSIBLE -- AND THE ONLY ROAD WINDS ALONG SHEER CLIFFS OVER BOTTOMLESS CANYONS.
YEAH. THIS IS DEFINITELY THE PLACE. SET US DOWN, MEZGRAF...
"...AND EVERYBODY PUT ON THOSE FANCY OUTFITS EMBER MADE FOR YOU."
YOU LOOK VERY LOVELY, EMBER. I MEAN, FOR A HUMAN.
I'M GUESSING.
UH, THANK YOU, RATTY...
THERE'S OUR RIDE.

WELCOME, GENTLE BEINGS. IT IS BUT A SHORT, SCENIC RIDE TO THE LUCKY TWI'LEK...

...WHERE ALL YOUR DREAMS MAY COME TRUE.

D-DRIVER, HOW F-FAR DOWN IS IT?

TO THE BOTTOM OF THE RAVINE? MANY KILOMETERS IN MOST PLACES...

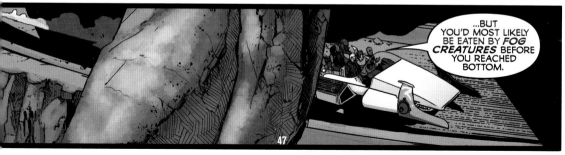

...BUT YOU'D MOST LIKELY BE EATEN BY *FOG CREATURES* BEFORE YOU REACHED BOTTOM.

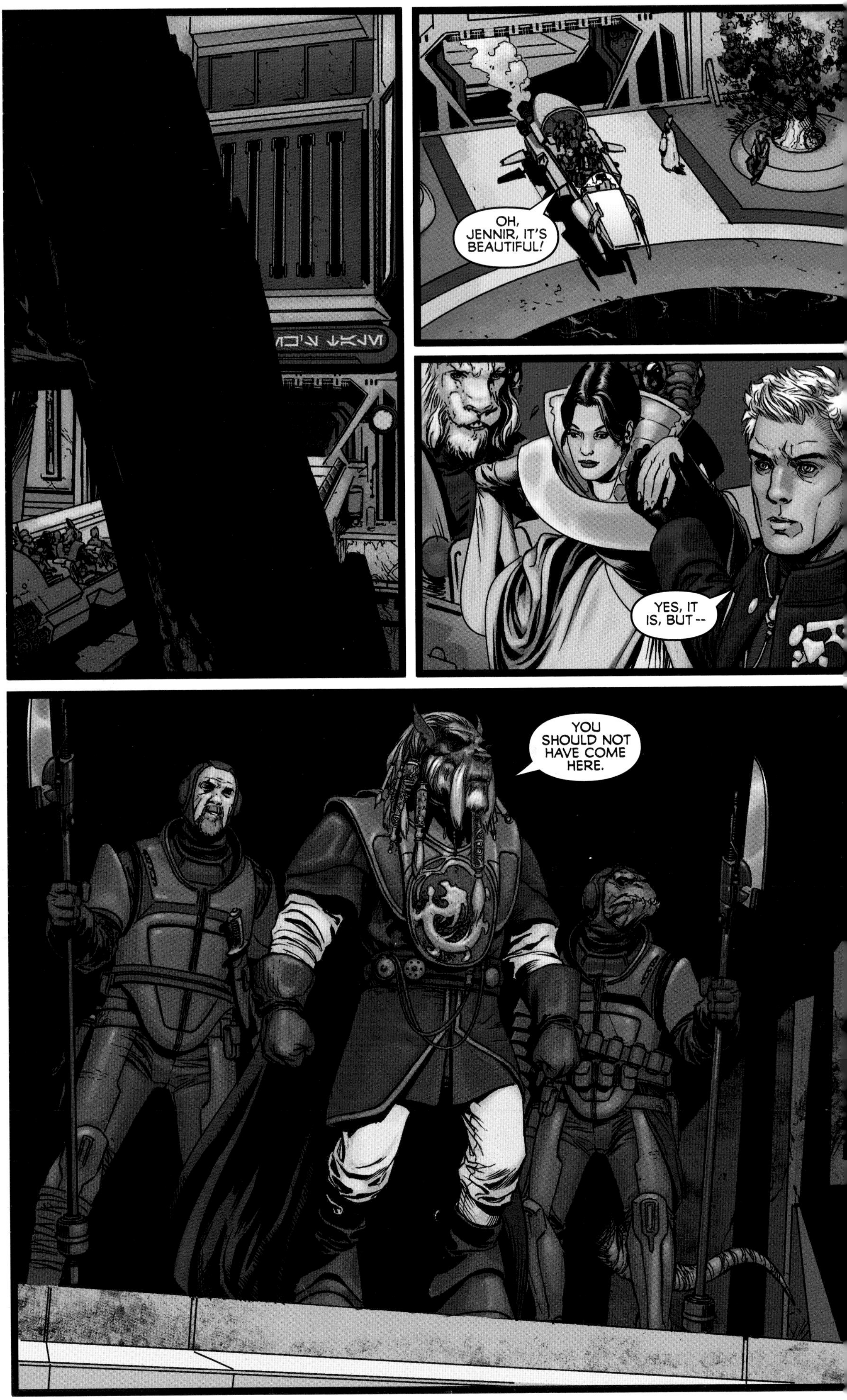
OH, JENNIR, IT'S BEAUTIFUL!
YES, IT IS, BUT --
YOU SHOULD NOT HAVE COME HERE.

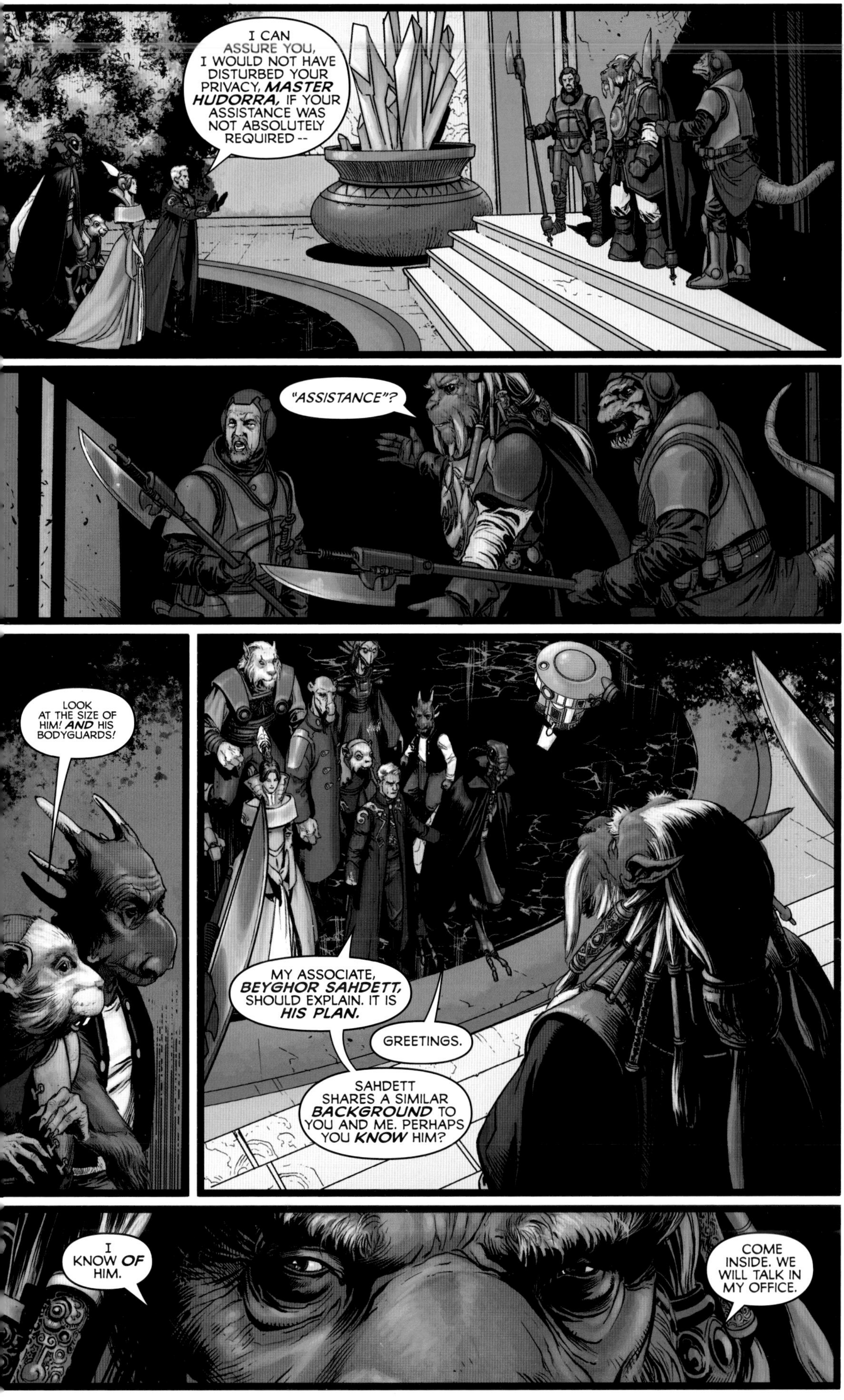
I CAN ASSURE YOU, I WOULD NOT HAVE DISTURBED YOUR PRIVACY, MASTER HUDORRA, IF YOUR ASSISTANCE WAS NOT ABSOLUTELY REQUIRED --
"ASSISTANCE"?
LOOK AT THE SIZE OF HIM! AND HIS BODYGUARDS!
MY ASSOCIATE, BEYGHOR SAHDETT, SHOULD EXPLAIN. IT IS HIS PLAN.
GREETINGS.
SAHDETT SHARES A SIMILAR BACKGROUND TO YOU AND ME. PERHAPS YOU KNOW HIM?
I KNOW OF HIM.
COME INSIDE. WE WILL TALK IN MY OFFICE.

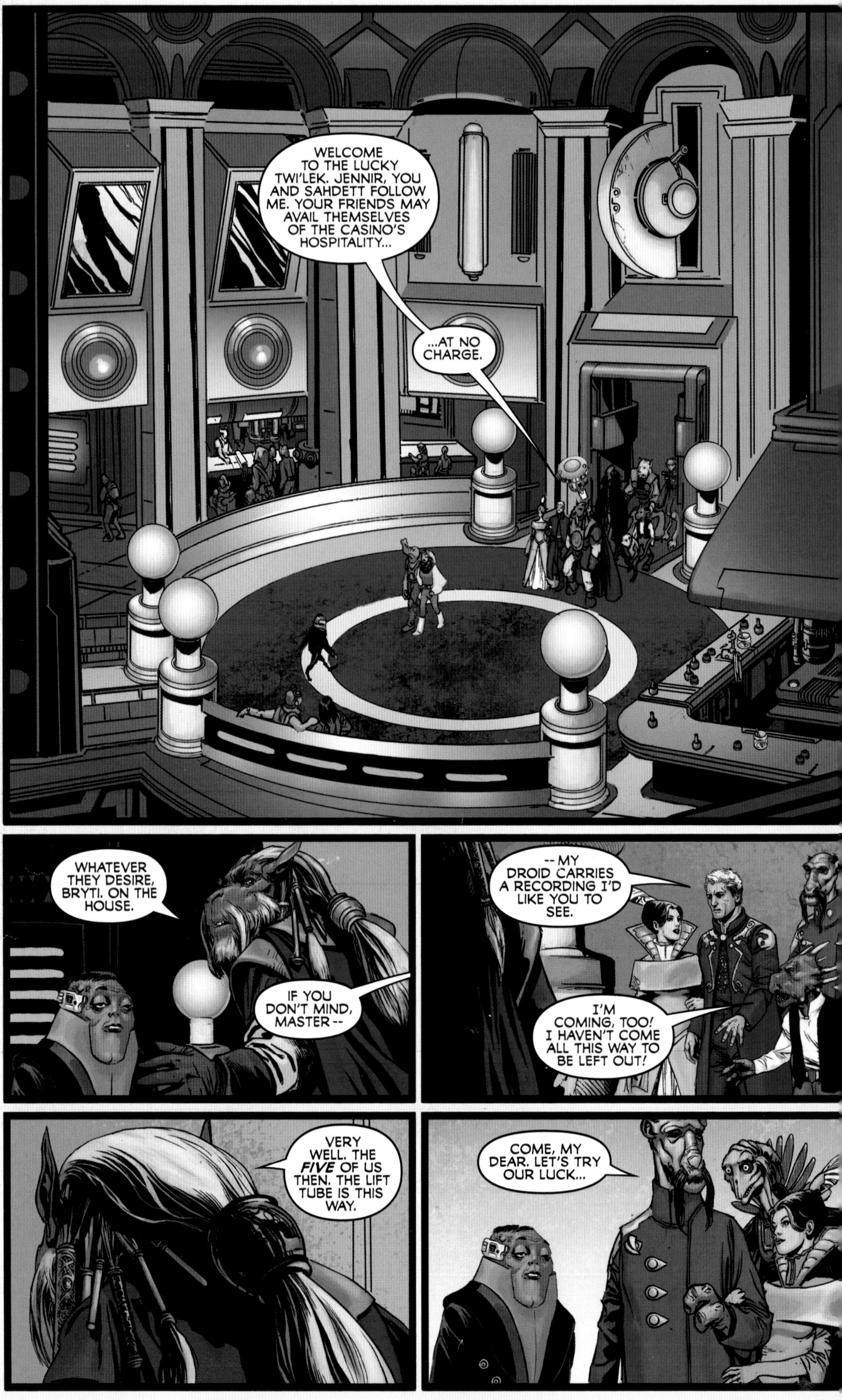

WELCOME TO THE LUCKY TWI'LEK. JENNIR, YOU AND SAHDETT FOLLOW ME. YOUR FRIENDS MAY AVAIL THEMSELVES OF THE CASINO'S HOSPITALITY...
...AT NO CHARGE.
WHATEVER THEY DESIRE, BRYTI. ON THE HOUSE.
IF YOU DON'T MIND, MASTER --
-- MY DROID CARRIES A RECORDING I'D LIKE YOU TO SEE.
I'M COMING, TOO! I HAVEN'T COME ALL THIS WAY TO BE LEFT OUT!
VERY WELL. THE *FIVE* OF US THEN. THE LIFT TUBE IS THIS WAY.
COME, MY DEAR. LET'S TRY OUR LUCK...

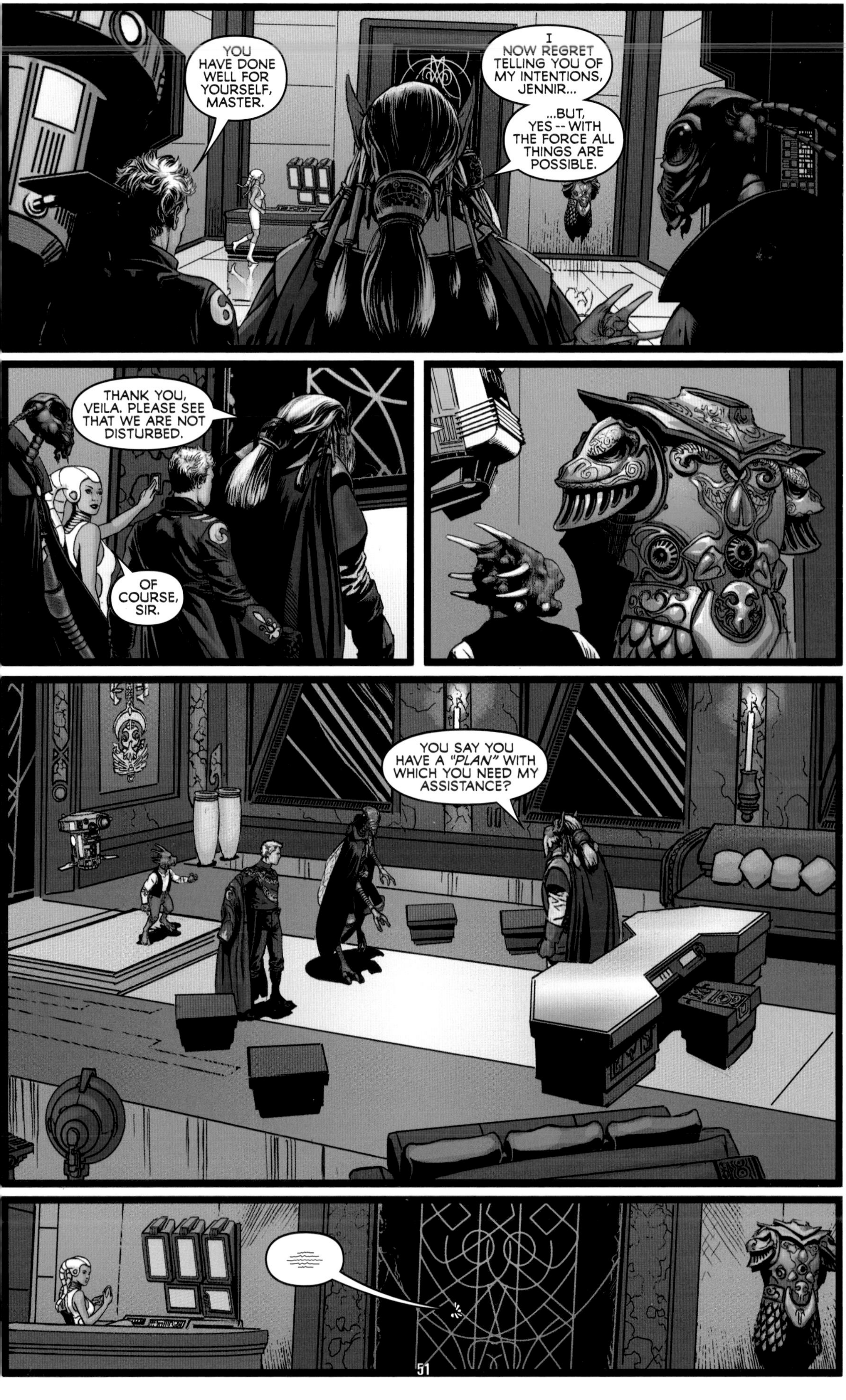
YOU HAVE DONE WELL FOR YOURSELF, MASTER.
I NOW REGRET TELLING YOU OF MY INTENTIONS, JENNIR...
...BUT, YES -- WITH THE FORCE ALL THINGS ARE POSSIBLE.
THANK YOU, VEILA. PLEASE SEE THAT WE ARE NOT DISTURBED.
OF COURSE, SIR.
YOU SAY YOU HAVE A *"PLAN"* WITH WHICH YOU NEED MY ASSISTANCE?

...A SURPRISE BY WHICH WE WILL OVERCOME THE ENEMY AND SIGNIFICANTLY WEAKEN THE EMPIRE.

YOU WOULD HAVE US SELL OUR LIVES -- BUT *DEARLY?*

YES. IF IT COMES TO THAT. THERE MAY BE NO OTHER WAY TO ACCOMPLISH OUR ENDS.

A BOLD PLAN, MASTER SAHDETT.

YOU KNOW HE'S *LYING,* DON'T YOU, JENNIR?

YES.

WHAT?!

I'VE KNOWN FOR SOME TIME. BUT I ALSO KNOW HIS REPUTATION WITH A LIGHTSABER. I KNEW I COULDN'T TAKE HIM MYSELF.

THAT'S WHY I NEEDED *YOUR* ASSISTANCE.

krik!

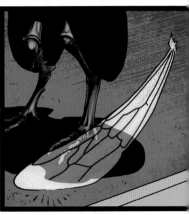

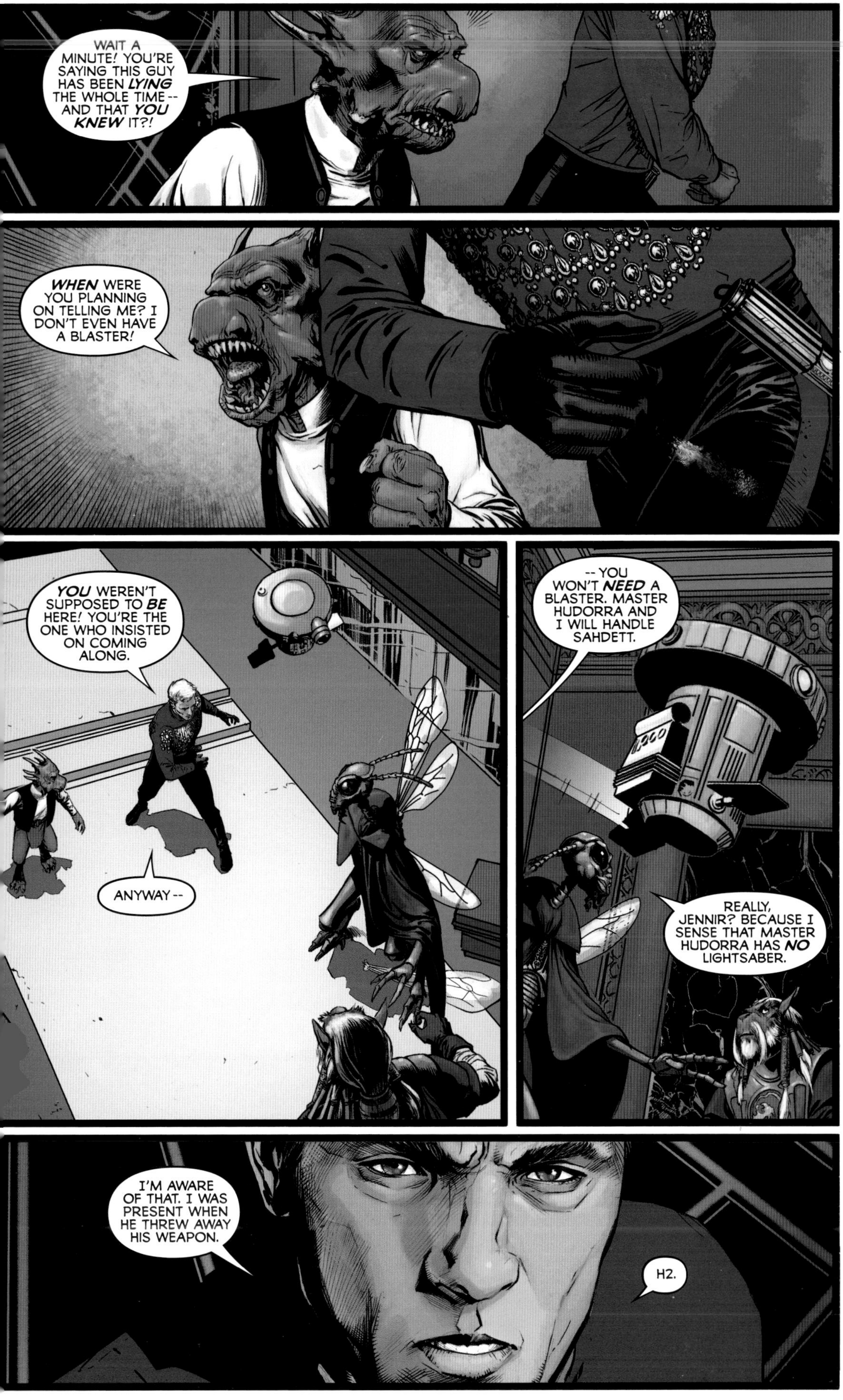
WAIT A MINUTE! YOU'RE SAYING THIS GUY HAS BEEN *LYING* THE WHOLE TIME -- AND THAT *YOU KNEW* IT?!
WHEN WERE YOU PLANNING ON TELLING ME? I DON'T EVEN HAVE A BLASTER!
YOU WEREN'T SUPPOSED TO *BE* HERE! YOU'RE THE ONE WHO INSISTED ON COMING ALONG.
ANYWAY --
-- YOU WON'T *NEED* A BLASTER. MASTER HUDORRA AND I WILL HANDLE SAHDETT.
REALLY, JENNIR? BECAUSE I SENSE THAT MASTER HUDORRA HAS *NO* LIGHTSABER.
I'M AWARE OF THAT. I WAS PRESENT WHEN HE THREW AWAY HIS WEAPON.
H2.

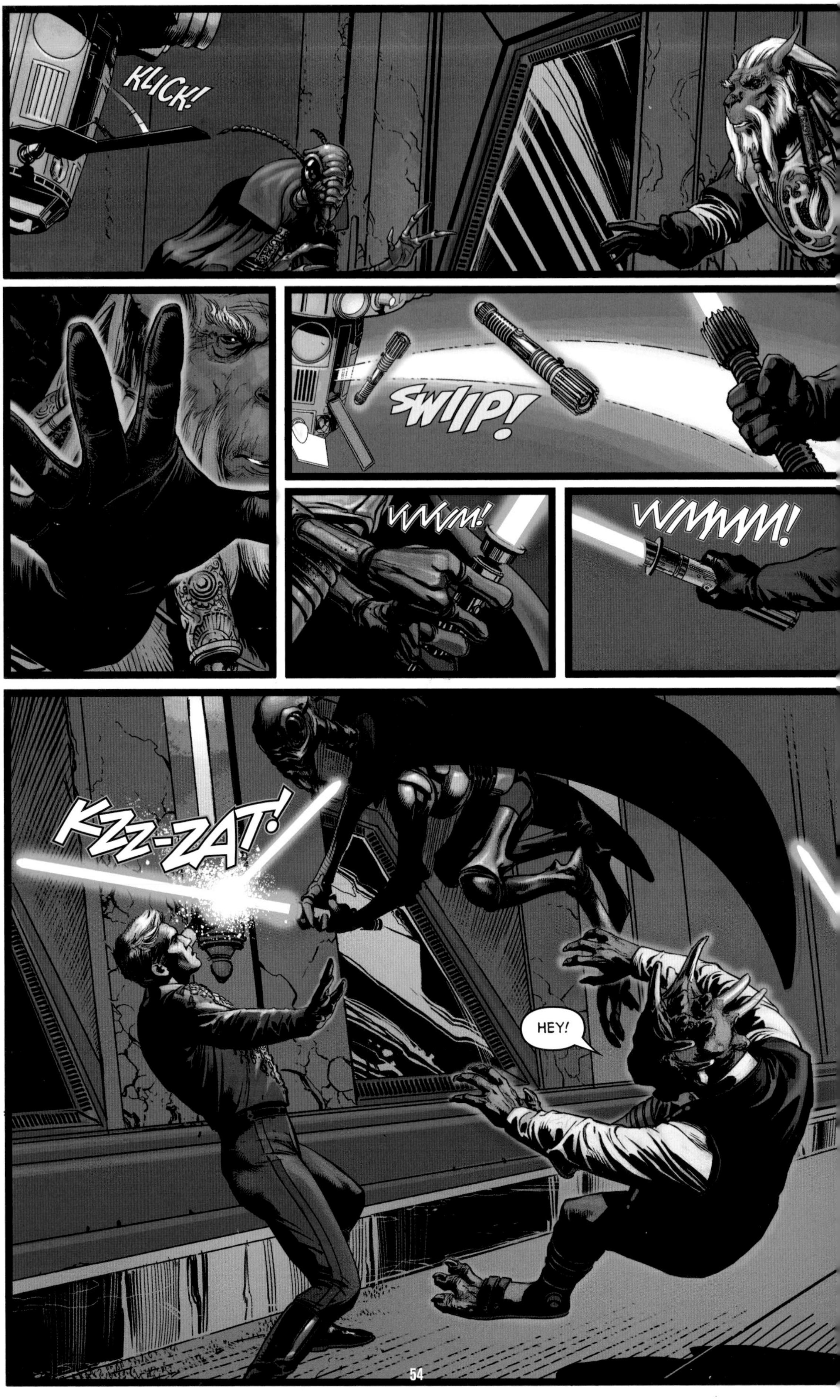
KLICK!
SWIP!
VVVVM!
VVMMM!
KZZ-ZAT!
HEY!

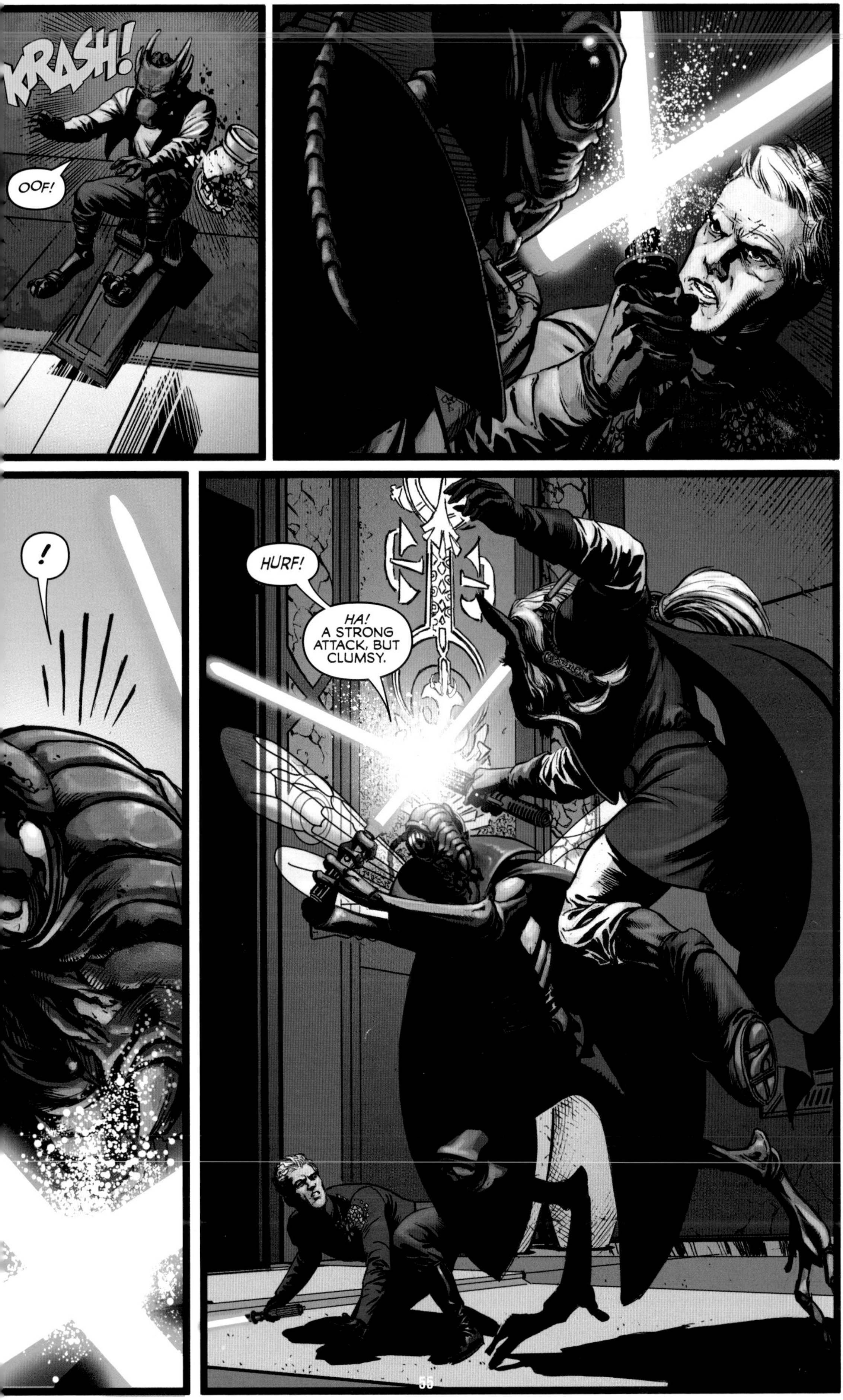
KRASH!
OOF!
!
HURF!
HA! A STRONG ATTACK, BUT CLUMSY.

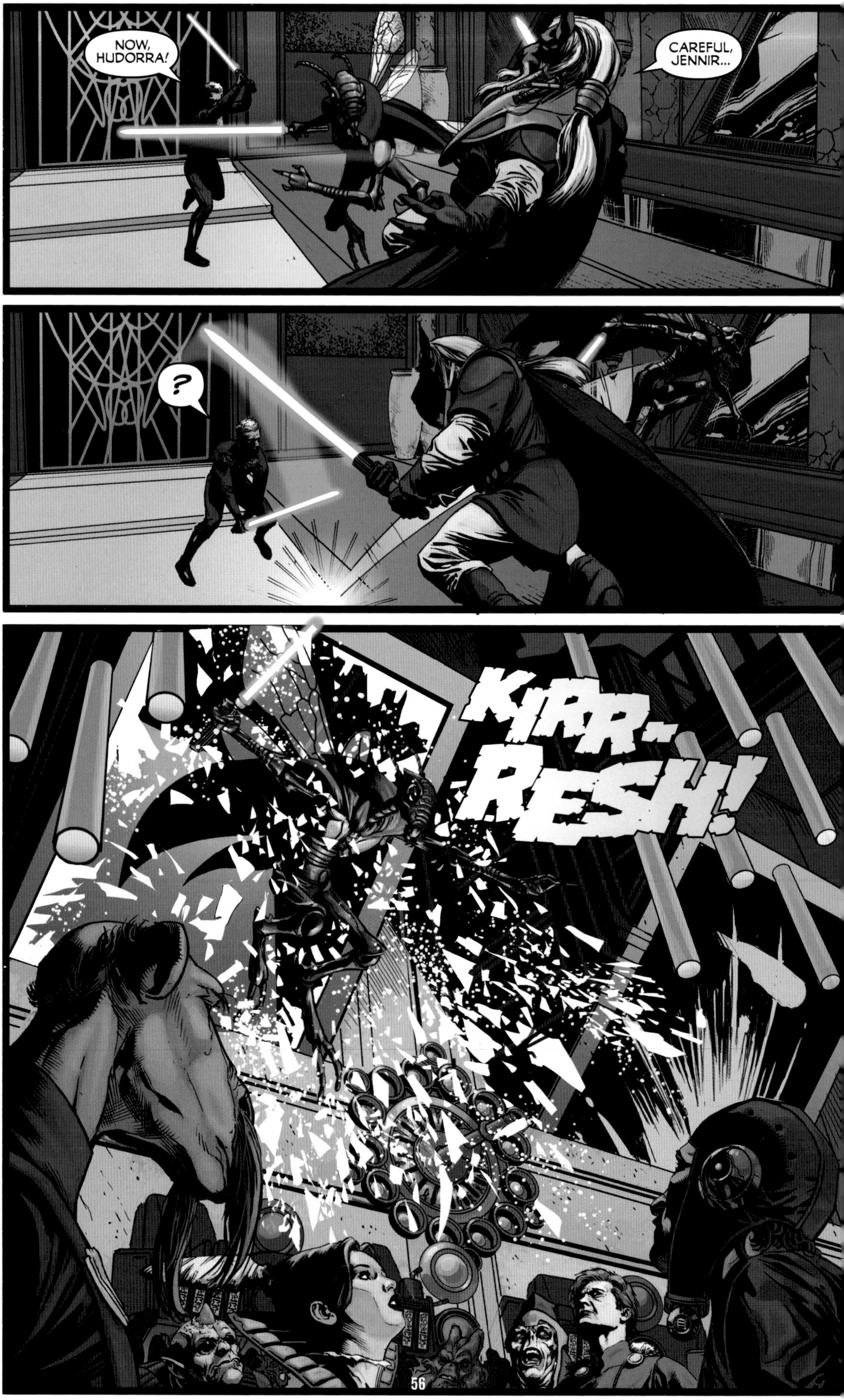
NOW, HUDORRA!
CAREFUL, JENNIR...
?
KIRR-RESH!

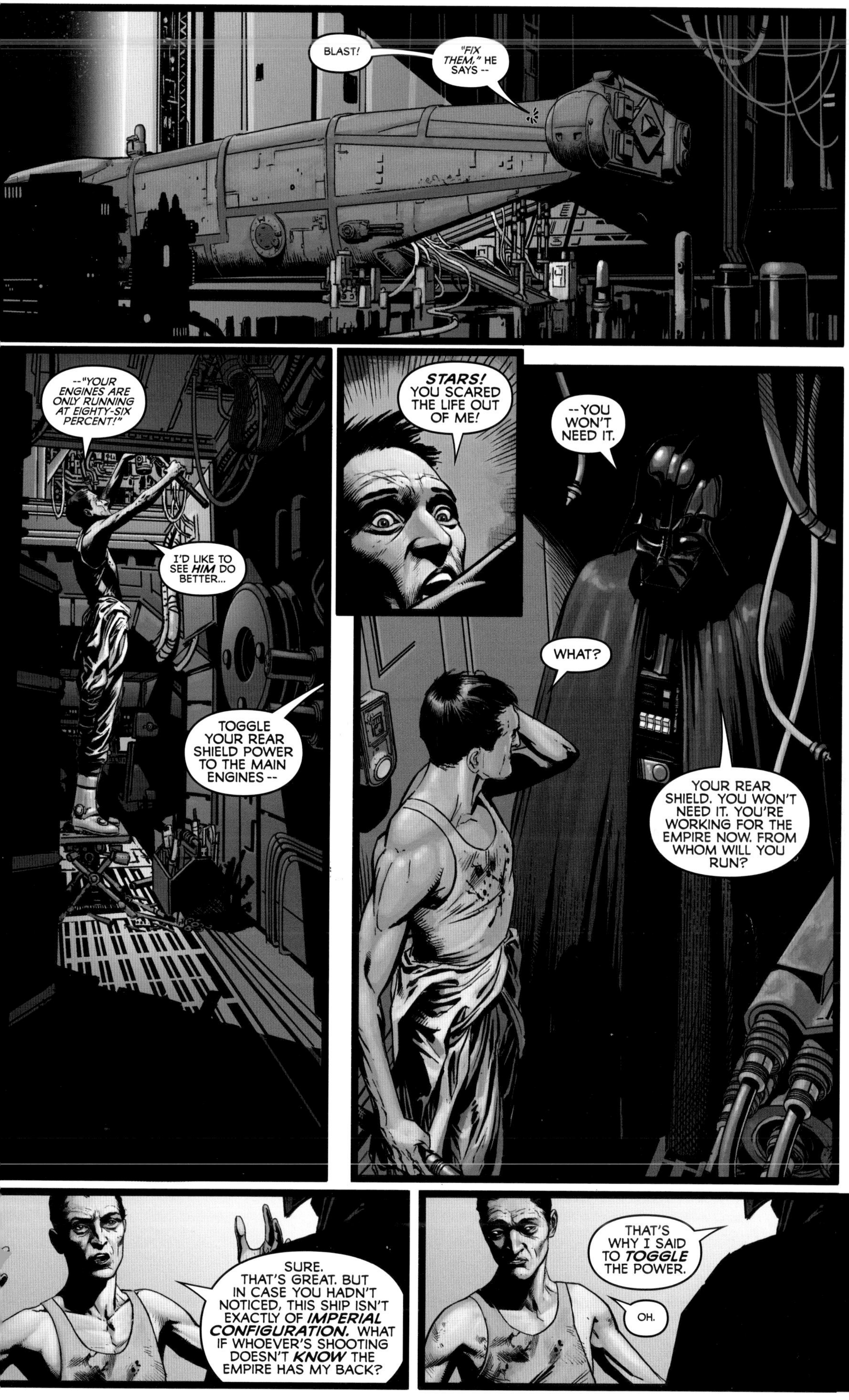
BLAST!
"FIX THEM," HE SAYS --
--"YOUR ENGINES ARE ONLY RUNNING AT EIGHTY-SIX PERCENT!"
I'D LIKE TO SEE HIM DO BETTER...
TOGGLE YOUR REAR SHIELD POWER TO THE MAIN ENGINES --
STARS! YOU SCARED THE LIFE OUT OF ME!
--YOU WON'T NEED IT.
WHAT?
YOUR REAR SHIELD. YOU WON'T NEED IT. YOU'RE WORKING FOR THE EMPIRE NOW. FROM WHOM WILL YOU RUN?
SURE. THAT'S GREAT. BUT IN CASE YOU HADN'T NOTICED, THIS SHIP ISN'T EXACTLY OF IMPERIAL CONFIGURATION. WHAT IF WHOEVER'S SHOOTING DOESN'T KNOW THE EMPIRE HAS MY BACK?
THAT'S WHY I SAID TO TOGGLE THE POWER.
OH.

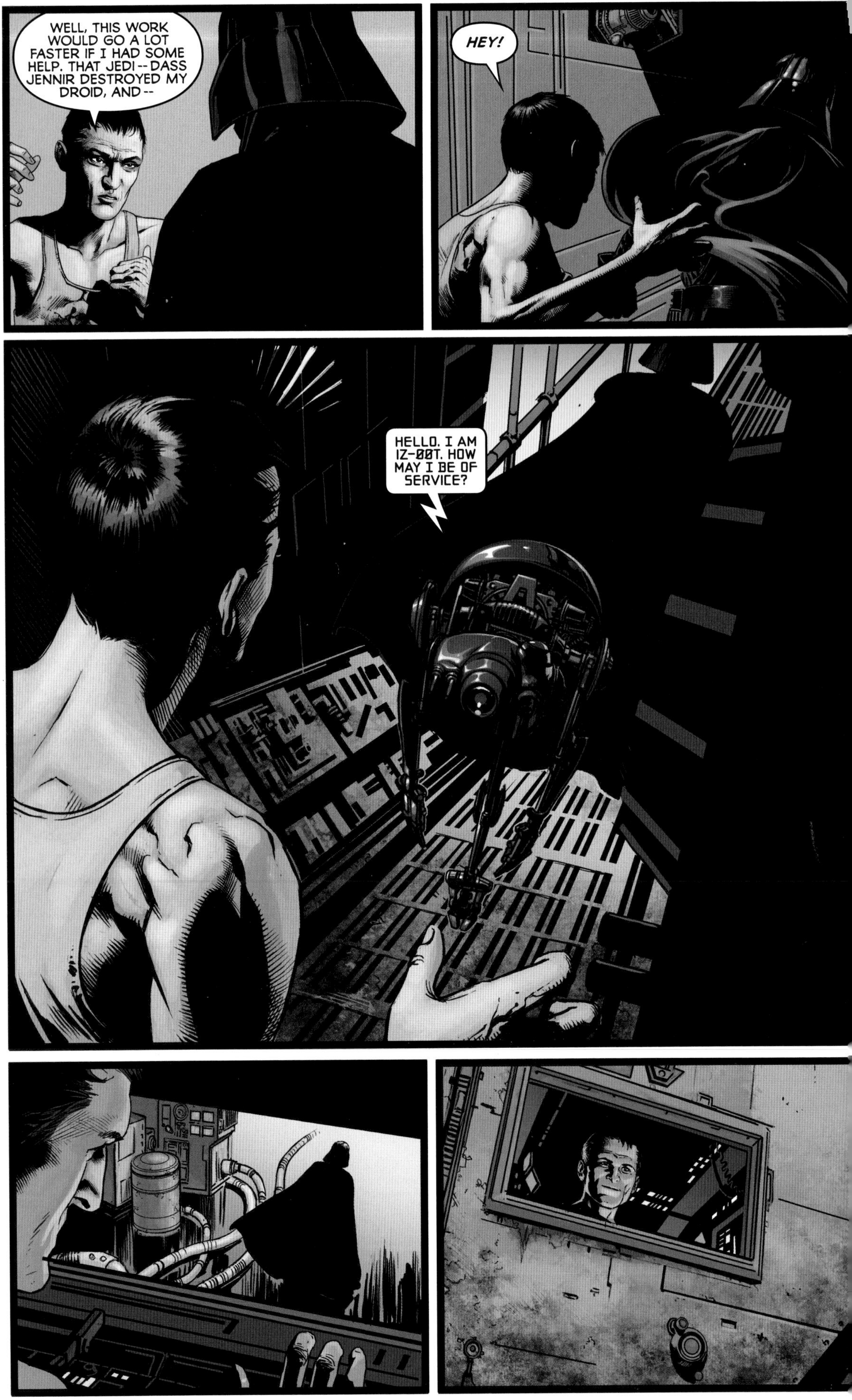
WELL, THIS WORK WOULD GO A LOT FASTER IF I HAD SOME HELP. THAT JEDI--DASS JENNIR DESTROYED MY DROID, AND--
HEY!
HELLO. I AM IZ-ØØT. HOW MAY I BE OF SERVICE?

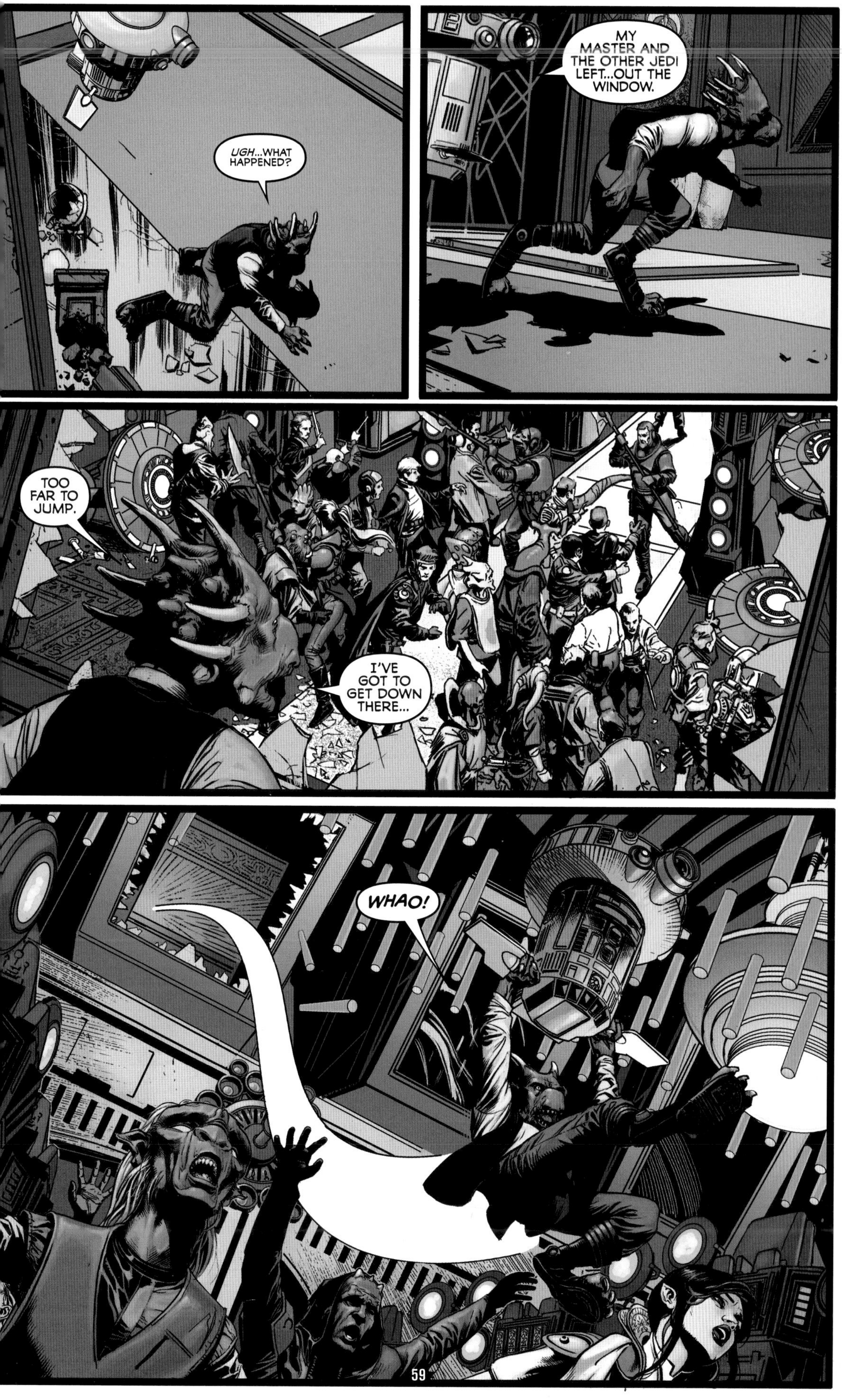
UGH...WHAT HAPPENED?
MY MASTER AND THE OTHER JEDI LEFT...OUT THE WINDOW.
TOO FAR TO JUMP.
I'VE GOT TO GET DOWN THERE...
WHAO!

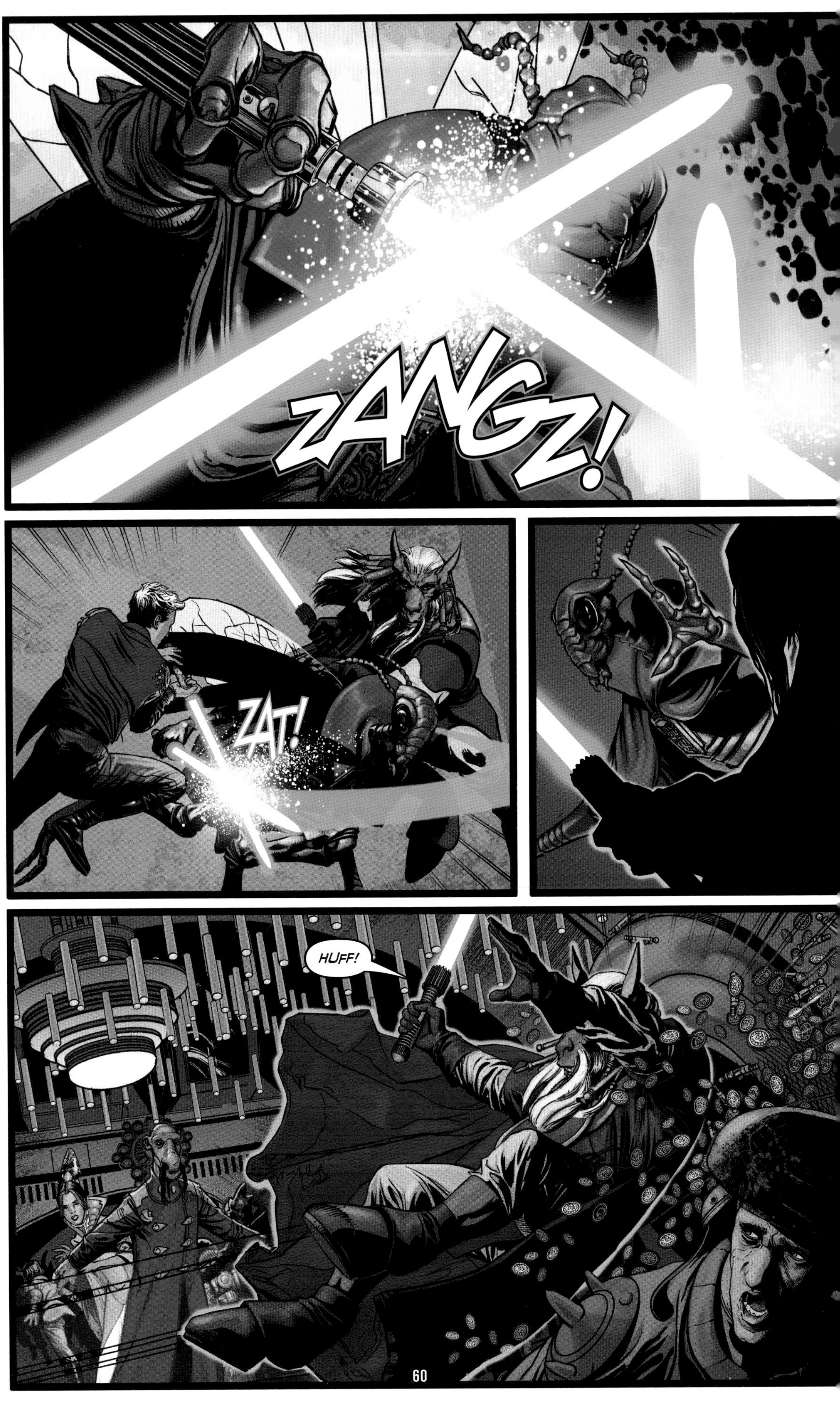
ZANGZ!
ZAT!
HUFF!

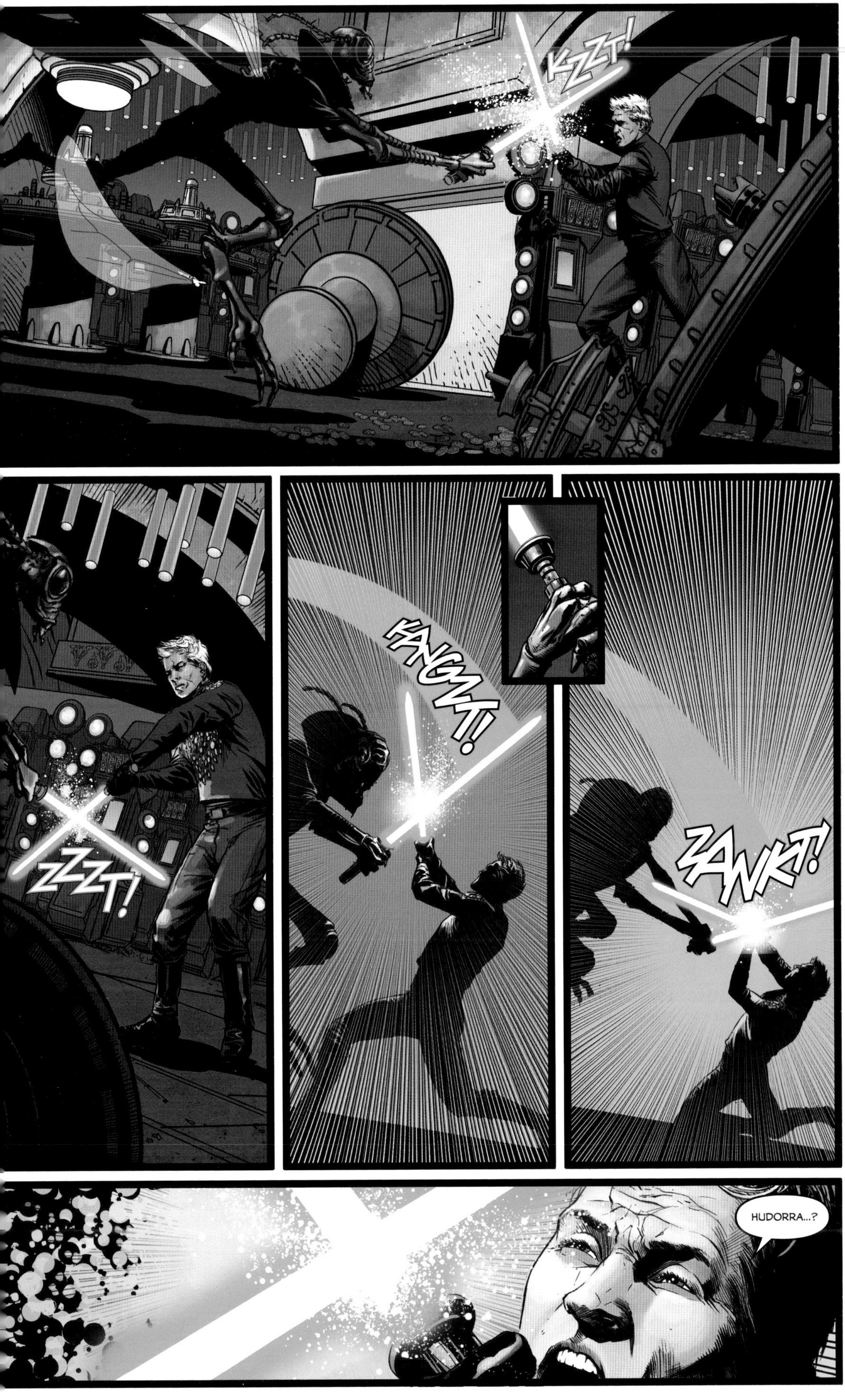

KZZZT!
ZZZZT!
KANGZAT!!
ZANKT!
HUDORRA...?

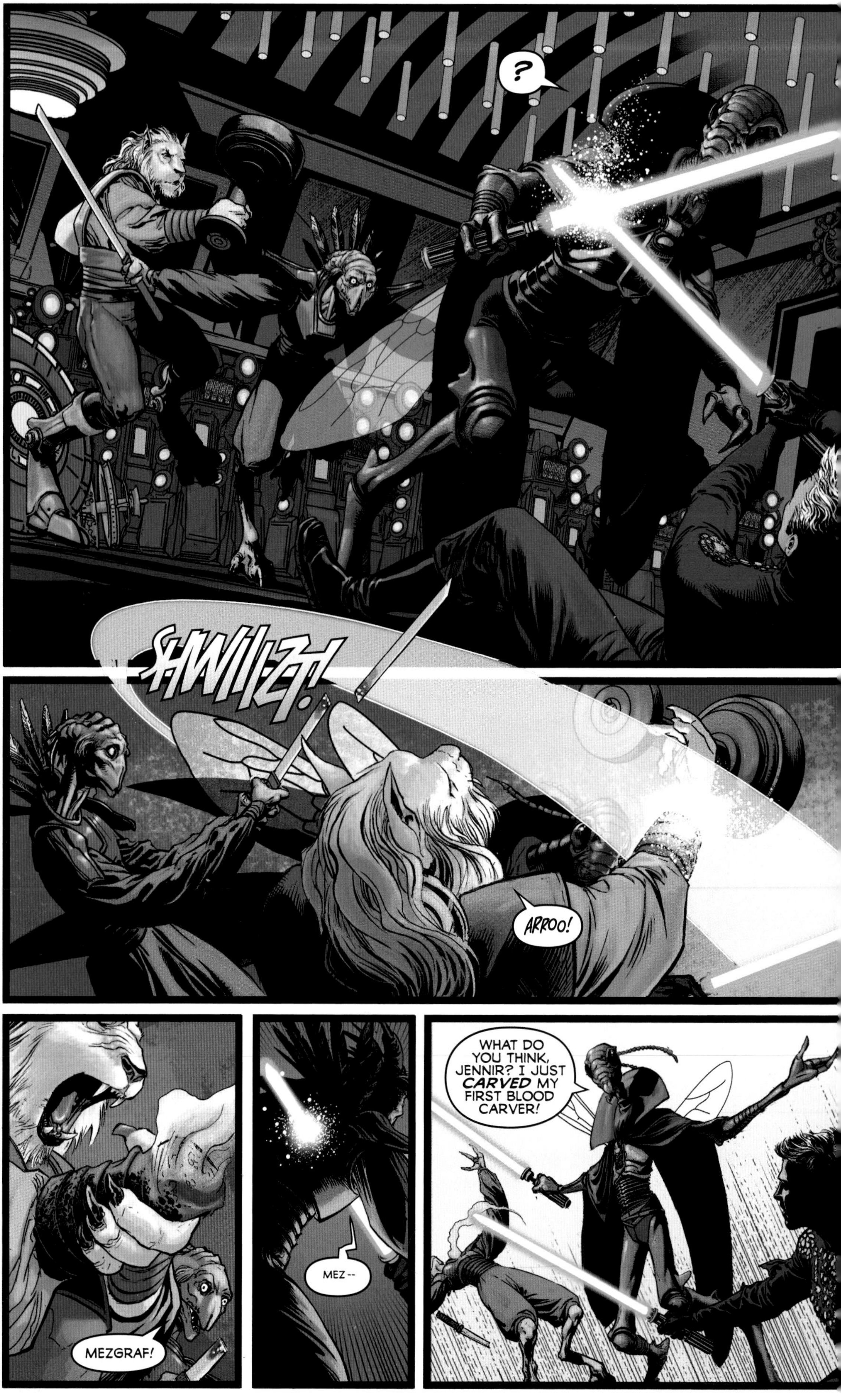

?
SHWIIZT!
ARROO!
MEZGRAF!
MEZ --
WHAT DO YOU THINK, JENNIR? I JUST CARVED MY FIRST BLOOD CARVER!

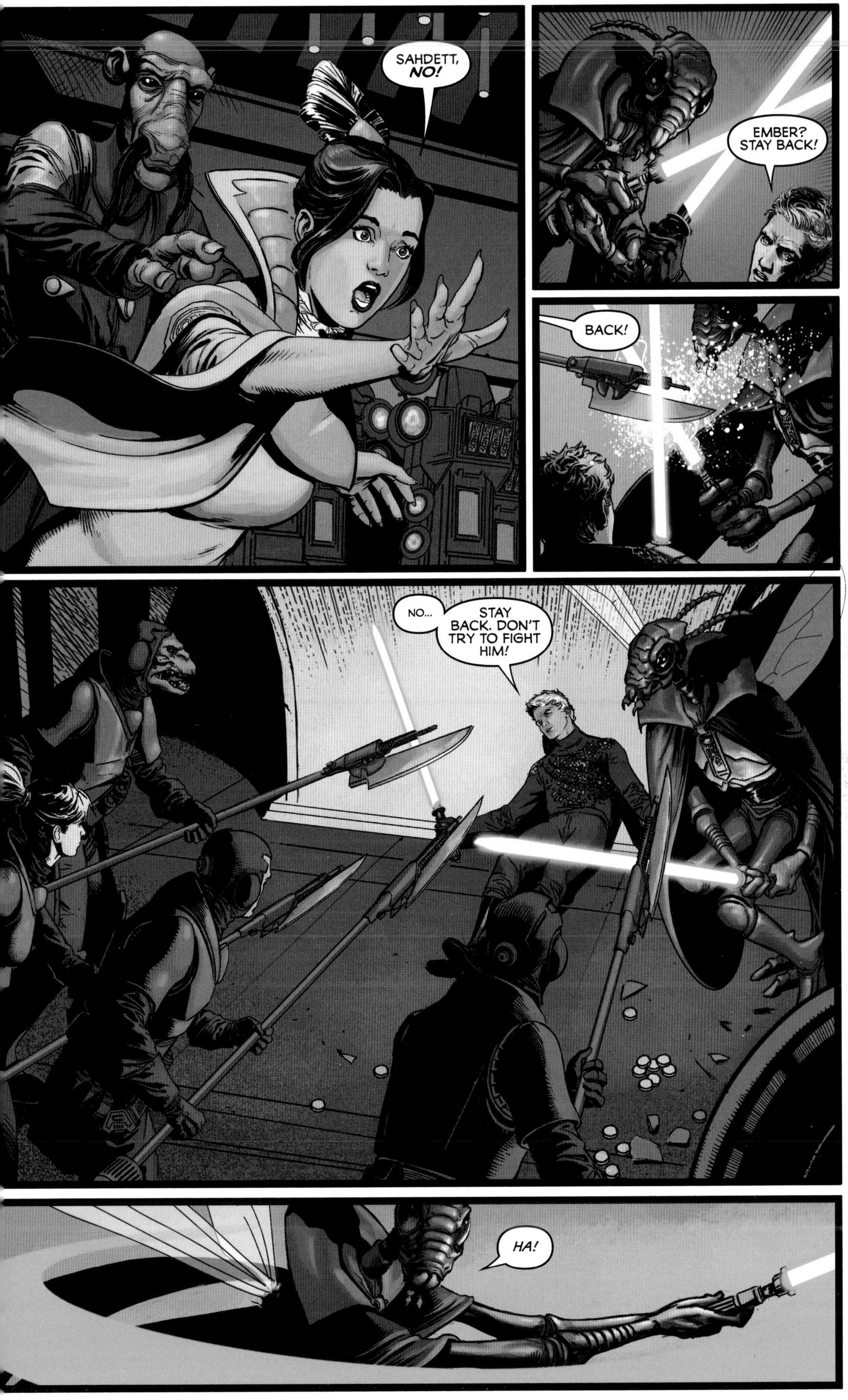
SAHDETT, NO!
EMBER? STAY BACK!
BACK!
NO...
STAY BACK. DON'T TRY TO FIGHT HIM!
HA!

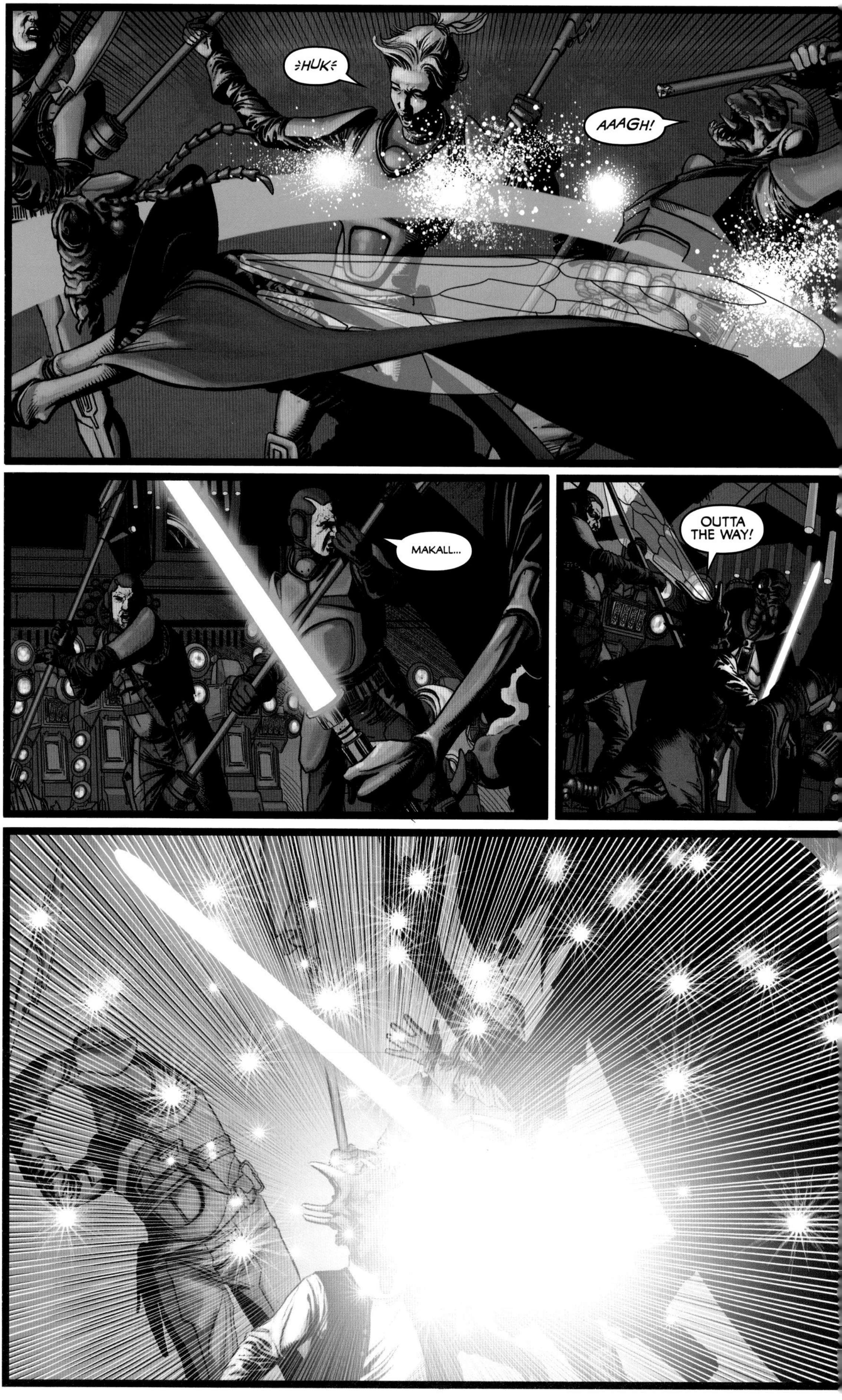
HUK
AAAGH!
MAKALL...
OUTTA THE WAY!

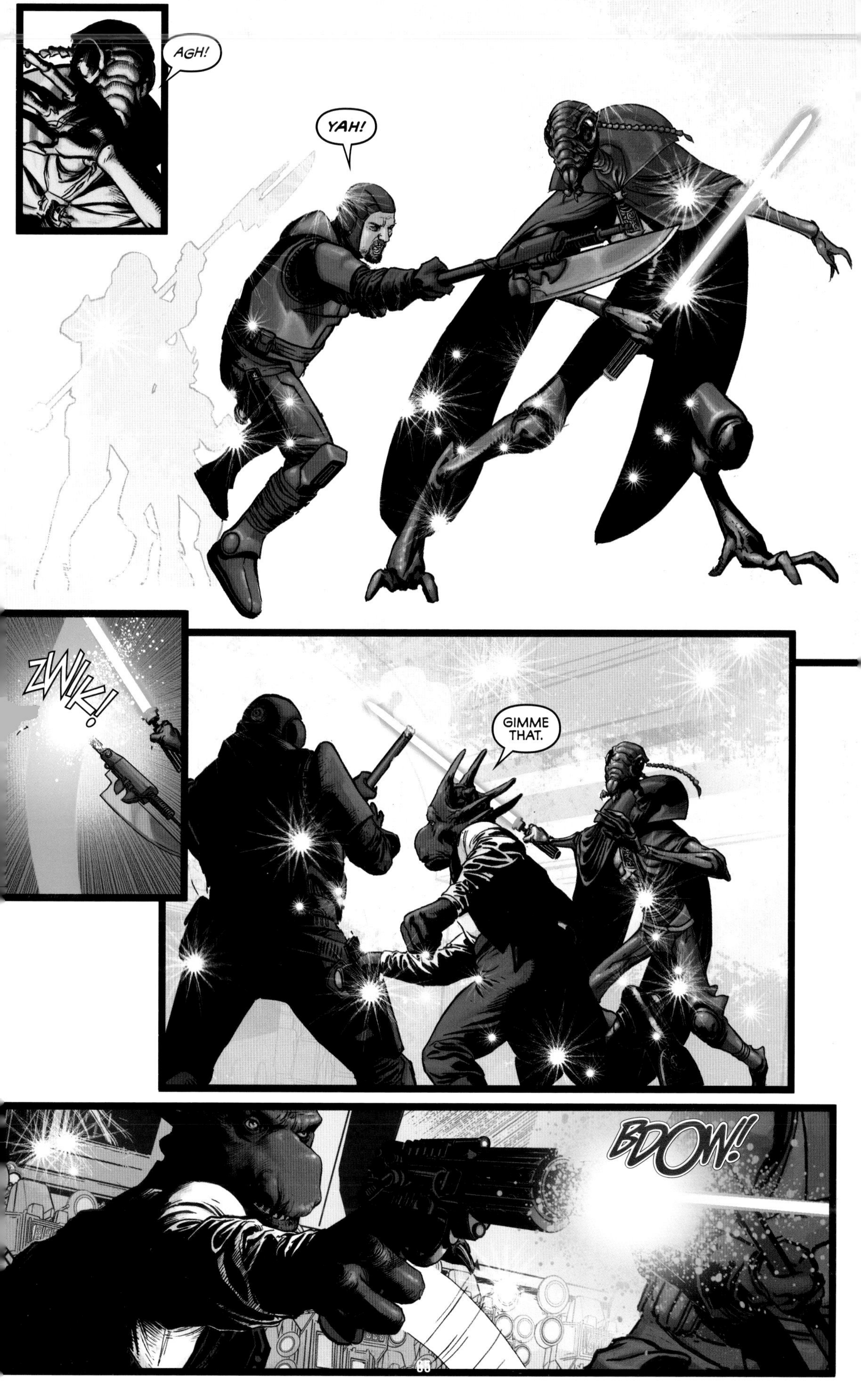
AGH!
YAH!
ZWIK!
GIMME THAT.
BDOW!

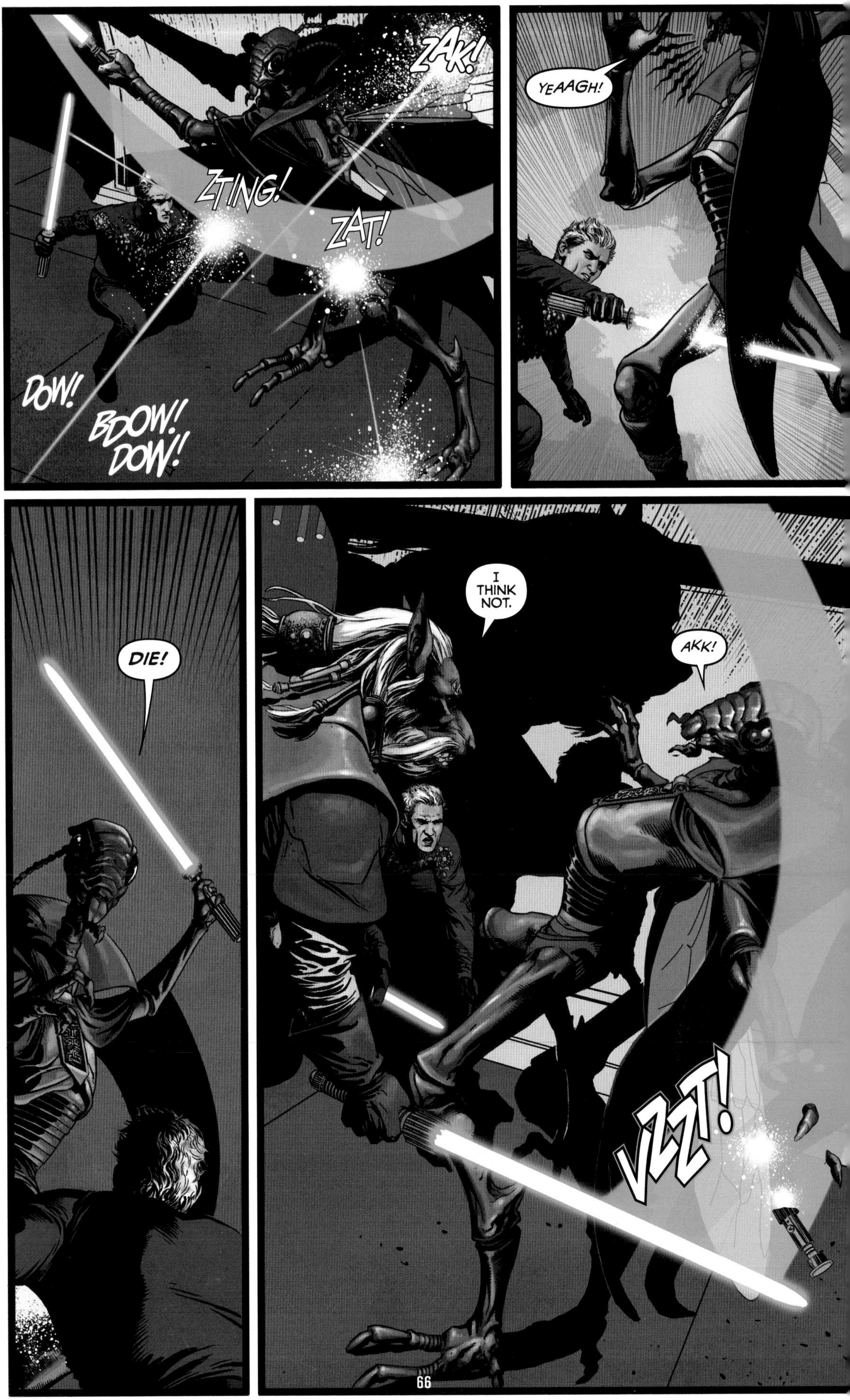
ZAK!
ZTING!
ZAT!
DOW!
BDOW!
DOW!
YEAAGH!
DIE!
I THINK NOT.
AKK!
VZZT!

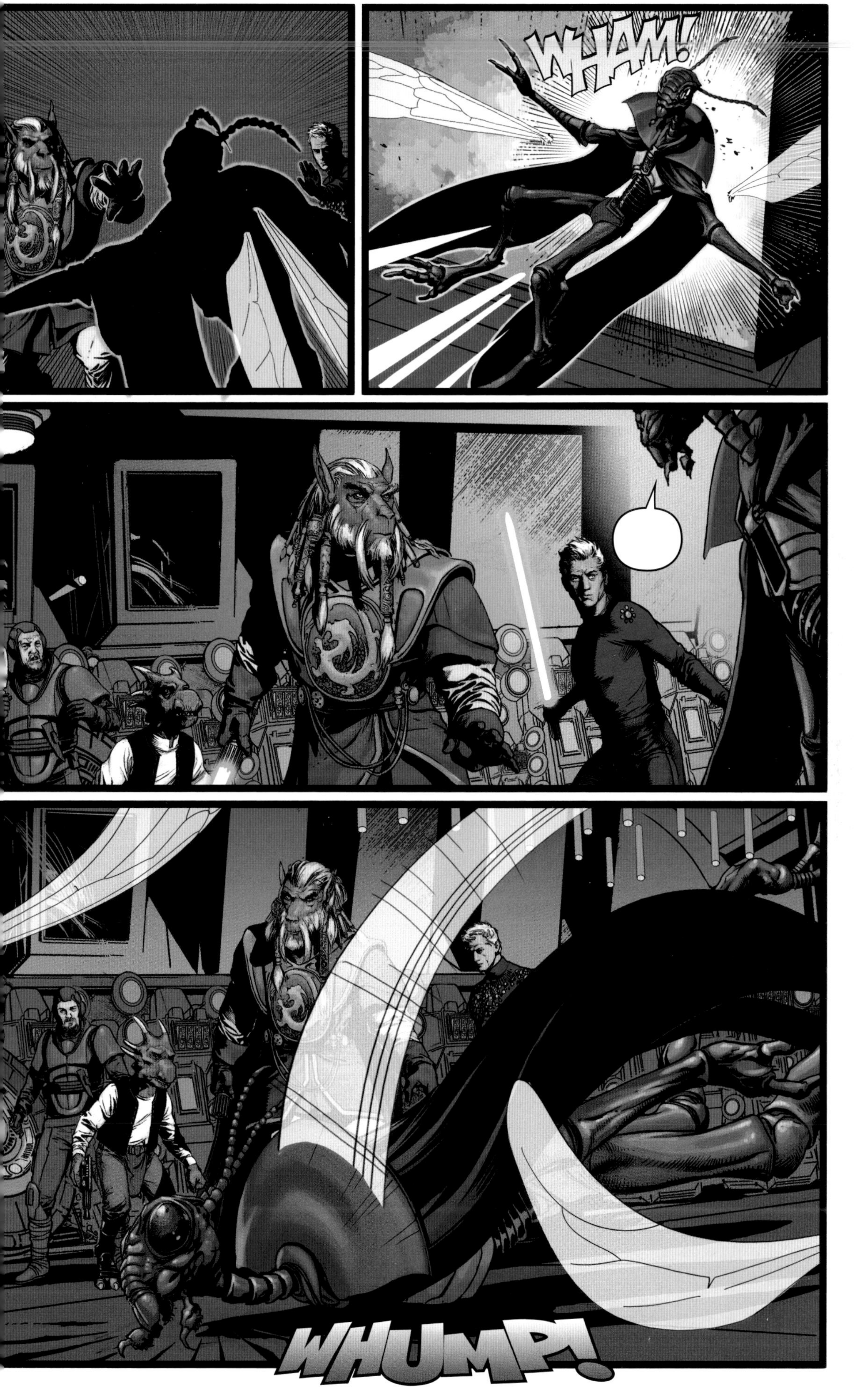
WHAM!
WHUMP!

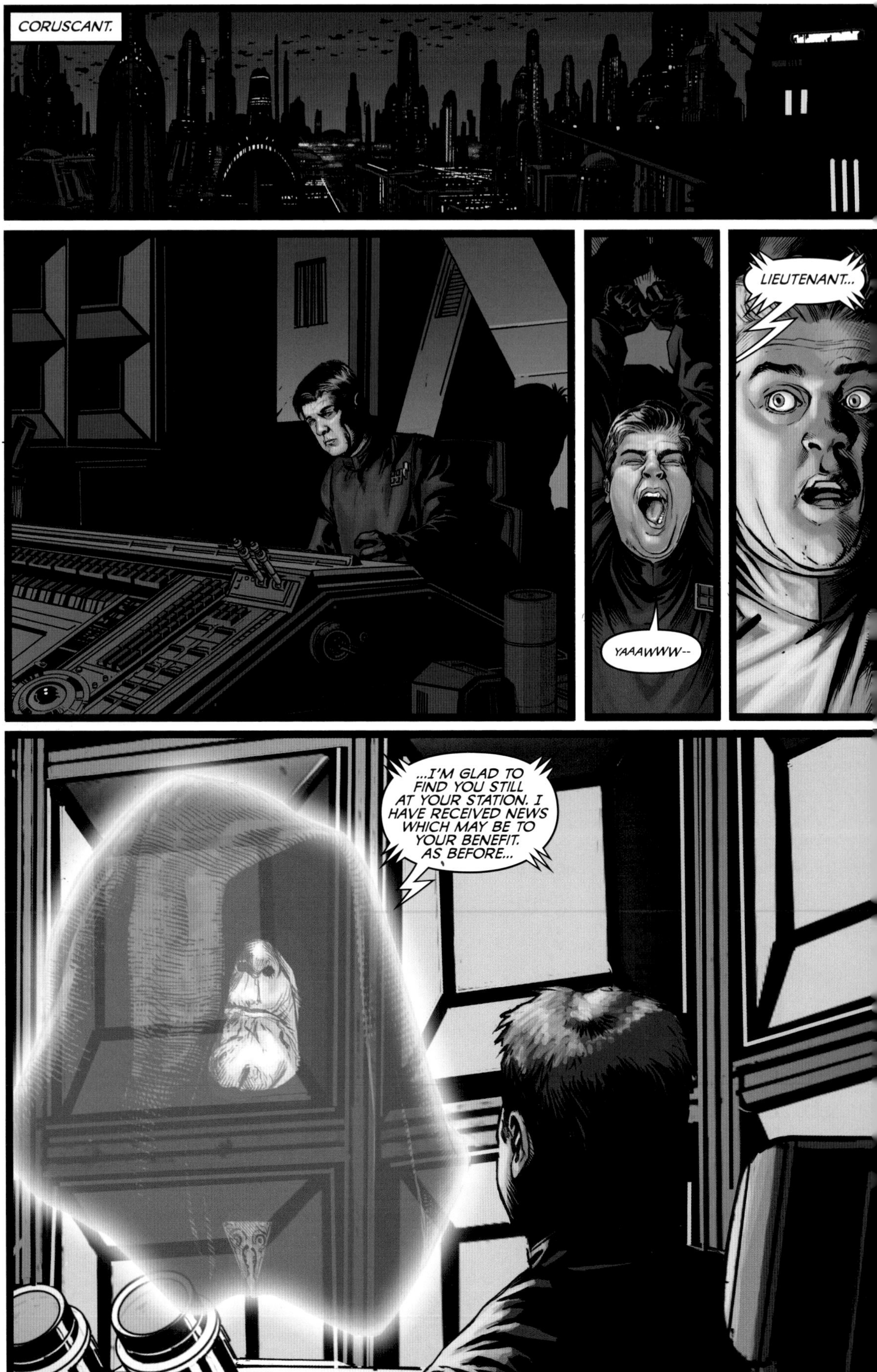
CORUSCANT.
YAAAWWW--
LIEUTENANT...
...I'M GLAD TO FIND YOU STILL AT YOUR STATION. I HAVE RECEIVED NEWS WHICH MAY BE TO YOUR BENEFIT. AS BEFORE...

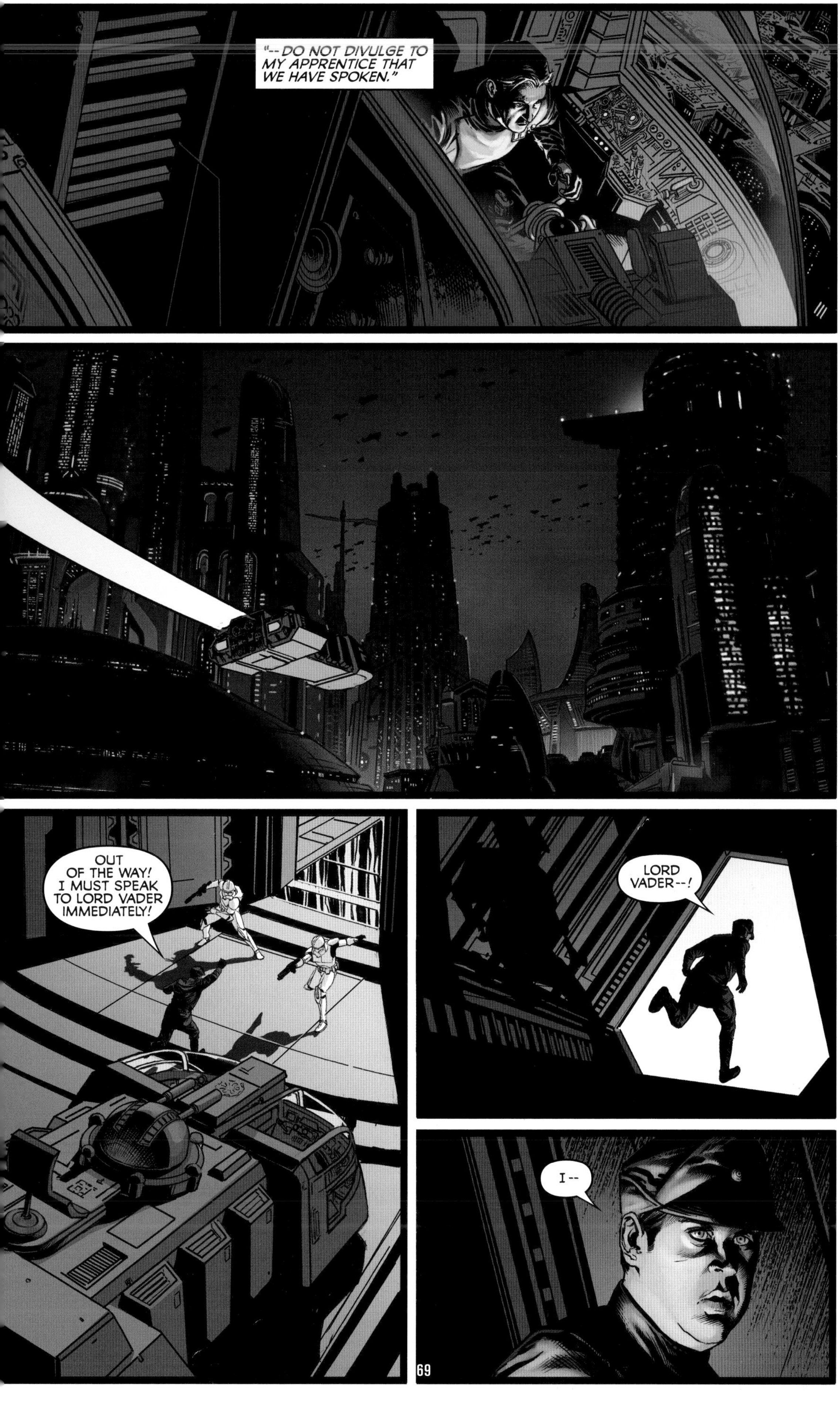
"-- DO NOT DIVULGE TO MY APPRENTICE THAT WE HAVE SPOKEN."
OUT OF THE WAY! I MUST SPEAK TO LORD VADER IMMEDIATELY!
LORD VADER--!
I --

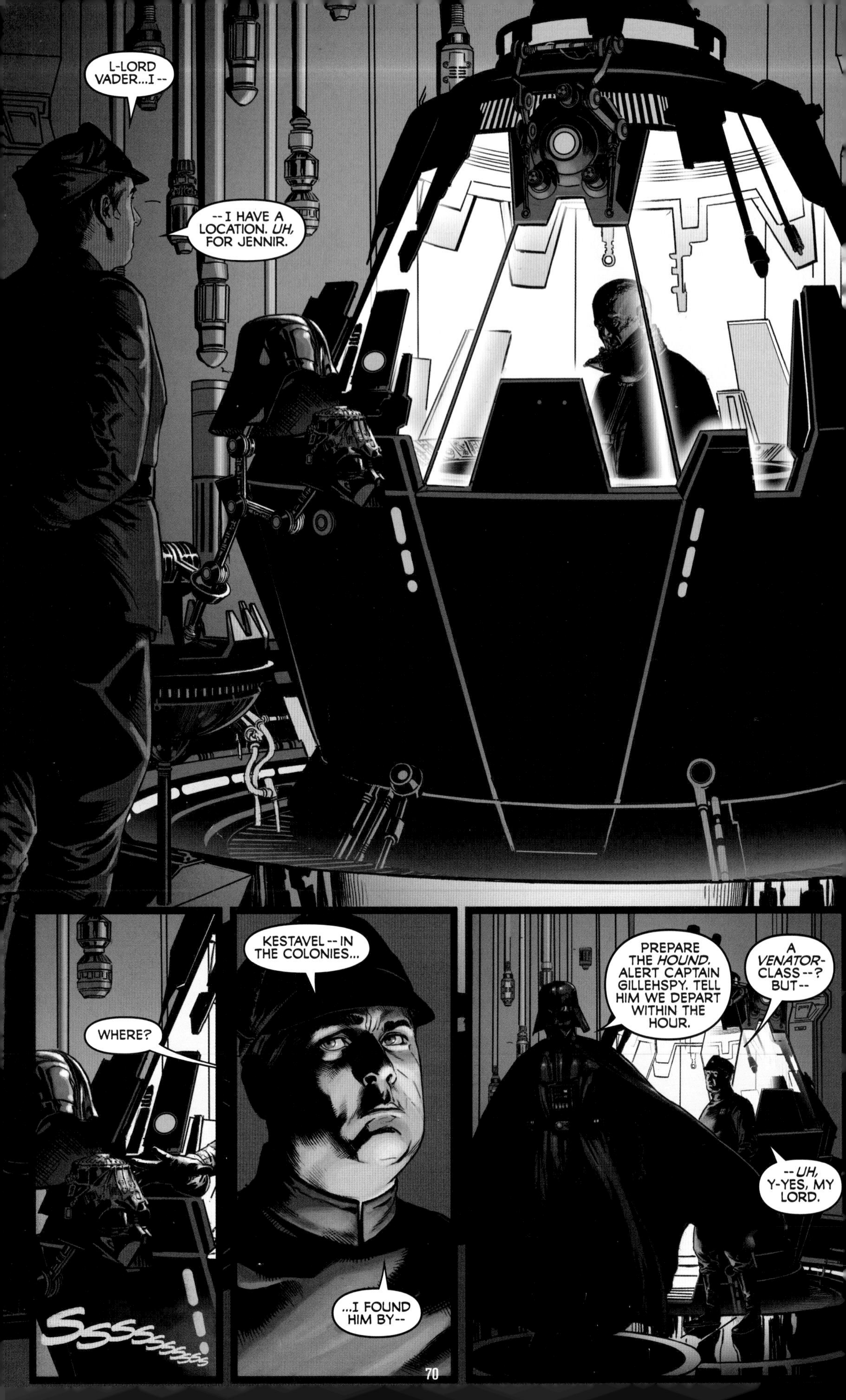
L-LORD VADER...I --
-- I HAVE A LOCATION. UH, FOR JENNIR.
WHERE?
SSSSSSSSSS
KESTAVEL -- IN THE COLONIES...
...I FOUND HIM BY--
PREPARE THE HOUND. ALERT CAPTAIN GILLEHSPY. TELL HIM WE DEPART WITHIN THE HOUR.
A VENATOR-CLASS --? BUT--
-- UH, Y-YES, MY LORD.

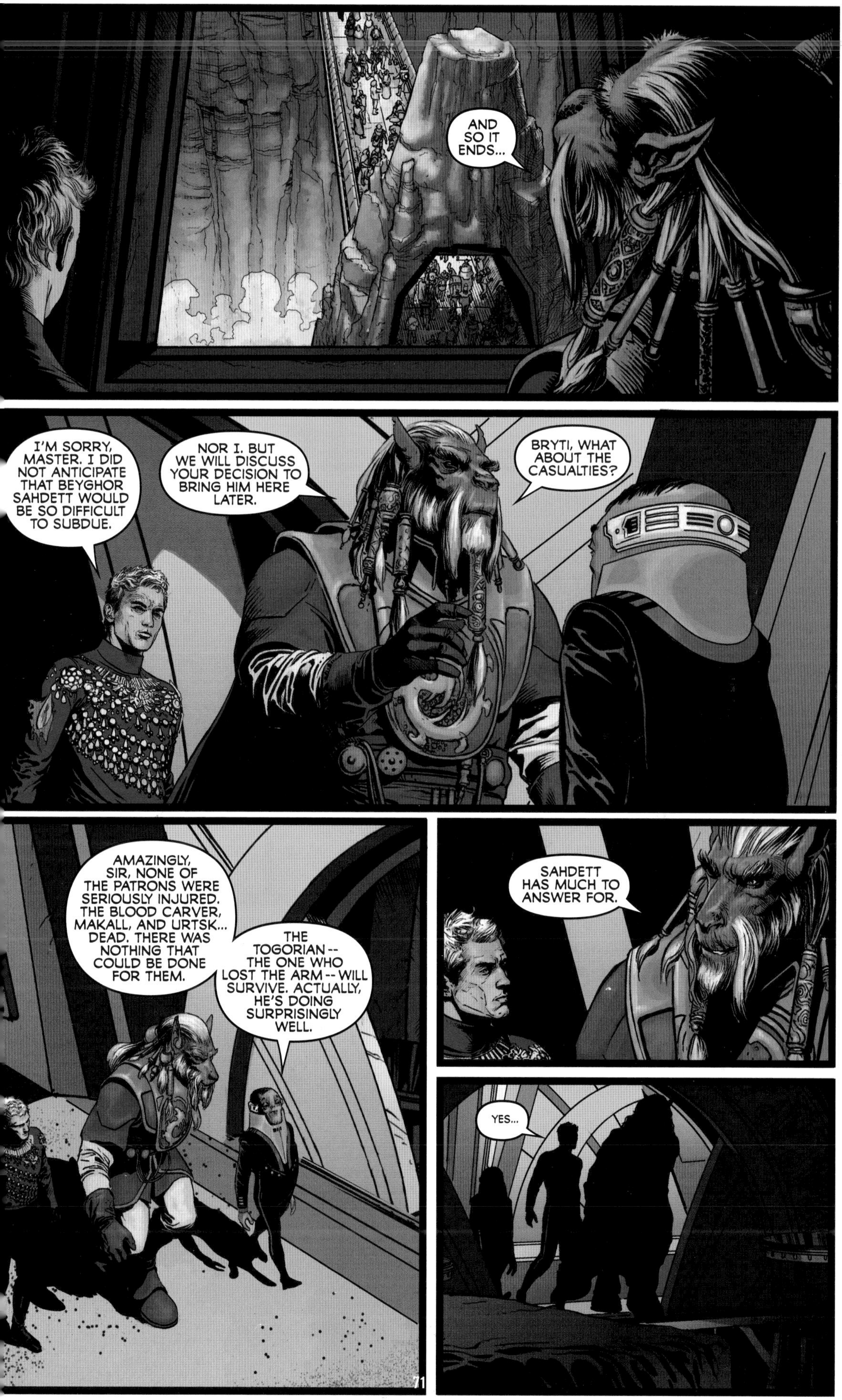
AND SO IT ENDS...
I'M SORRY, MASTER. I DID NOT ANTICIPATE THAT BEYGHOR SAHDETT WOULD BE SO DIFFICULT TO SUBDUE.
NOR I. BUT WE WILL DISCUSS YOUR DECISION TO BRING HIM HERE LATER.
BRYTI, WHAT ABOUT THE CASUALTIES?
AMAZINGLY, SIR, NONE OF THE PATRONS WERE SERIOUSLY INJURED. THE BLOOD CARVER, MAKALL, AND URTSK... DEAD. THERE WAS NOTHING THAT COULD BE DONE FOR THEM.
THE TOGORIAN -- THE ONE WHO LOST THE ARM -- WILL SURVIVE. ACTUALLY, HE'S DOING SURPRISINGLY WELL.
SAHDETT HAS MUCH TO ANSWER FOR.
YES...

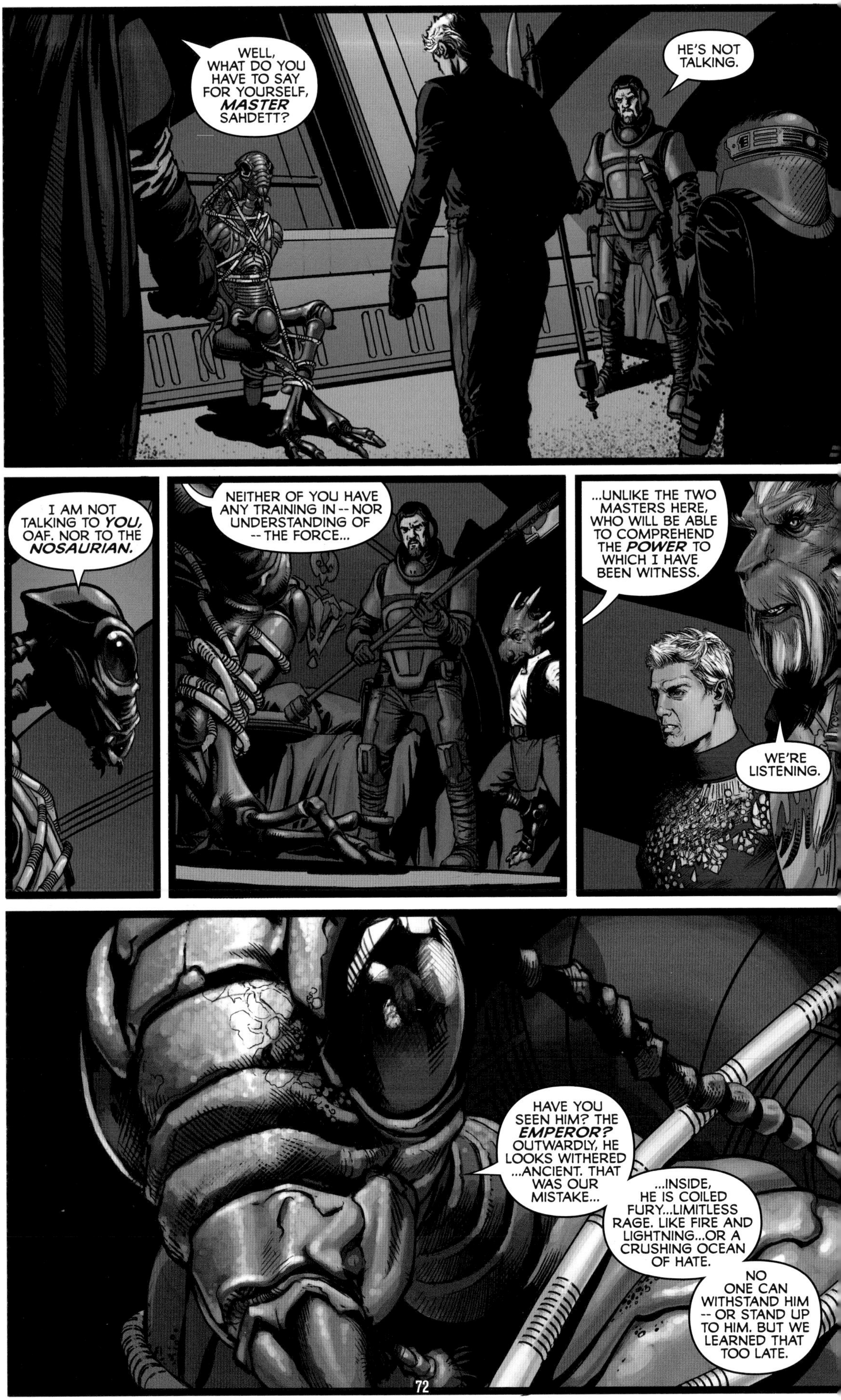
WELL, WHAT DO YOU HAVE TO SAY FOR YOURSELF, MASTER SAHDETT?
HE'S NOT TALKING.
I AM NOT TALKING TO YOU, OAF. NOR TO THE NOSAURIAN.
NEITHER OF YOU HAVE ANY TRAINING IN -- NOR UNDERSTANDING OF -- THE FORCE...
...UNLIKE THE TWO MASTERS HERE, WHO WILL BE ABLE TO COMPREHEND THE POWER TO WHICH I HAVE BEEN WITNESS.
WE'RE LISTENING.
HAVE YOU SEEN HIM? THE EMPEROR? OUTWARDLY, HE LOOKS WITHERED ...ANCIENT. THAT WAS OUR MISTAKE...
...INSIDE, HE IS COILED FURY...LIMITLESS RAGE. LIKE FIRE AND LIGHTNING...OR A CRUSHING OCEAN OF HATE.
NO ONE CAN WITHSTAND HIM -- OR STAND UP TO HIM. BUT WE LEARNED THAT TOO LATE.

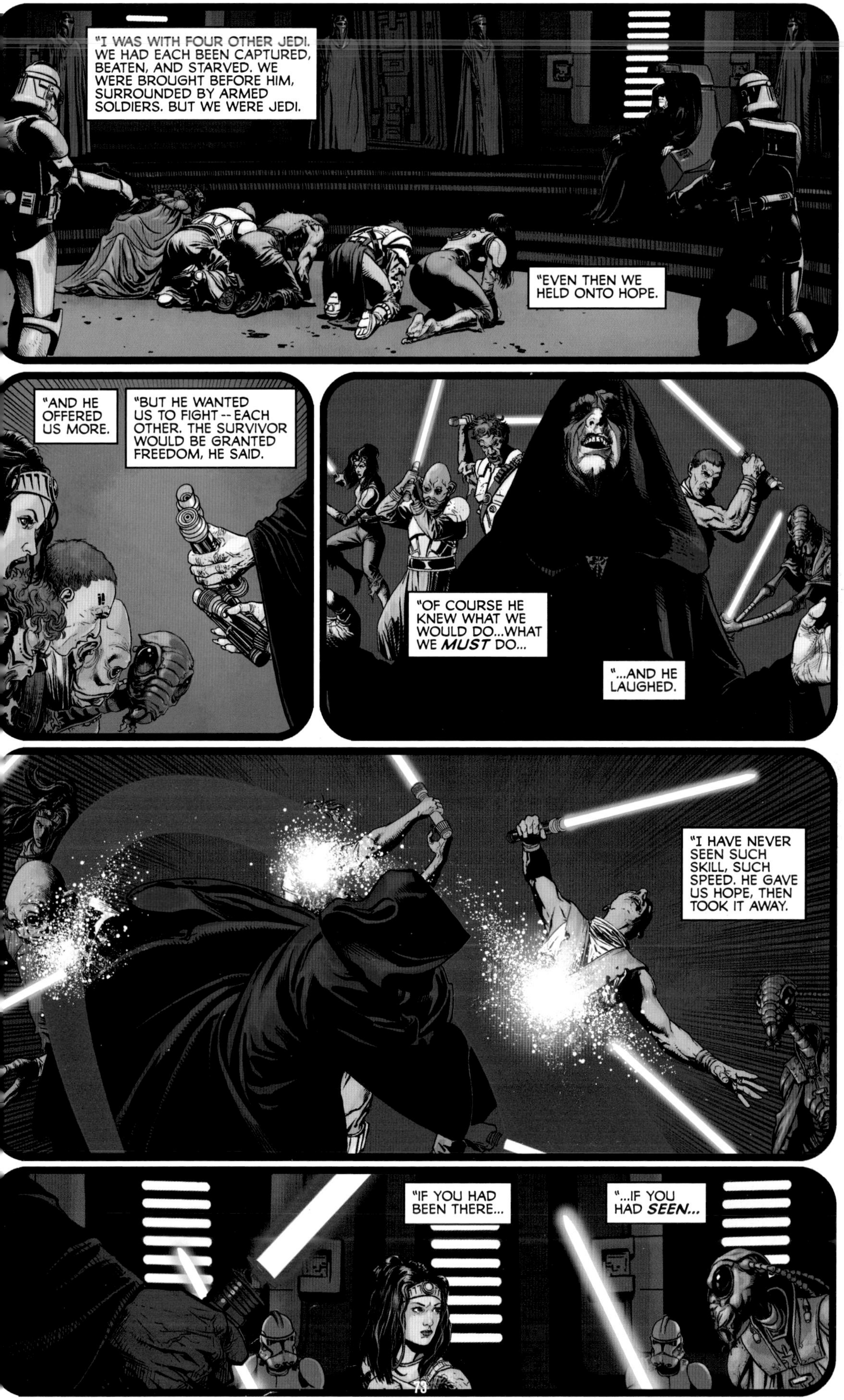
"I WAS WITH FOUR OTHER JEDI. WE HAD EACH BEEN CAPTURED, BEATEN, AND STARVED. WE WERE BROUGHT BEFORE HIM, SURROUNDED BY ARMED SOLDIERS. BUT WE WERE JEDI.
"EVEN THEN WE HELD ONTO HOPE.
"AND HE OFFERED US MORE.
"BUT HE WANTED US TO FIGHT -- EACH OTHER. THE SURVIVOR WOULD BE GRANTED FREEDOM, HE SAID.
"OF COURSE HE KNEW WHAT WE WOULD DO...WHAT WE *MUST* DO...
"...AND HE LAUGHED.
"I HAVE NEVER SEEN SUCH SKILL, SUCH SPEED. HE GAVE US HOPE, THEN TOOK IT AWAY.
"IF YOU HAD BEEN THERE...
"...IF YOU HAD ***SEEN...***

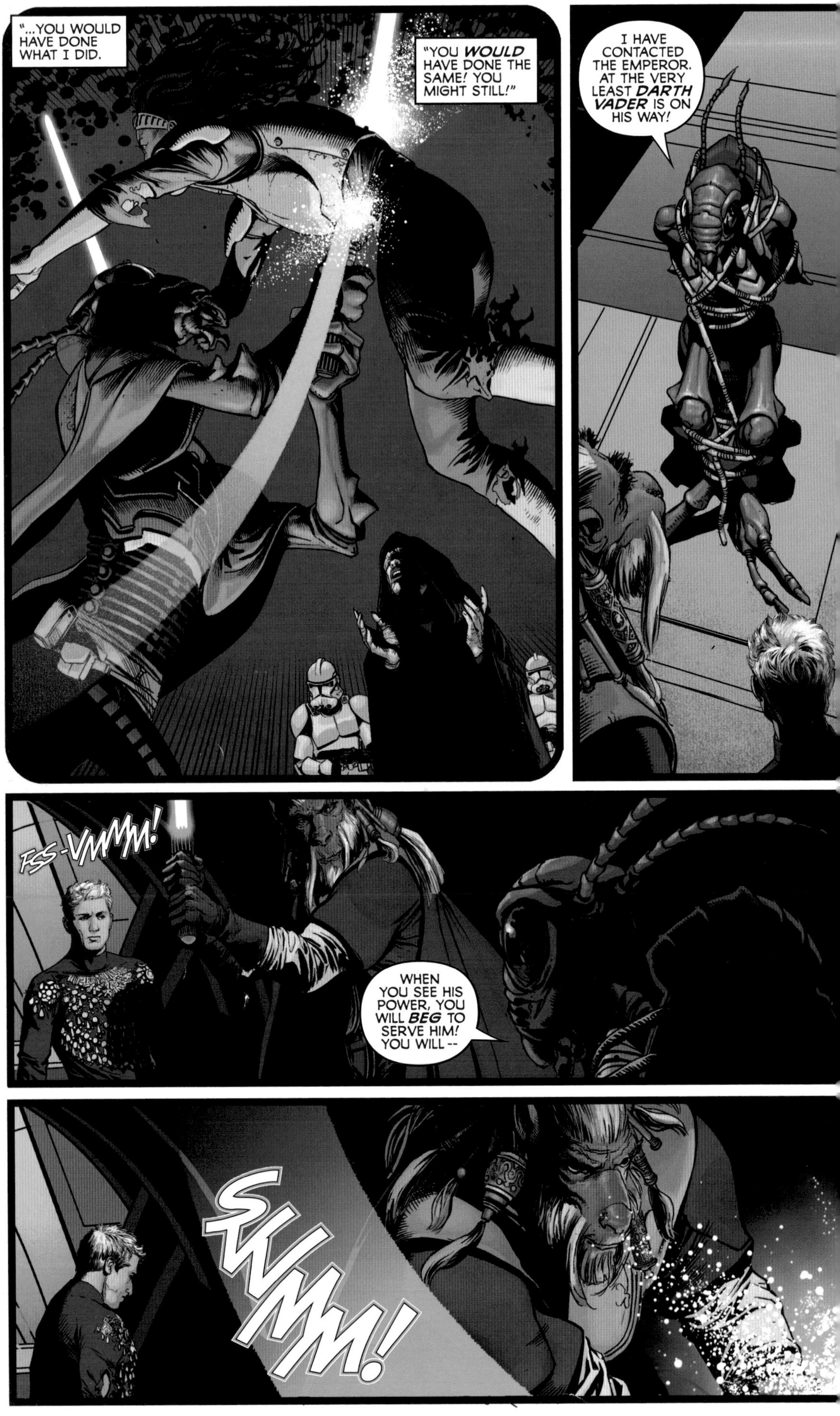
"...YOU WOULD HAVE DONE WHAT I DID.
"YOU *WOULD* HAVE DONE THE SAME! YOU MIGHT STILL!"
I HAVE CONTACTED THE EMPEROR. AT THE VERY LEAST *DARTH VADER* IS ON HIS WAY!
FSS-VMMM!
WHEN YOU SEE HIS POWER, YOU WILL *BEG* TO SERVE HIM! YOU WILL --
SKWMM!

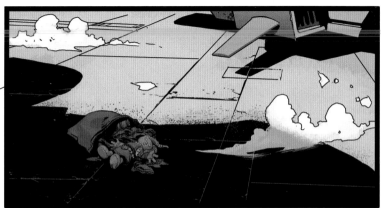

"WHAT DO YOU THINK, DASS JENNIR? WILL THIS *'DARTH VADER'* COME?"

I DON'T KNOW, KAI. I ONLY LEARNED ABOUT HIM RECENTLY. BOMO HAS SEEN HIM IN ACTION.

AND I'M NOT ANXIOUS TO SEE HIM *AGAIN*. BUT IF SAHDETT SAID HE'D COME, I WOULDN'T DOUBT IT.

THEN WE MUST PREPARE.

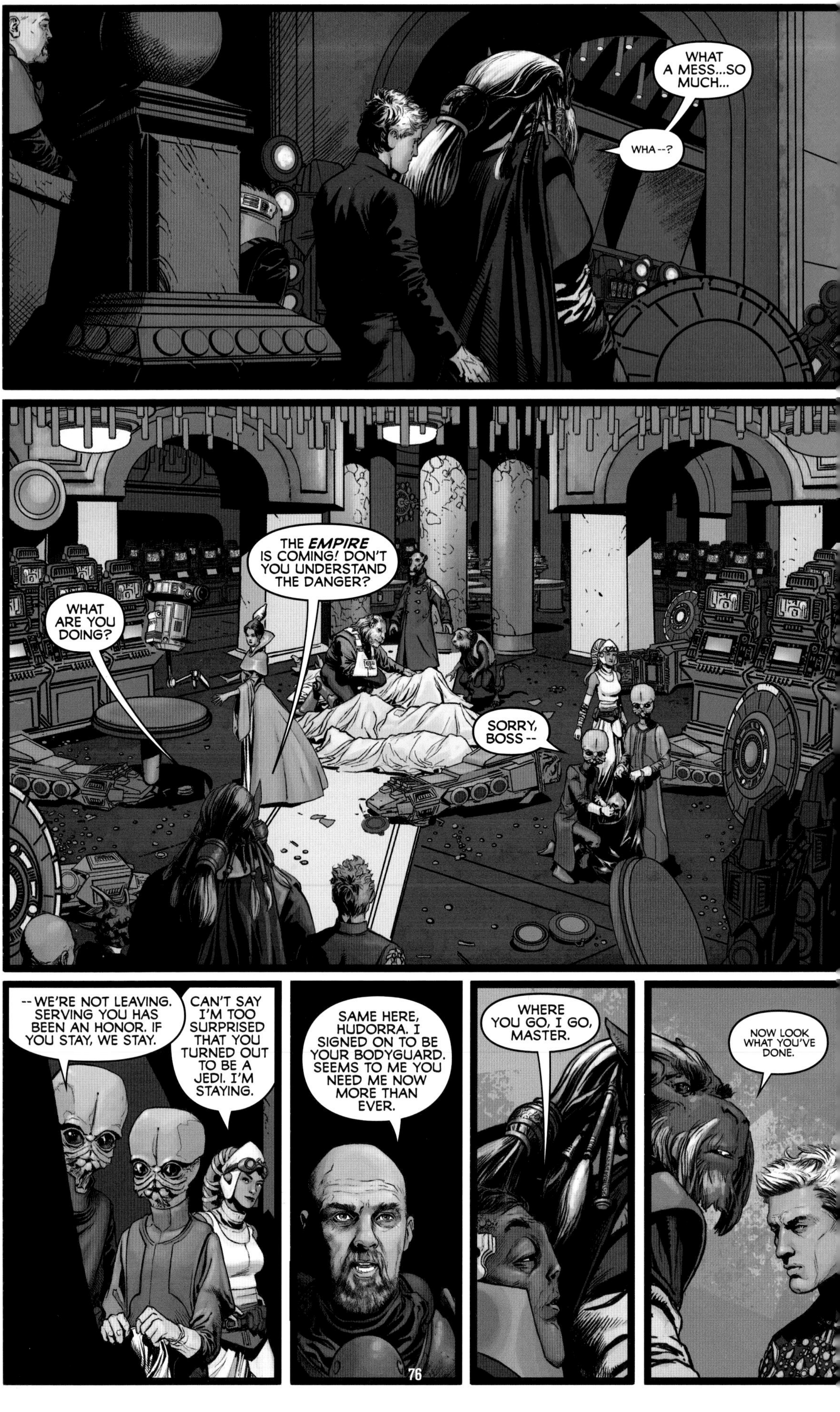
WHAT A MESS...SO MUCH...
WHA--?
WHAT ARE YOU DOING?
THE *EMPIRE* IS COMING! DON'T YOU UNDERSTAND THE DANGER?
SORRY, BOSS--
--WE'RE NOT LEAVING. SERVING YOU HAS BEEN AN HONOR. IF YOU STAY, WE STAY.
CAN'T SAY I'M TOO SURPRISED THAT YOU TURNED OUT TO BE A JEDI. I'M STAYING.
SAME HERE, HUDORRA. I SIGNED ON TO BE YOUR BODYGUARD. SEEMS TO ME YOU NEED ME NOW MORE THAN EVER.
WHERE YOU GO, I GO, MASTER.
NOW LOOK WHAT YOU'VE DONE.

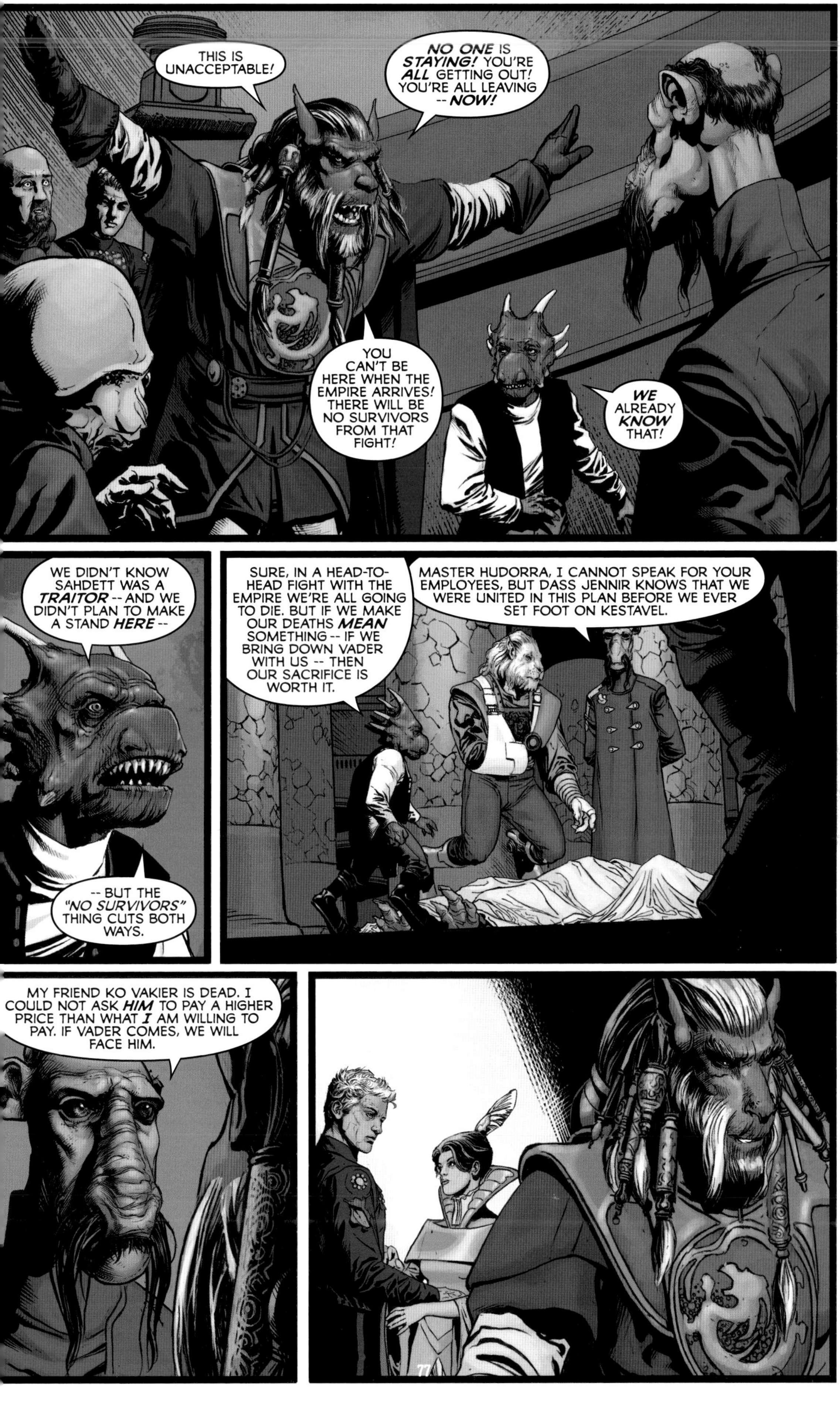

THIS IS UNACCEPTABLE!
NO ONE IS STAYING! YOU'RE ALL GETTING OUT! YOU'RE ALL LEAVING -- NOW!
YOU CAN'T BE HERE WHEN THE EMPIRE ARRIVES! THERE WILL BE NO SURVIVORS FROM THAT FIGHT!
WE ALREADY KNOW THAT!
WE DIDN'T KNOW SAHDETT WAS A TRAITOR -- AND WE DIDN'T PLAN TO MAKE A STAND HERE --
-- BUT THE "NO SURVIVORS" THING CUTS BOTH WAYS.
SURE, IN A HEAD-TO-HEAD FIGHT WITH THE EMPIRE WE'RE ALL GOING TO DIE. BUT IF WE MAKE OUR DEATHS MEAN SOMETHING -- IF WE BRING DOWN VADER WITH US -- THEN OUR SACRIFICE IS WORTH IT.
MASTER HUDORRA, I CANNOT SPEAK FOR YOUR EMPLOYEES, BUT DASS JENNIR KNOWS THAT WE WERE UNITED IN THIS PLAN BEFORE WE EVER SET FOOT ON KESTAVEL.
MY FRIEND KO VAKIER IS DEAD. I COULD NOT ASK HIM TO PAY A HIGHER PRICE THAN WHAT I AM WILLING TO PAY. IF VADER COMES, WE WILL FACE HIM.

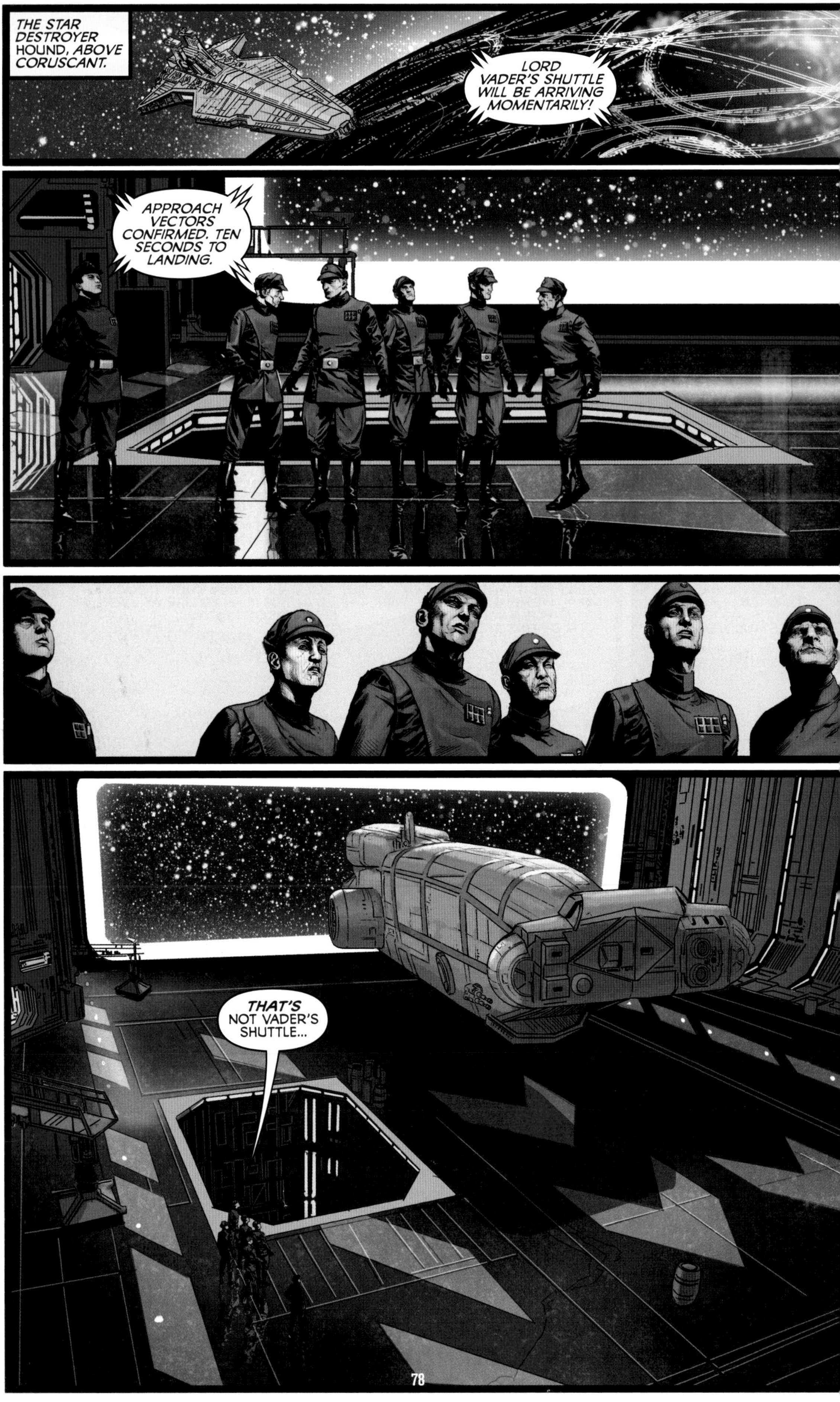
THE STAR DESTROYER HOUND, ABOVE CORUSCANT.
LORD VADER'S SHUTTLE WILL BE ARRIVING MOMENTARILY!
APPROACH VECTORS CONFIRMED. TEN SECONDS TO LANDING.
THAT'S NOT VADER'S SHUTTLE...

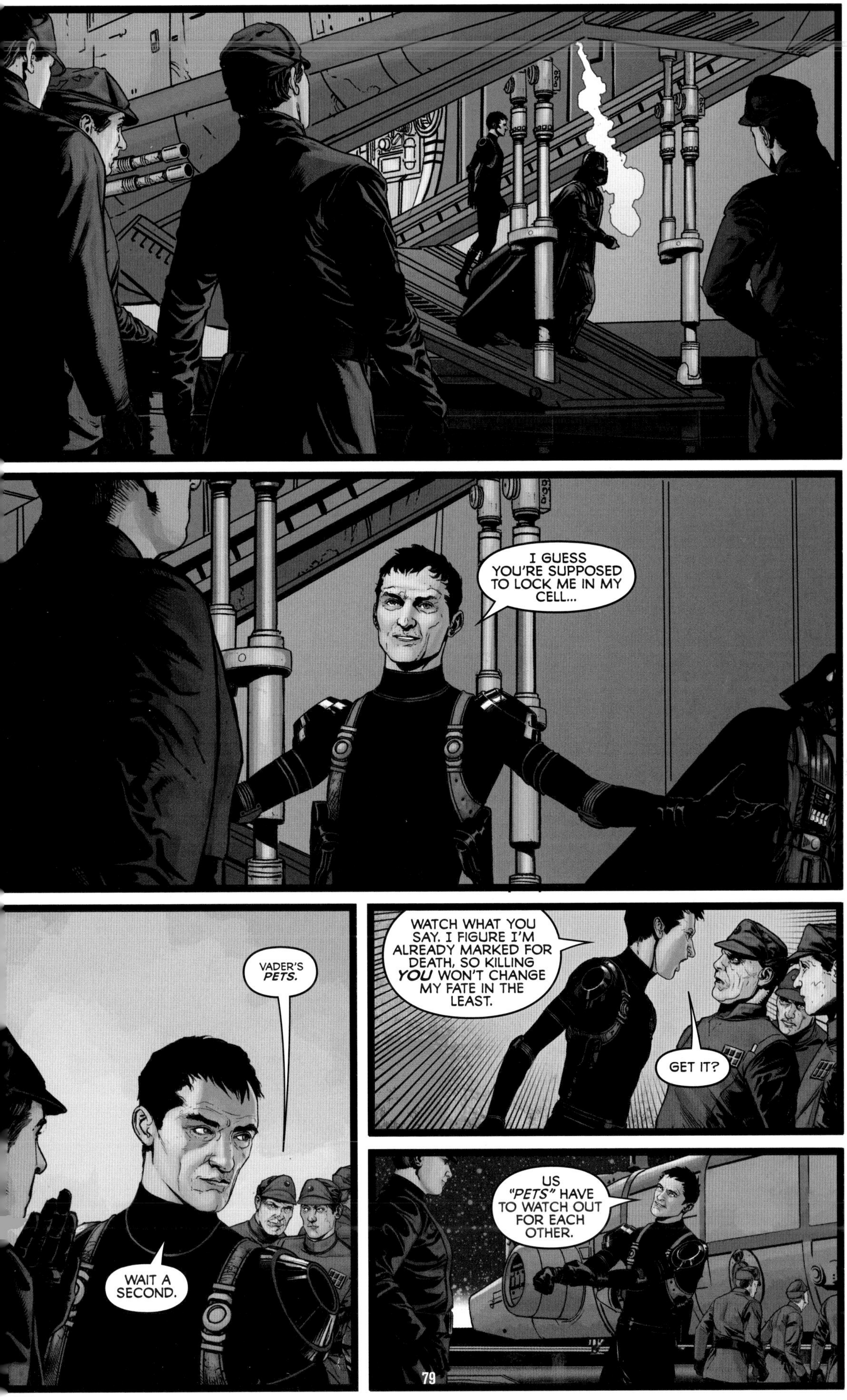
I GUESS YOU'RE SUPPOSED TO LOCK ME IN MY CELL...
VADER'S *PETS.*
WAIT A SECOND.
WATCH WHAT YOU SAY. I FIGURE I'M ALREADY MARKED FOR DEATH, SO KILLING ***YOU*** WON'T CHANGE MY FATE IN THE LEAST.
GET IT?
US *"PETS"* HAVE TO WATCH OUT FOR EACH OTHER.

WHERE -- *WHEN* -- DID YOU GET ALL OF THIS, HEREN? I DON'T BELIEVE IT!

I PICKED THINGS UP HERE AND THERE, BOMO. AFTER THE WAY YOU SAVED ALL OF US ON MIMBAN --

-- IT OCCURRED TO ME THAT HAVING A CACHE OF EXPLOSIVES ON HAND MIGHT BE USEFUL.

I'LL MAKE SURE OF IT.

THE ARCHWAY TUNNEL JUST BEFORE YOU REACH THE CASINO IS AN OBVIOUS CHOKE-POINT.

AS ARE THE TWO BRIDGES NEAR THE SPACEPORT. BUT I WOULD SUGGEST WE LEAVE THE FIRST BRIDGE ALONE -- LET THEM REACH THE SECOND BRIDGE BEFORE WE STRIKE...

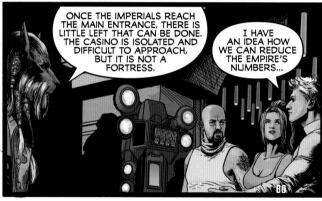

ONCE THE IMPERIALS REACH THE MAIN ENTRANCE, THERE IS LITTLE LEFT THAT CAN BE DONE. THE CASINO IS ISOLATED AND DIFFICULT TO APPROACH, BUT IT IS NOT A FORTRESS.

I HAVE AN IDEA HOW WE CAN REDUCE THE EMPIRE'S NUMBERS...

KAL, COME WITH ME.

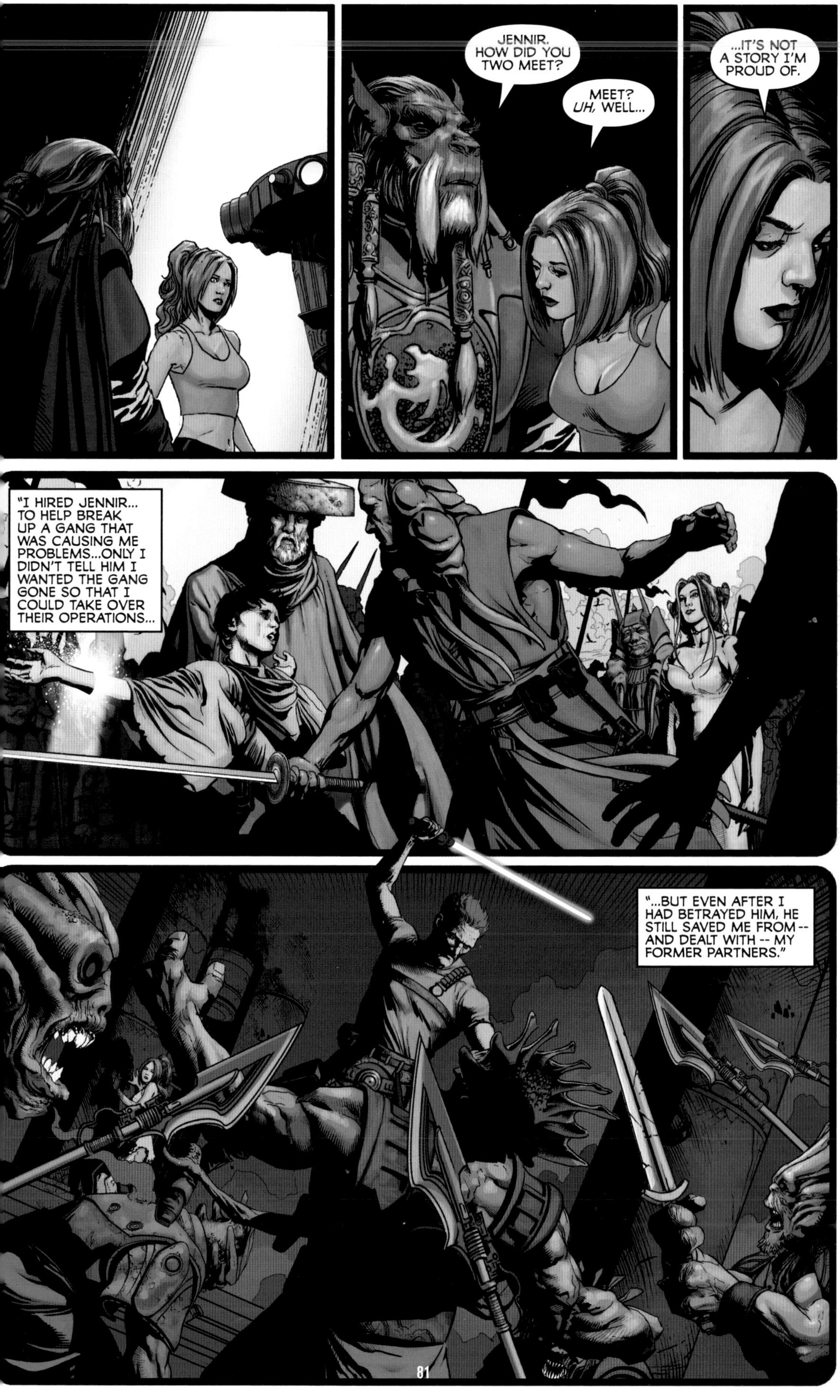
JENNIR. HOW DID YOU TWO MEET?
MEET? UH, WELL...
...IT'S NOT A STORY I'M PROUD OF.
"I HIRED JENNIR... TO HELP BREAK UP A GANG THAT WAS CAUSING ME PROBLEMS...ONLY I DIDN'T TELL HIM I WANTED THE GANG GONE SO THAT I COULD TAKE OVER THEIR OPERATIONS...
"...BUT EVEN AFTER I HAD BETRAYED HIM, HE STILL SAVED ME FROM -- AND DEALT WITH -- MY FORMER PARTNERS."

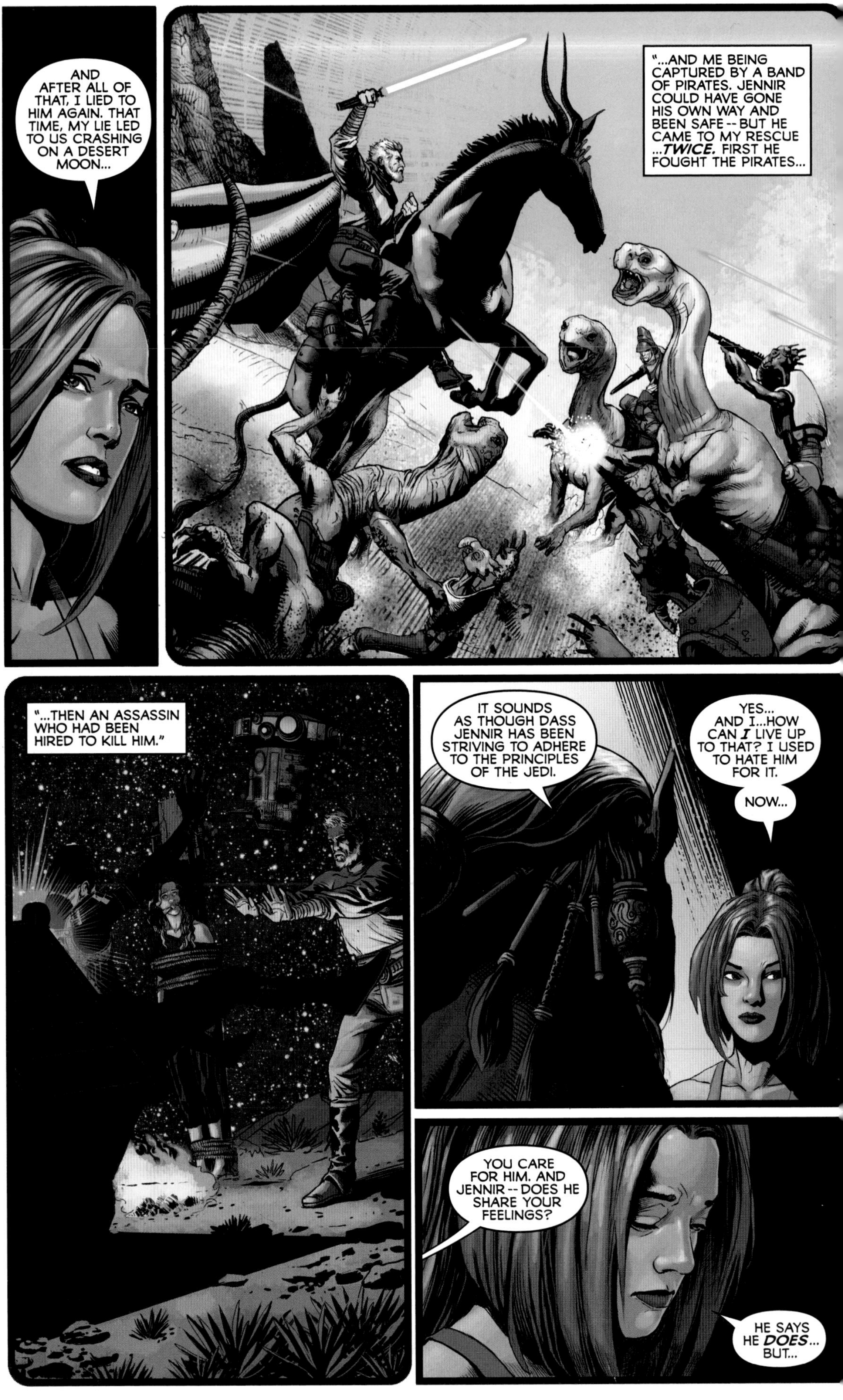
AND AFTER ALL OF THAT, I LIED TO HIM AGAIN. THAT TIME, MY LIE LED TO US CRASHING ON A DESERT MOON...
"...AND ME BEING CAPTURED BY A BAND OF PIRATES. JENNIR COULD HAVE GONE HIS OWN WAY AND BEEN SAFE -- BUT HE CAME TO MY RESCUE ...TWICE. FIRST HE FOUGHT THE PIRATES...
"...THEN AN ASSASSIN WHO HAD BEEN HIRED TO KILL HIM."
IT SOUNDS AS THOUGH DASS JENNIR HAS BEEN STRIVING TO ADHERE TO THE PRINCIPLES OF THE JEDI.
YES... AND I...HOW CAN I LIVE UP TO THAT? I USED TO HATE HIM FOR IT.
NOW...
YOU CARE FOR HIM. AND JENNIR -- DOES HE SHARE YOUR FEELINGS?
HE SAYS HE DOES... BUT...

...IF HE KEEPS FOLLOWING THE JEDI PATH, HE'S GOING TO GET HIMSELF KILLED. I DON'T WANT TO LOSE HIM --

-- BUT I HAVE NO RIGHT TO ASK HIM TO CHANGE. I OWE MY LIFE TO THE FACT THAT HE INSISTS ON BEING A JEDI. AND I LOVE HIM BECAUSE OF IT.

I AM ALSO GLAD MY MASTER IS A JEDI. I WAS WITH HIM WHEN HE FOUGHT THE GANGS --

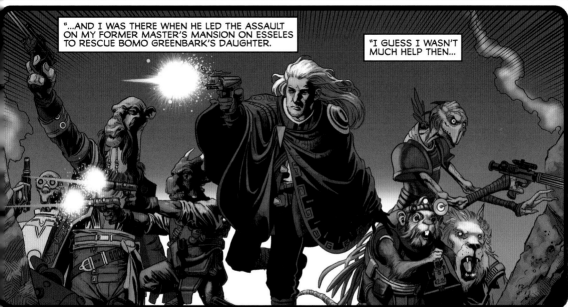

"...AND I WAS THERE WHEN HE LED THE ASSAULT ON MY FORMER MASTER'S MANSION ON ESSELES TO RESCUE BOMO GREENBARK'S DAUGHTER.

"I GUESS I WASN'T MUCH HELP THEN...

"...BUT I TRIED TO HELP WHEN HE FREED THE SLAVES ON THE MOON OF TELERATH."

MY MASTER IS A VERY GREAT JEDI!

SO IT WOULD SEEM.

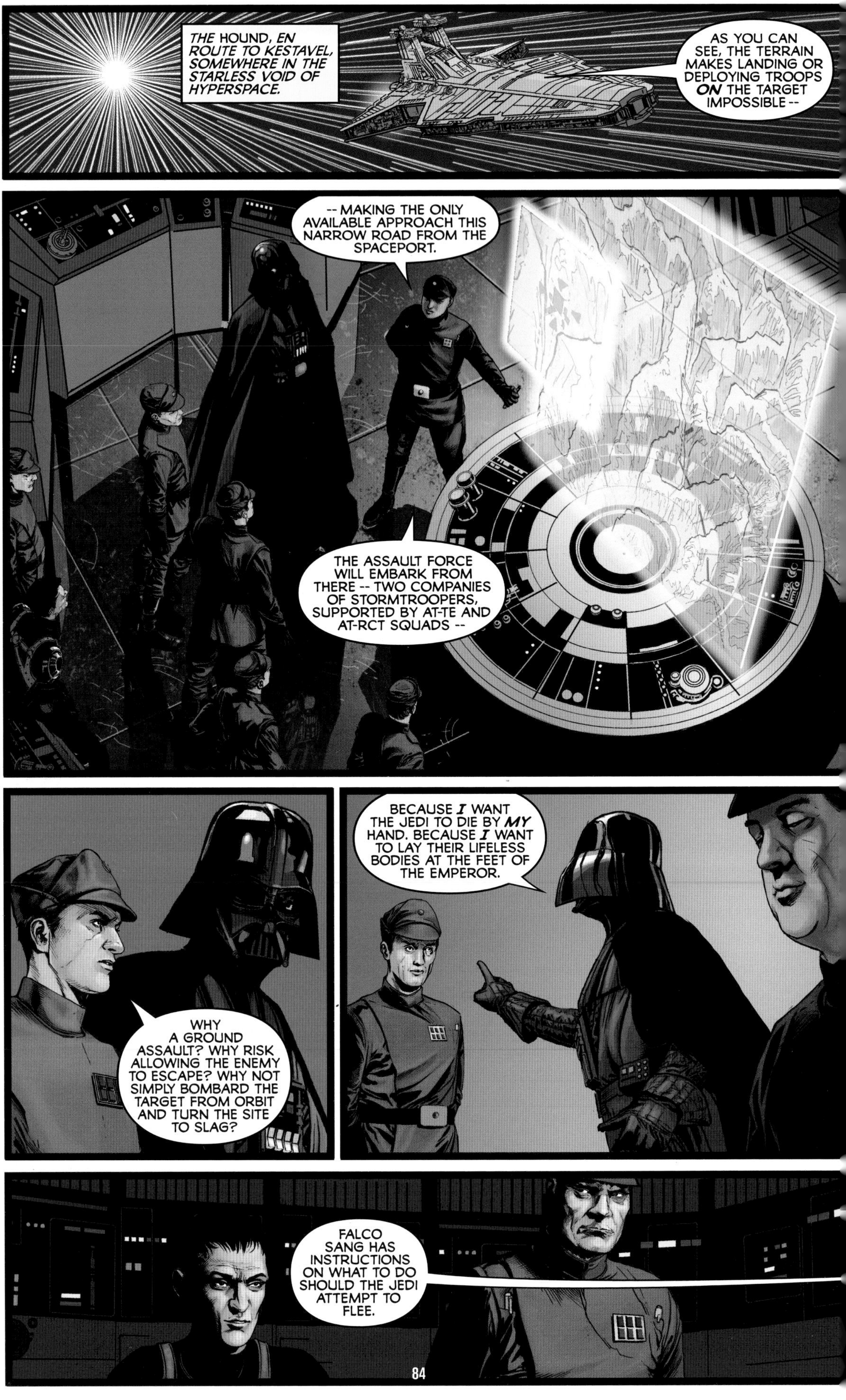
THE HOUND, EN ROUTE TO KESTAVEL, SOMEWHERE IN THE STARLESS VOID OF HYPERSPACE.
AS YOU CAN SEE, THE TERRAIN MAKES LANDING OR DEPLOYING TROOPS ON THE TARGET IMPOSSIBLE --
-- MAKING THE ONLY AVAILABLE APPROACH THIS NARROW ROAD FROM THE SPACEPORT.
THE ASSAULT FORCE WILL EMBARK FROM THERE -- TWO COMPANIES OF STORMTROOPERS, SUPPORTED BY AT-TE AND AT-RCT SQUADS --
WHY A GROUND ASSAULT? WHY RISK ALLOWING THE ENEMY TO ESCAPE? WHY NOT SIMPLY BOMBARD THE TARGET FROM ORBIT AND TURN THE SITE TO SLAG?
BECAUSE I WANT THE JEDI TO DIE BY MY HAND. BECAUSE I WANT TO LAY THEIR LIFELESS BODIES AT THE FEET OF THE EMPEROR.
FALCO SANG HAS INSTRUCTIONS ON WHAT TO DO SHOULD THE JEDI ATTEMPT TO FLEE.

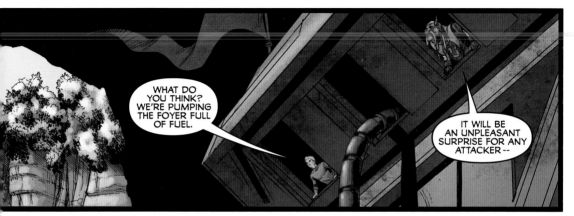

WHAT DO YOU THINK? WE'RE PUMPING THE FOYER FULL OF FUEL.

IT WILL BE AN UNPLEASANT SURPRISE FOR ANY ATTACKER --

-- AS LONG AS IT DOESN'T ALL LEAK OUT BEFORE THE IMPERIALS ARRIVE.

I'VE GOT THAT COVERED...BUT I'M MORE CONCERNED THAT CAPTAIN HEREN AND BOMO RETAIN ENOUGH FUEL...

...TO MAKE AN ESCAPE.

YOU MEAN FOR THEM TO DEPART -- EVEN THOUGH THIS PLAN WAS THEIRS?

WHAT IF THEY REFUSE? THE CAPTAIN SEEMED QUITE DETERMINED.

IF IT COMES TO IT, I'LL USE THE FORCE TO PERSUADE THEM.

I OWE THEM MORE THAN I CAN EVER REPAY. I WILL NOT PLACE MYSELF FURTHER IN THEIR DEBT -- ESPECIALLY OVER SOMETHING THAT IS, I THINK YOU'LL AGREE, A JEDI PROBLEM.

I AGREE THAT THE JEDI BEAR A GREAT RESPONSIBILITY. BUT THE *"PROBLEM"* -- THE EMPIRE -- AFFECTS ALL.

STILL, WHEN THE TIME COMES, MY PEOPLE WILL JOIN YOURS ON THE *UHUMELE.*

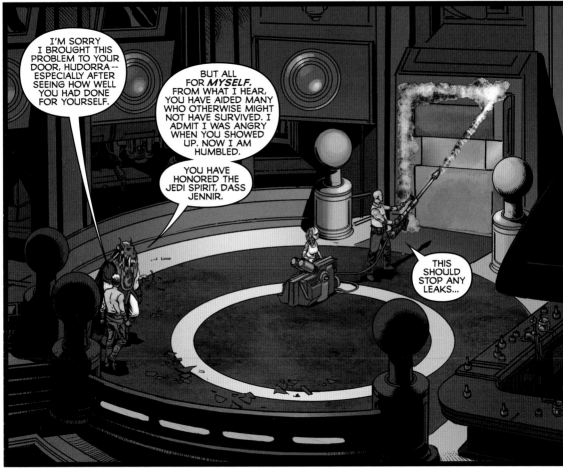

I'M SORRY I BROUGHT THIS PROBLEM TO YOUR DOOR, HUDORRA -- ESPECIALLY AFTER SEEING HOW WELL YOU HAD DONE FOR YOURSELF.

BUT ALL FOR *MYSELF.* FROM WHAT I HEAR, YOU HAVE AIDED MANY WHO OTHERWISE MIGHT NOT HAVE SURVIVED. I ADMIT I WAS ANGRY WHEN YOU SHOWED UP. NOW I AM HUMBLED.

YOU HAVE HONORED THE JEDI SPIRIT, DASS JENNIR.

THIS SHOULD STOP ANY LEAKS...

KAL, SHAYLAI -- YOU'VE DONE ENOUGH. GET CLEANED UP AND JOIN US IN THE DINING HALL. PASS THE WORD TO CAPTAIN HEREN AND BOMO GREENBARK.

I BELIEVE OUR CHEFS HAVE PREPARED A FEAST.

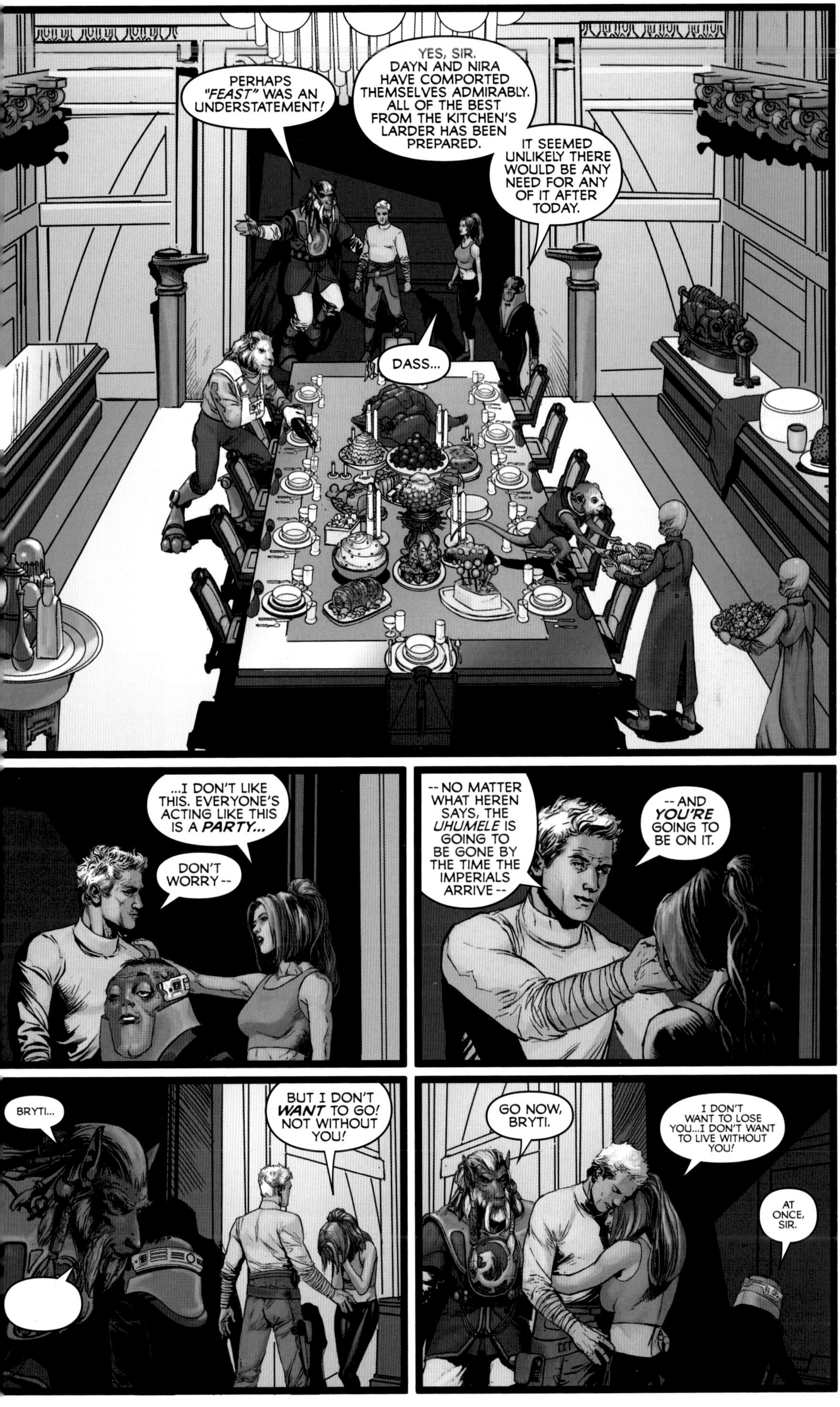
PERHAPS "FEAST" WAS AN UNDERSTATEMENT!
YES, SIR. DAYN AND NIRA HAVE COMPORTED THEMSELVES ADMIRABLY. ALL OF THE BEST FROM THE KITCHEN'S LARDER HAS BEEN PREPARED.
IT SEEMED UNLIKELY THERE WOULD BE ANY NEED FOR ANY OF IT AFTER TODAY.
DASS...
...I DON'T LIKE THIS. EVERYONE'S ACTING LIKE THIS IS A PARTY...
DON'T WORRY--
--NO MATTER WHAT HEREN SAYS, THE UHUMELE IS GOING TO BE GONE BY THE TIME THE IMPERIALS ARRIVE--
--AND YOU'RE GOING TO BE ON IT.
BRYTI...
BUT I DON'T WANT TO GO! NOT WITHOUT YOU!
GO NOW, BRYTI.
I DON'T WANT TO LOSE YOU...I DON'T WANT TO LIVE WITHOUT YOU!
AT ONCE, SIR.

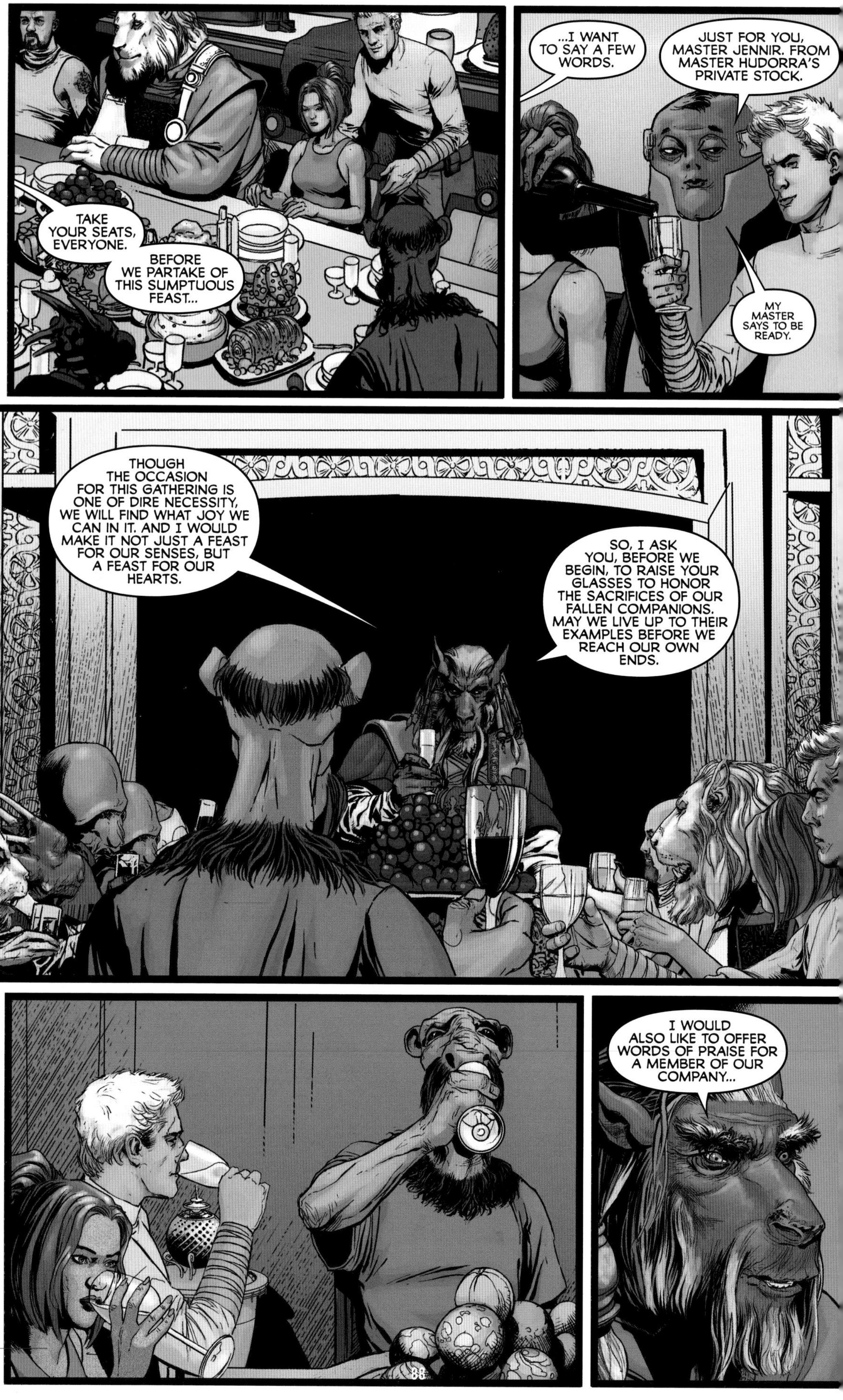
TAKE YOUR SEATS, EVERYONE.
BEFORE WE PARTAKE OF THIS SUMPTUOUS FEAST...
...I WANT TO SAY A FEW WORDS.
JUST FOR YOU, MASTER JENNIR. FROM MASTER HUDORRA'S PRIVATE STOCK.
MY MASTER SAYS TO BE READY.
THOUGH THE OCCASION FOR THIS GATHERING IS ONE OF DIRE NECESSITY, WE WILL FIND WHAT JOY WE CAN IN IT. AND I WOULD MAKE IT NOT JUST A FEAST FOR OUR SENSES, BUT A FEAST FOR OUR HEARTS.
SO, I ASK YOU, BEFORE WE BEGIN, TO RAISE YOUR GLASSES TO HONOR THE SACRIFICES OF OUR FALLEN COMPANIONS. MAY WE LIVE UP TO THEIR EXAMPLES BEFORE WE REACH OUR OWN ENDS.
I WOULD ALSO LIKE TO OFFER WORDS OF PRAISE FOR A MEMBER OF OUR COMPANY...

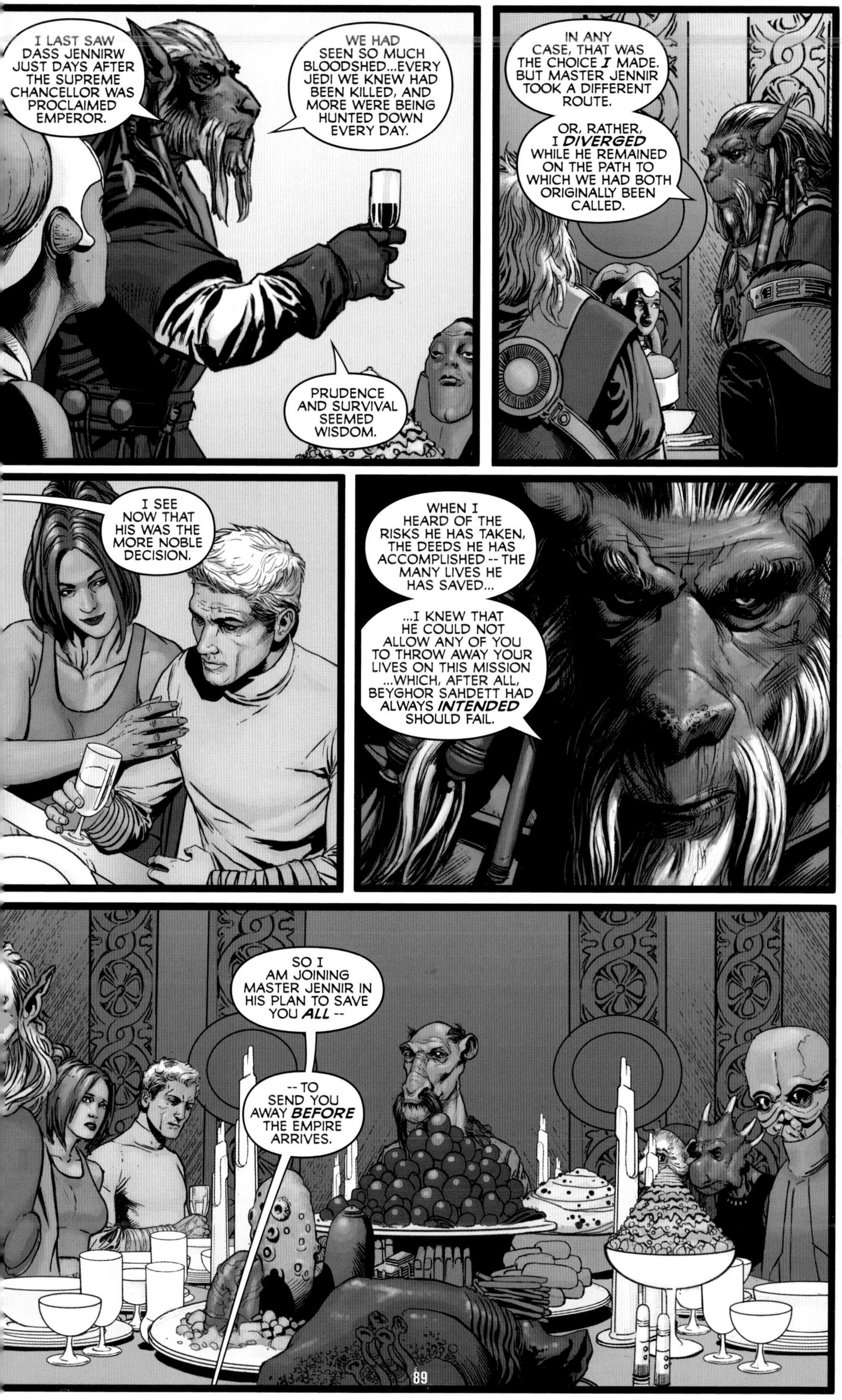
I LAST SAW DASS JENNIRW JUST DAYS AFTER THE SUPREME CHANCELLOR WAS PROCLAIMED EMPEROR.
WE HAD SEEN SO MUCH BLOODSHED...EVERY JEDI WE KNEW HAD BEEN KILLED, AND MORE WERE BEING HUNTED DOWN EVERY DAY.
PRUDENCE AND SURVIVAL SEEMED WISDOM.
IN ANY CASE, THAT WAS THE CHOICE *I* MADE. BUT MASTER JENNIR TOOK A DIFFERENT ROUTE.
OR, RATHER, I ***DIVERGED*** WHILE HE REMAINED ON THE PATH TO WHICH WE HAD BOTH ORIGINALLY BEEN CALLED.
I SEE NOW THAT HIS WAS THE MORE NOBLE DECISION.
WHEN I HEARD OF THE RISKS HE HAS TAKEN, THE DEEDS HE HAS ACCOMPLISHED -- THE MANY LIVES HE HAS SAVED...
...I KNEW THAT HE COULD NOT ALLOW ANY OF YOU TO THROW AWAY YOUR LIVES ON THIS MISSION ...WHICH, AFTER ALL, BEYGHOR SAHDETT HAD ALWAYS ***INTENDED*** SHOULD FAIL.
SO I AM JOINING MASTER JENNIR IN HIS PLAN TO SAVE YOU ***ALL*** --
-- TO SEND YOU AWAY ***BEFORE*** THE EMPIRE ARRIVES.

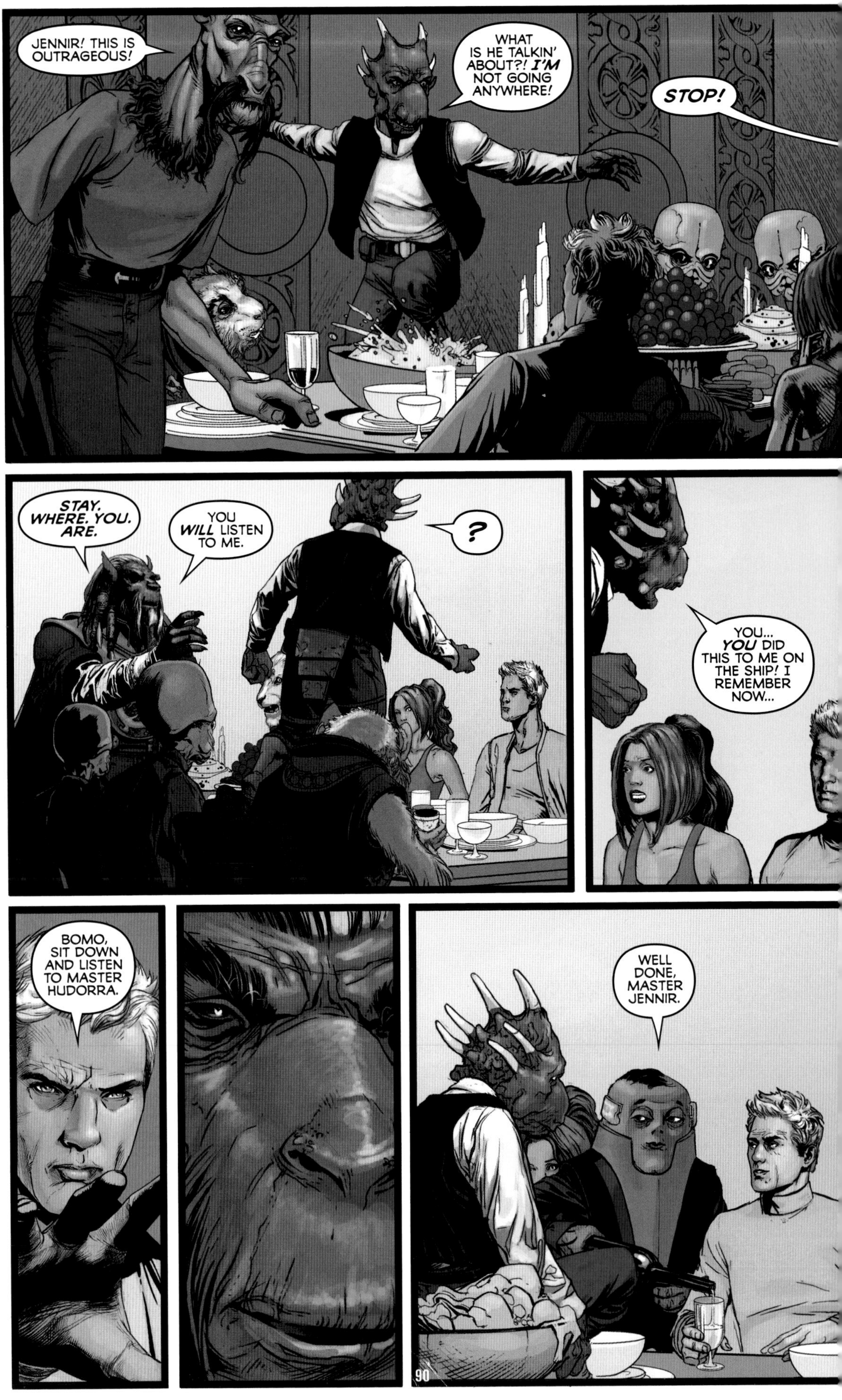
JENNIR! THIS IS OUTRAGEOUS!
WHAT IS HE TALKIN' ABOUT?! I'M NOT GOING ANYWHERE!
STOP!
STAY. WHERE. YOU. ARE.
YOU WILL LISTEN TO ME.
?
YOU... YOU DID THIS TO ME ON THE SHIP! I REMEMBER NOW...
BOMO, SIT DOWN AND LISTEN TO MASTER HUDORRA.
WELL DONE, MASTER JENNIR.

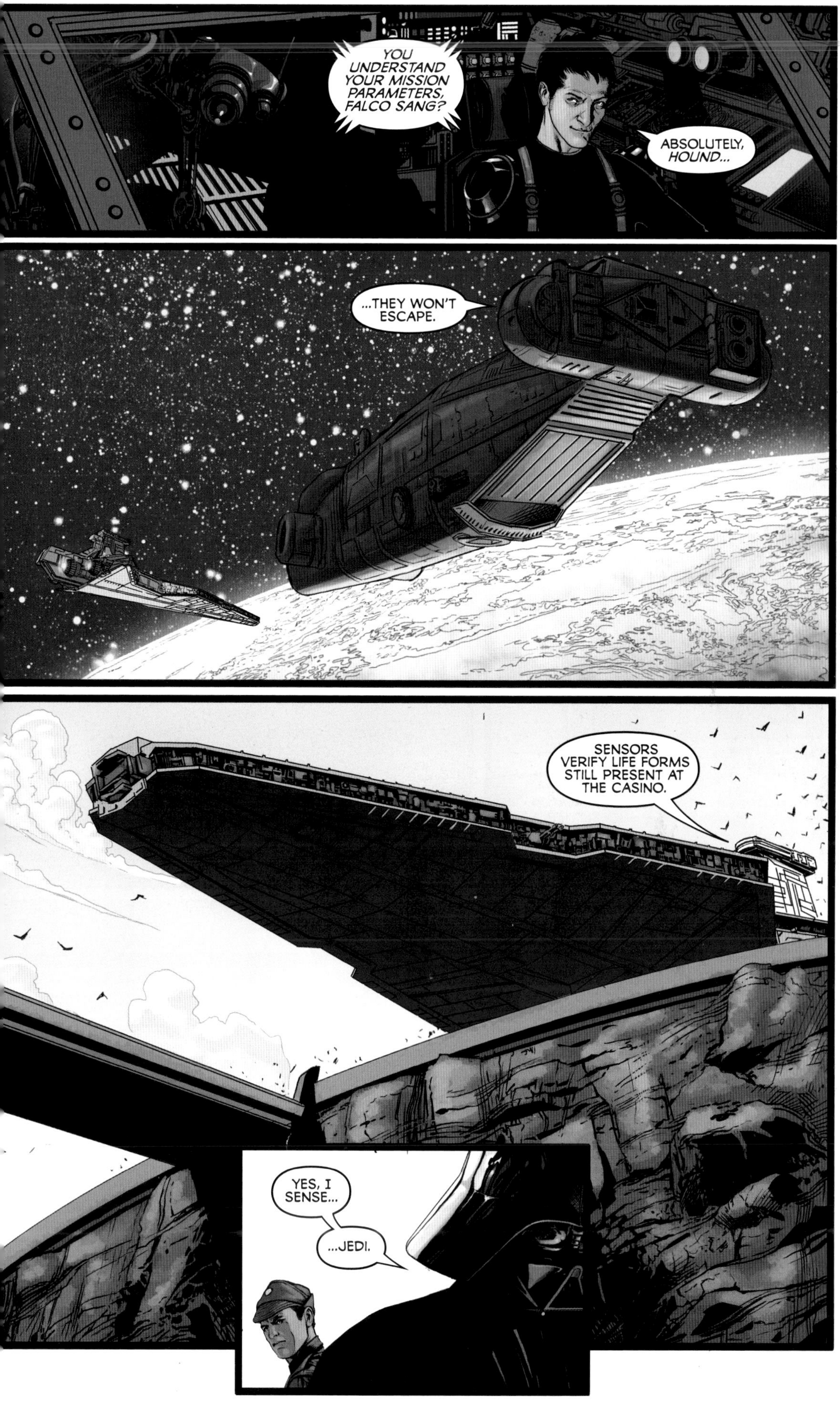
YOU UNDERSTAND YOUR MISSION PARAMETERS, FALCO SANG?
ABSOLUTELY, HOUND...
...THEY WON'T ESCAPE.
SENSORS VERIFY LIFE FORMS STILL PRESENT AT THE CASINO.
YES, I SENSE...
...JEDI.

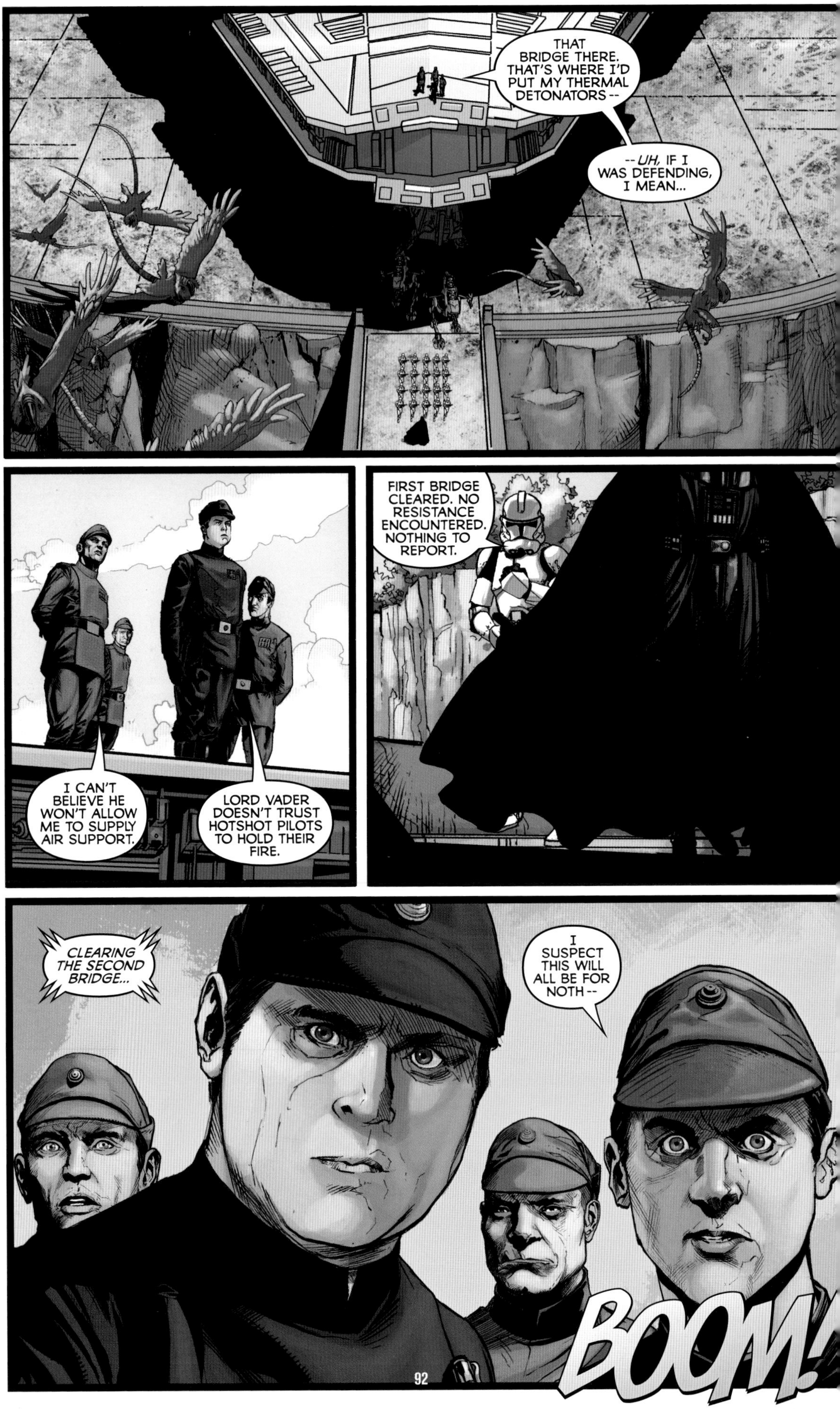

THAT BRIDGE THERE. THAT'S WHERE I'D PUT MY THERMAL DETONATORS --
-- *UH,* IF I WAS DEFENDING, I MEAN...
I CAN'T BELIEVE HE WON'T ALLOW ME TO SUPPLY AIR SUPPORT.
LORD VADER DOESN'T TRUST HOTSHOT PILOTS TO HOLD THEIR FIRE.
FIRST BRIDGE CLEARED. NO RESISTANCE ENCOUNTERED. NOTHING TO REPORT.
CLEARING THE SECOND BRIDGE...
I SUSPECT THIS WILL ALL BE FOR NOTH --
BOOM!

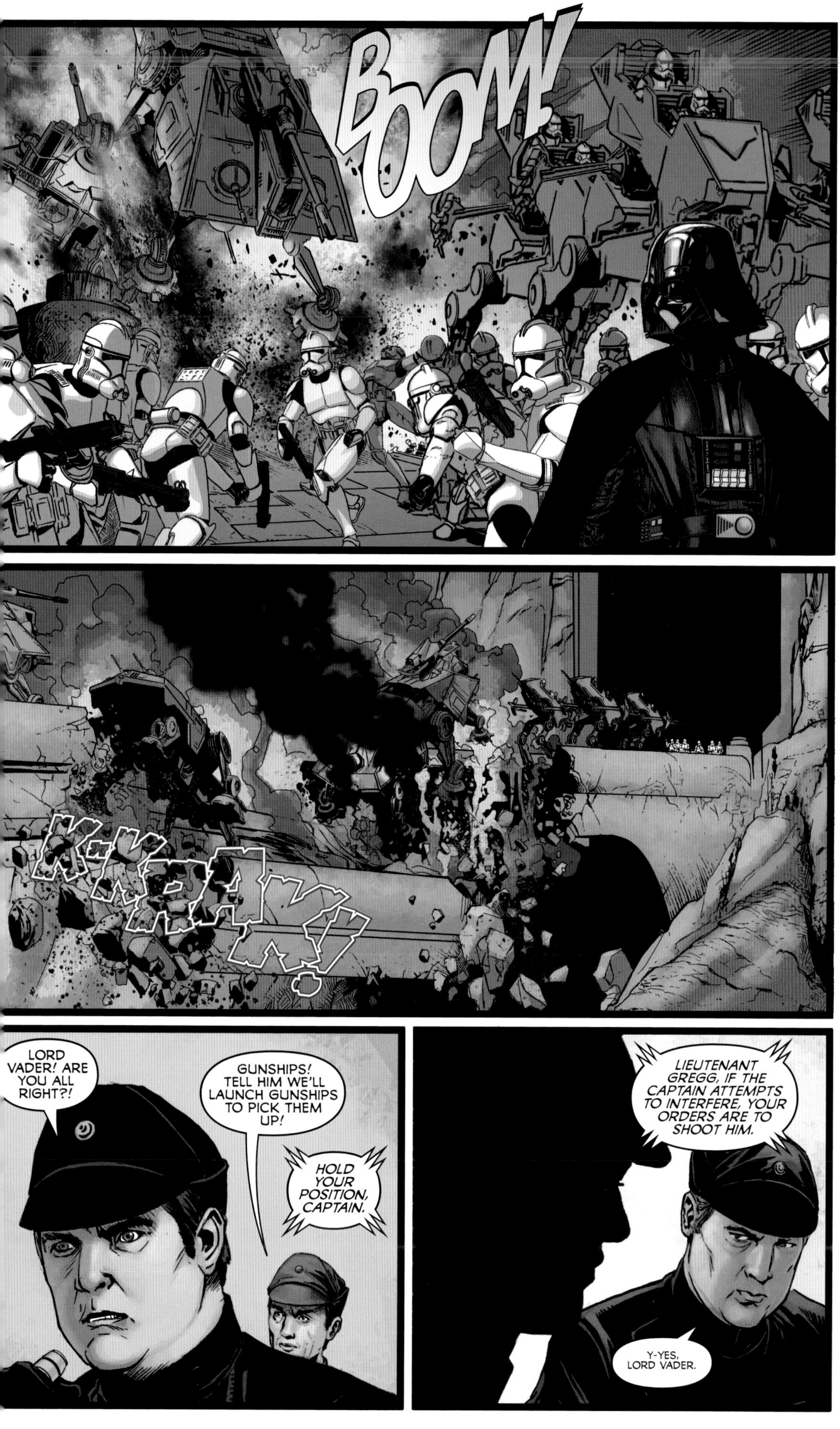
BOOM!
K-KRAKA!
LORD VADER! ARE YOU ALL RIGHT?!
GUNSHIPS! TELL HIM WE'LL LAUNCH GUNSHIPS TO PICK THEM UP!
HOLD YOUR POSITION, CAPTAIN.
LIEUTENANT GREGG, IF THE CAPTAIN ATTEMPTS TO INTERFERE, YOUR ORDERS ARE TO SHOOT HIM.
Y-YES, LORD VADER.

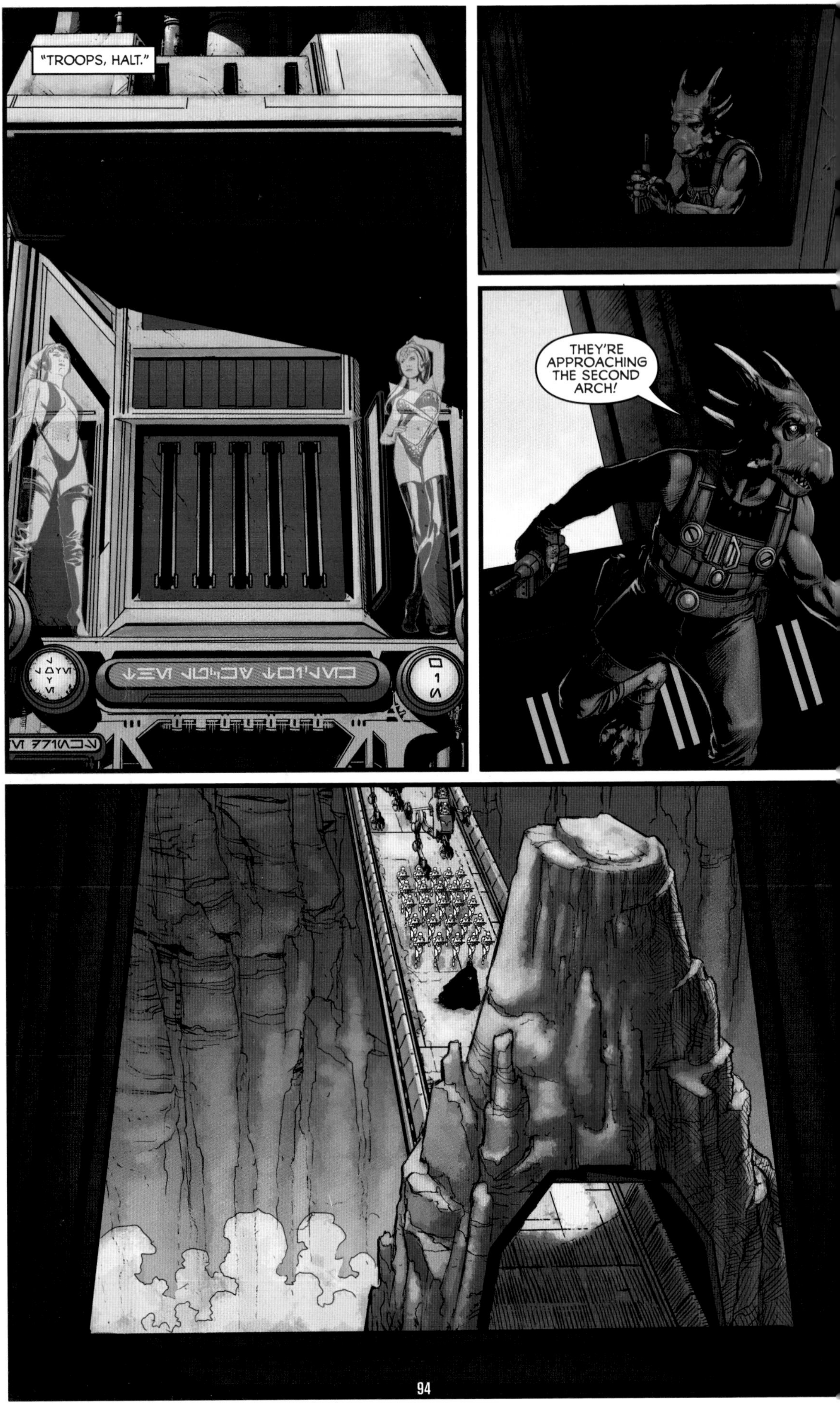
"TROOPS, HALT."
THEY'RE APPROACHING THE SECOND ARCH!

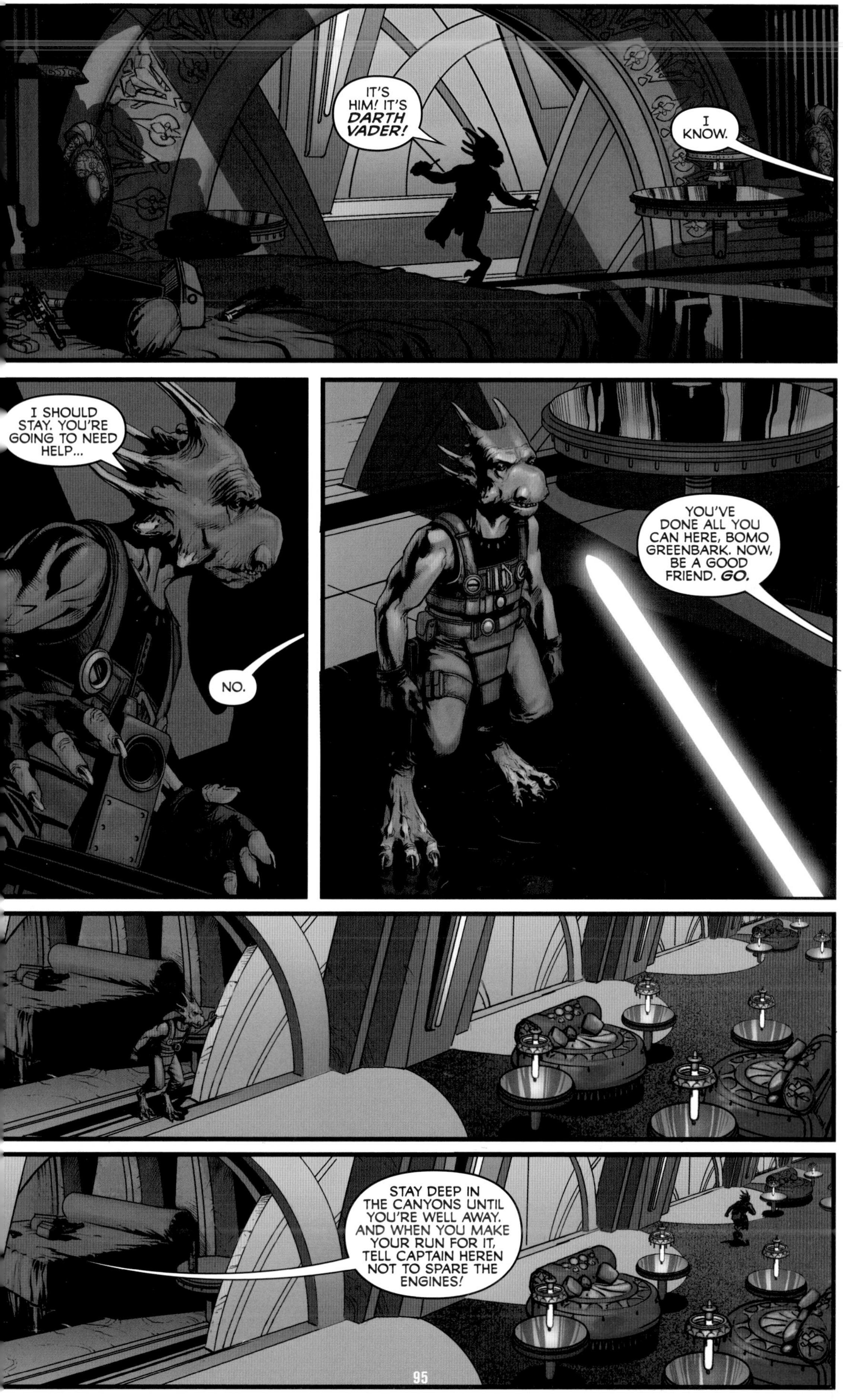
IT'S HIM! IT'S *DARTH VADER!*
I KNOW.
I SHOULD STAY. YOU'RE GOING TO NEED HELP...
NO.
YOU'VE DONE ALL YOU CAN HERE, BOMO GREENBARK. NOW, BE A GOOD FRIEND. *GO.*
STAY DEEP IN THE CANYONS UNTIL YOU'RE WELL AWAY. AND WHEN YOU MAKE YOUR RUN FOR IT, TELL CAPTAIN HEREN NOT TO SPARE THE ENGINES!

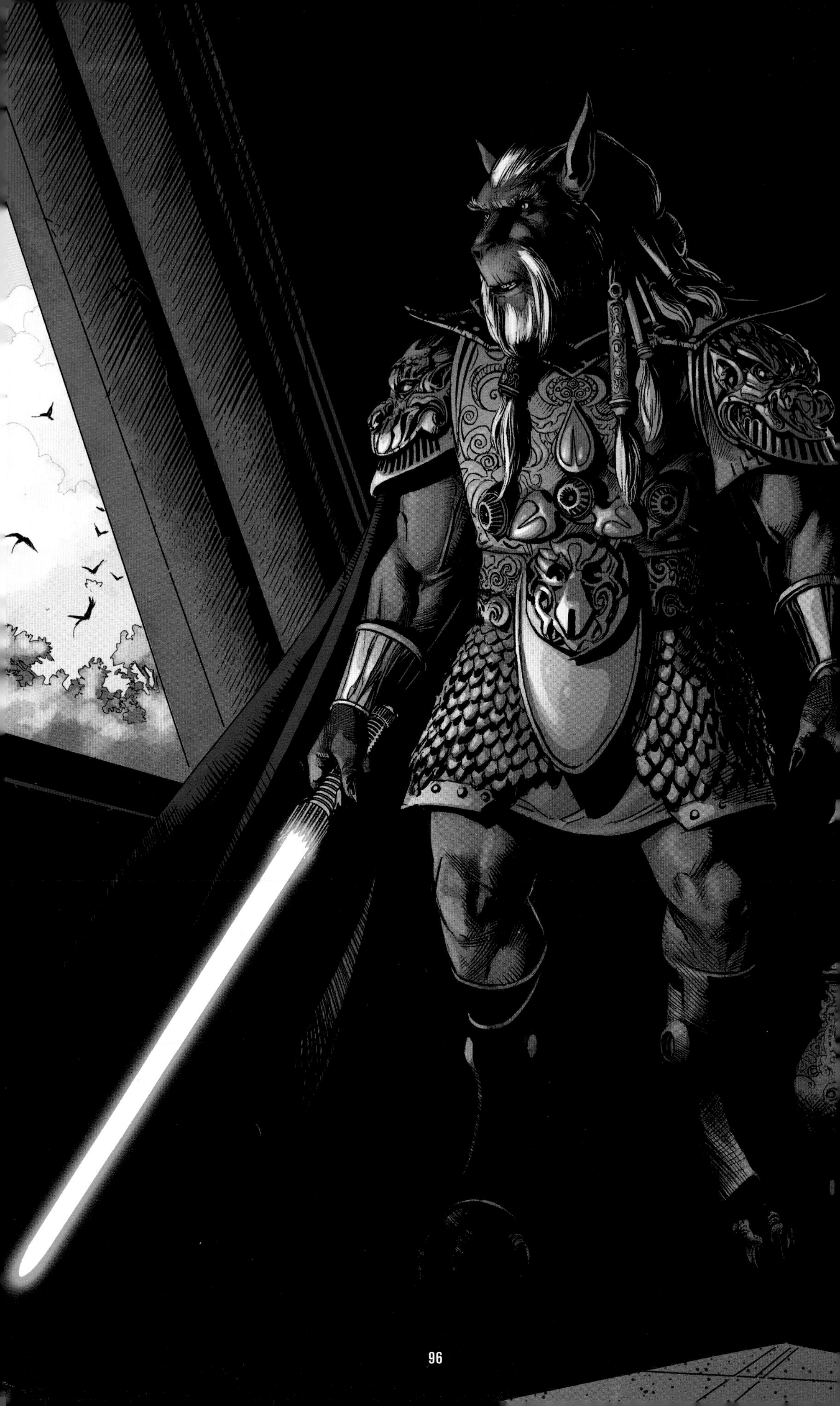

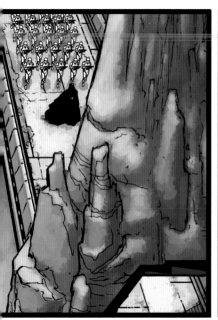

SIR?

SEND MEN TO SWEEP THAT ARCHWAY FOR BOOBY TRAPS.

YES, SIR.

ENGINEERS FORWARD! SWEEP THAT TUNNEL!

CHI-CHIK

WHOOOAAAOOOO!

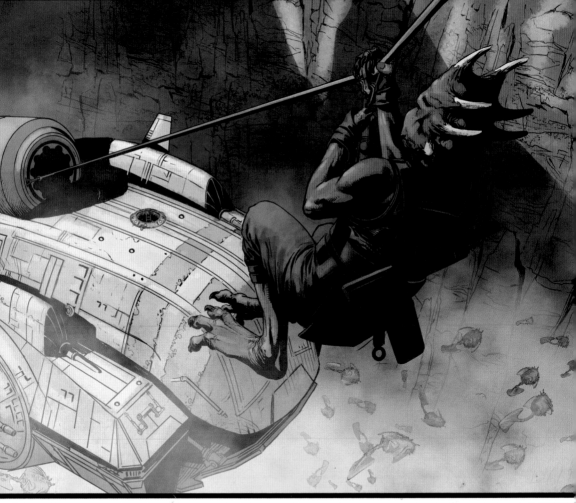

OOF!

WELCOME ABOARD, BOMO.

C'MON, YOU TWO. LET'S GET INSIDE BEFORE THE MIST CREATURES DISCOVER US.

WE DISCOVERED EXPLOSIVES, LORD VADER -- BUT THE TUNNEL IS CLEAR NOW.

PROCEED.

WELL. WE COULDN'T EXPECT YOU TO FALL FOR *EVERY* TRAP, COULD WE?

FORWARD!

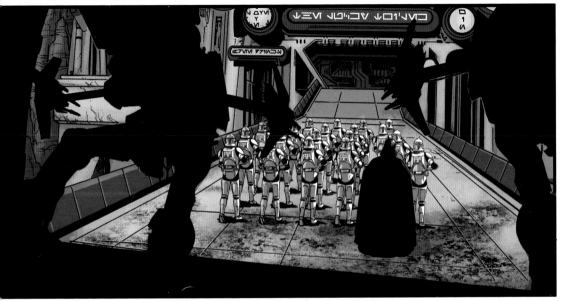

?...

JEDI... *TWO* OF THEM!

SO, DASS JENNIR HAS ENLISTED AN ALLY...

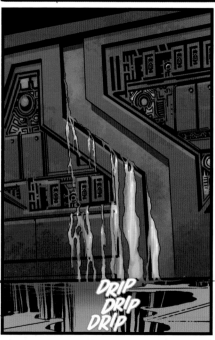

DRIP
DRIP
DRIP

FOOSH!

SPLOOSH! !

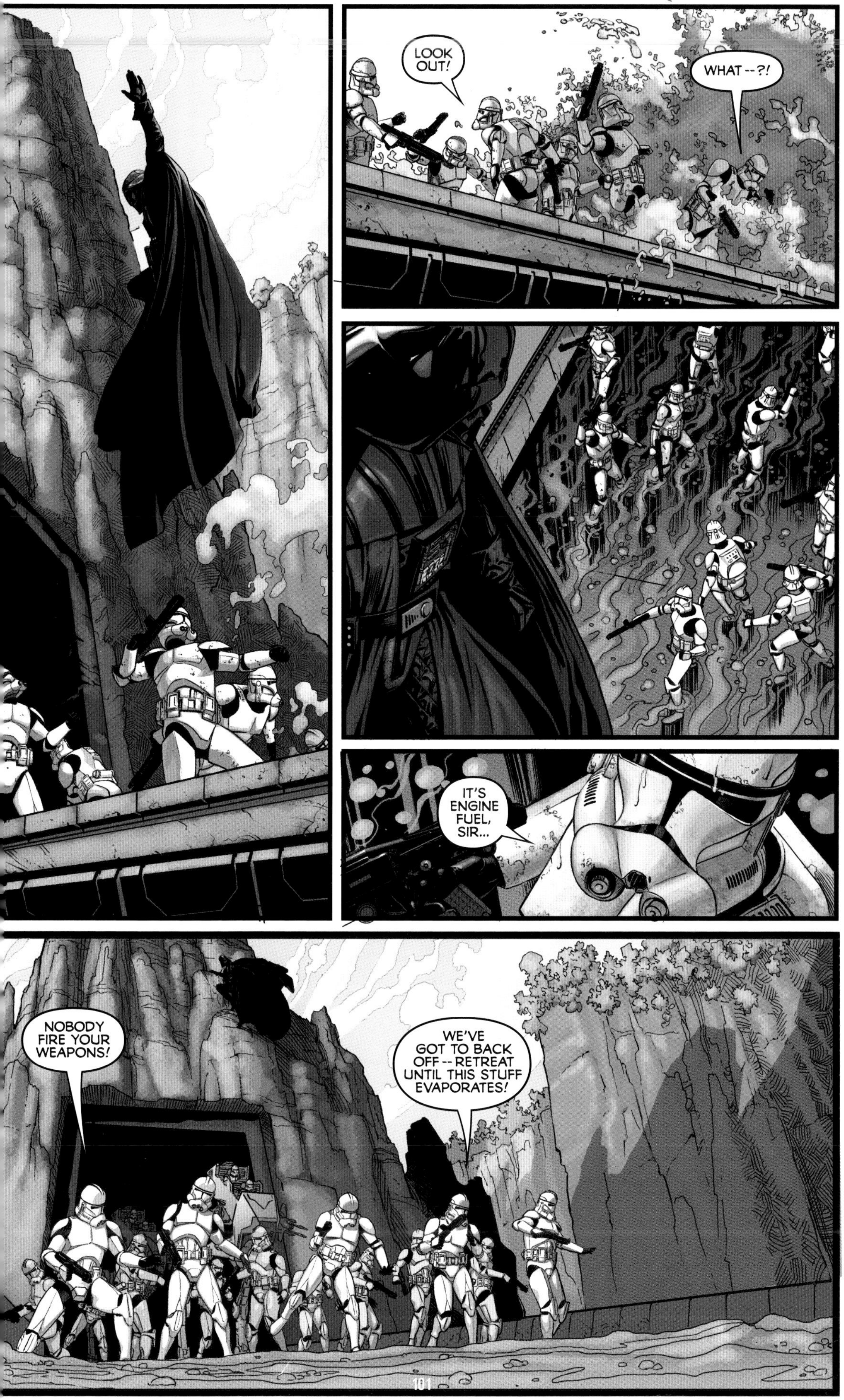
LOOK OUT!
WHAT --?!
IT'S ENGINE FUEL, SIR...
NOBODY FIRE YOUR WEAPONS!
WE'VE GOT TO BACK OFF -- RETREAT UNTIL THIS STUFF EVAPORATES!

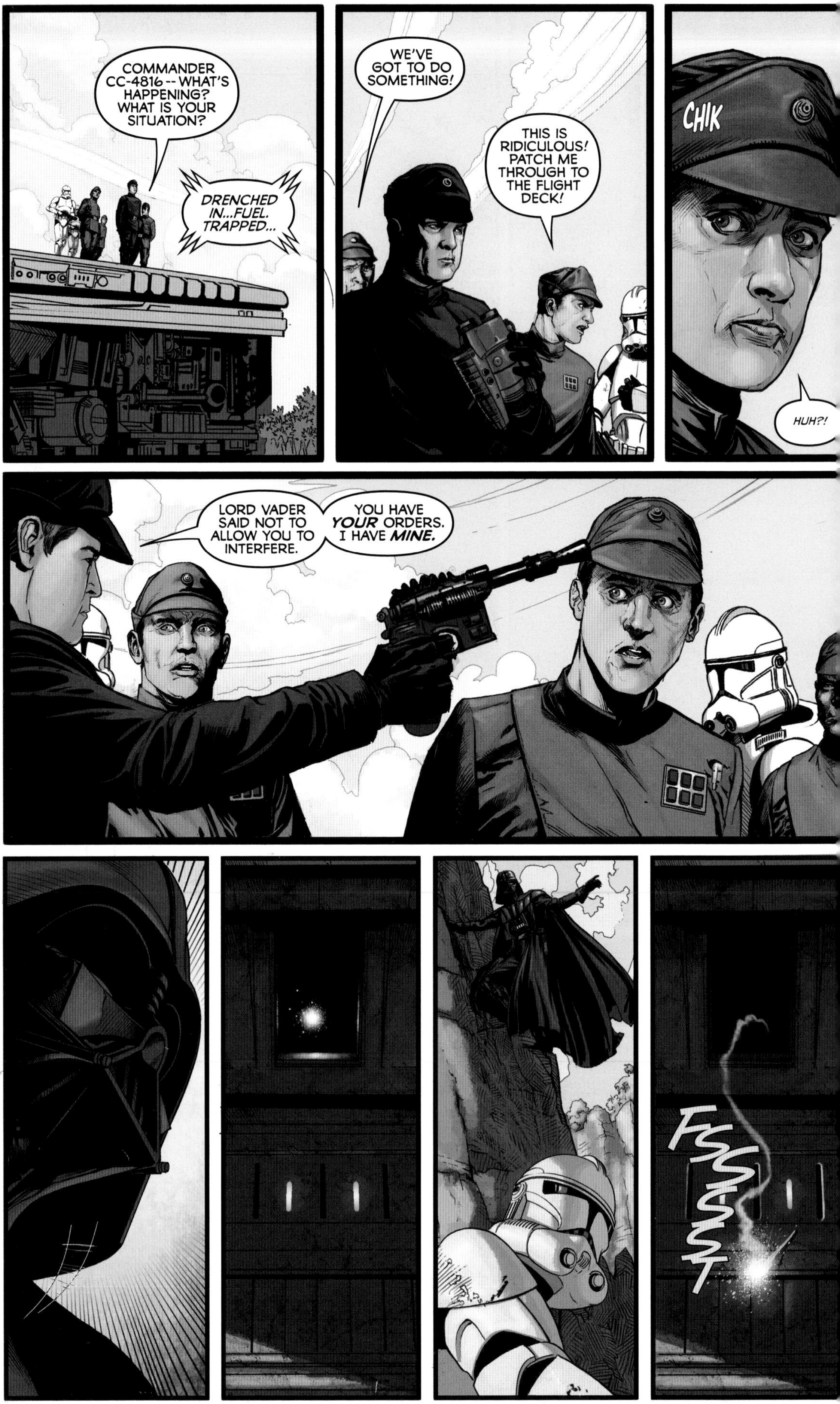
COMMANDER CC-4816 -- WHAT'S HAPPENING? WHAT IS YOUR SITUATION?
DRENCHED IN...FUEL. TRAPPED...
WE'VE GOT TO DO SOMETHING!
THIS IS RIDICULOUS! PATCH ME THROUGH TO THE FLIGHT DECK!
CHIK
HUH?!
LORD VADER SAID NOT TO ALLOW YOU TO INTERFERE.
YOU HAVE YOUR ORDERS. I HAVE MINE.
FSSSST

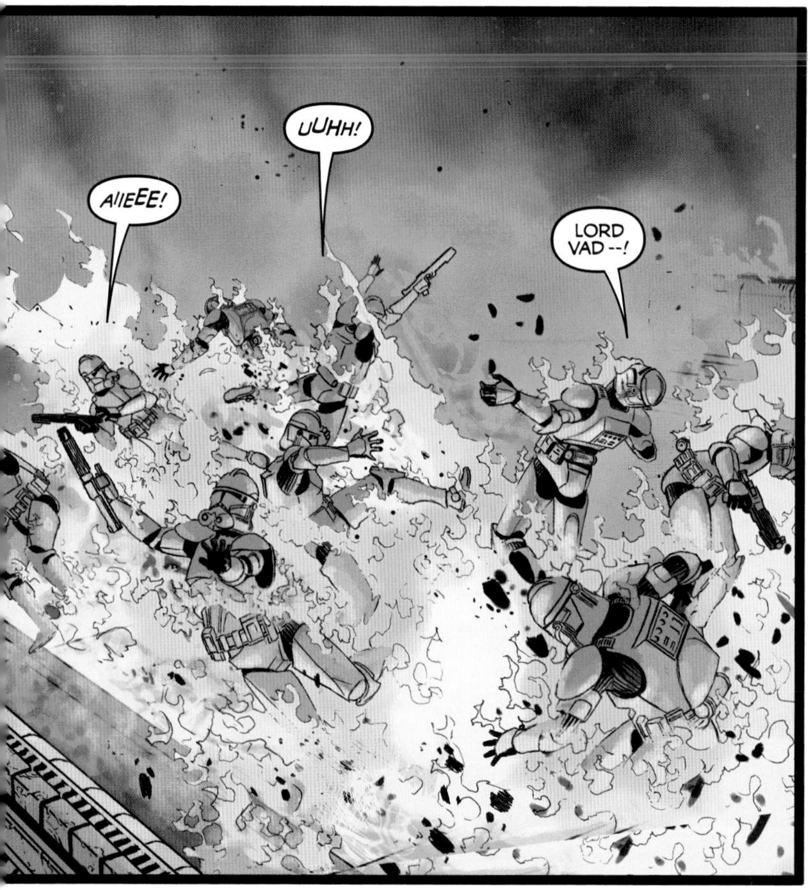
AIIEEE!
UUHH!
LORD VAD --!

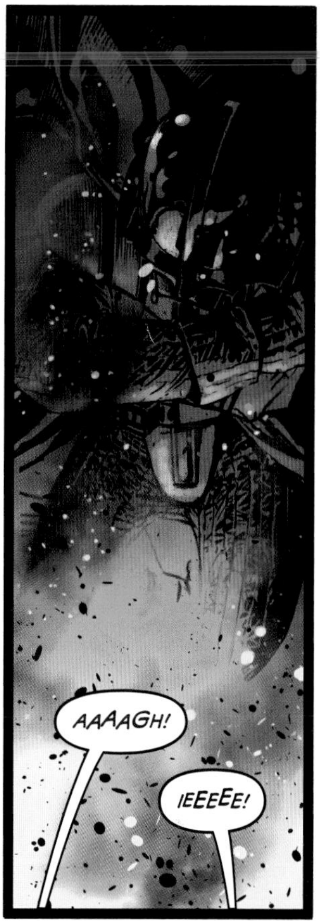
AAAAGH!
IEEEEE!

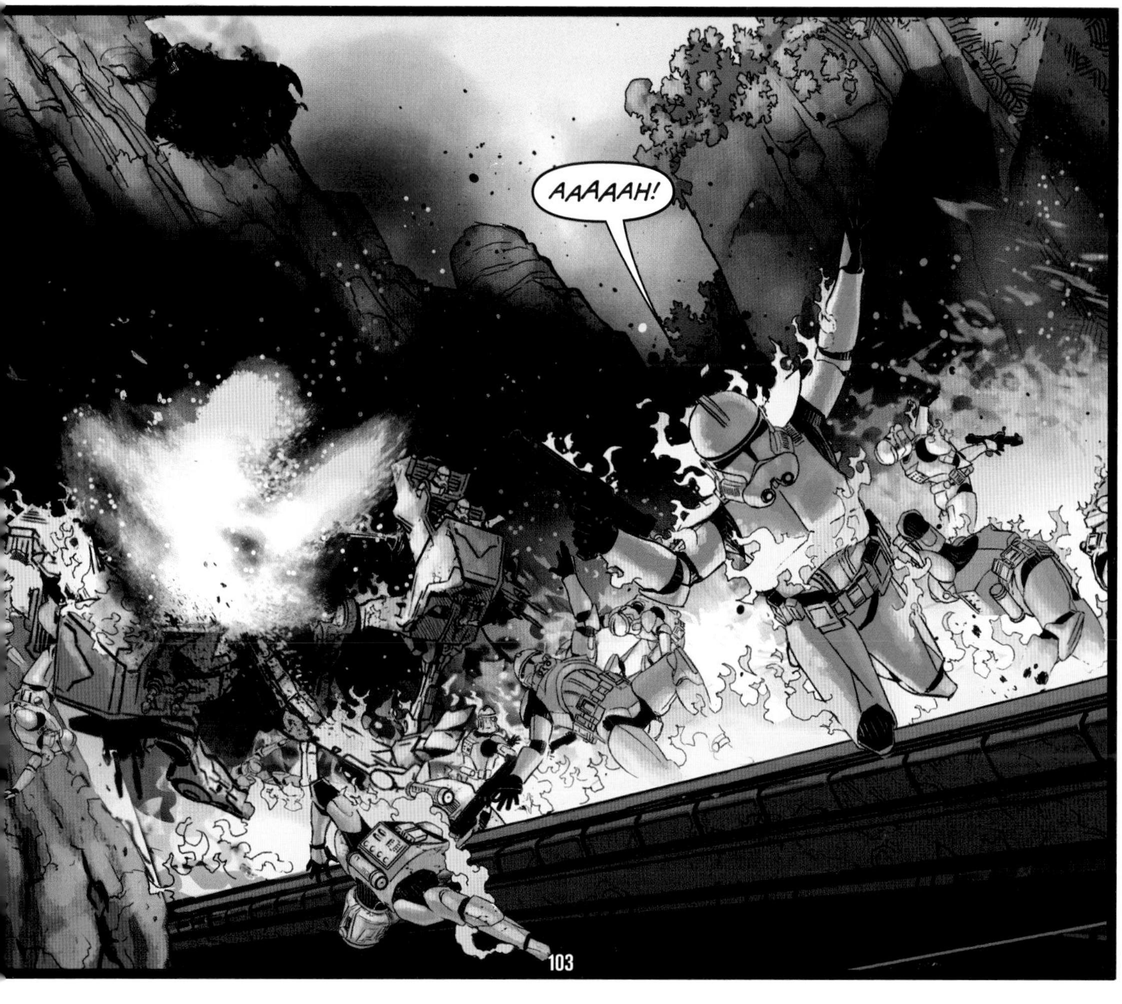
AAAAAH!

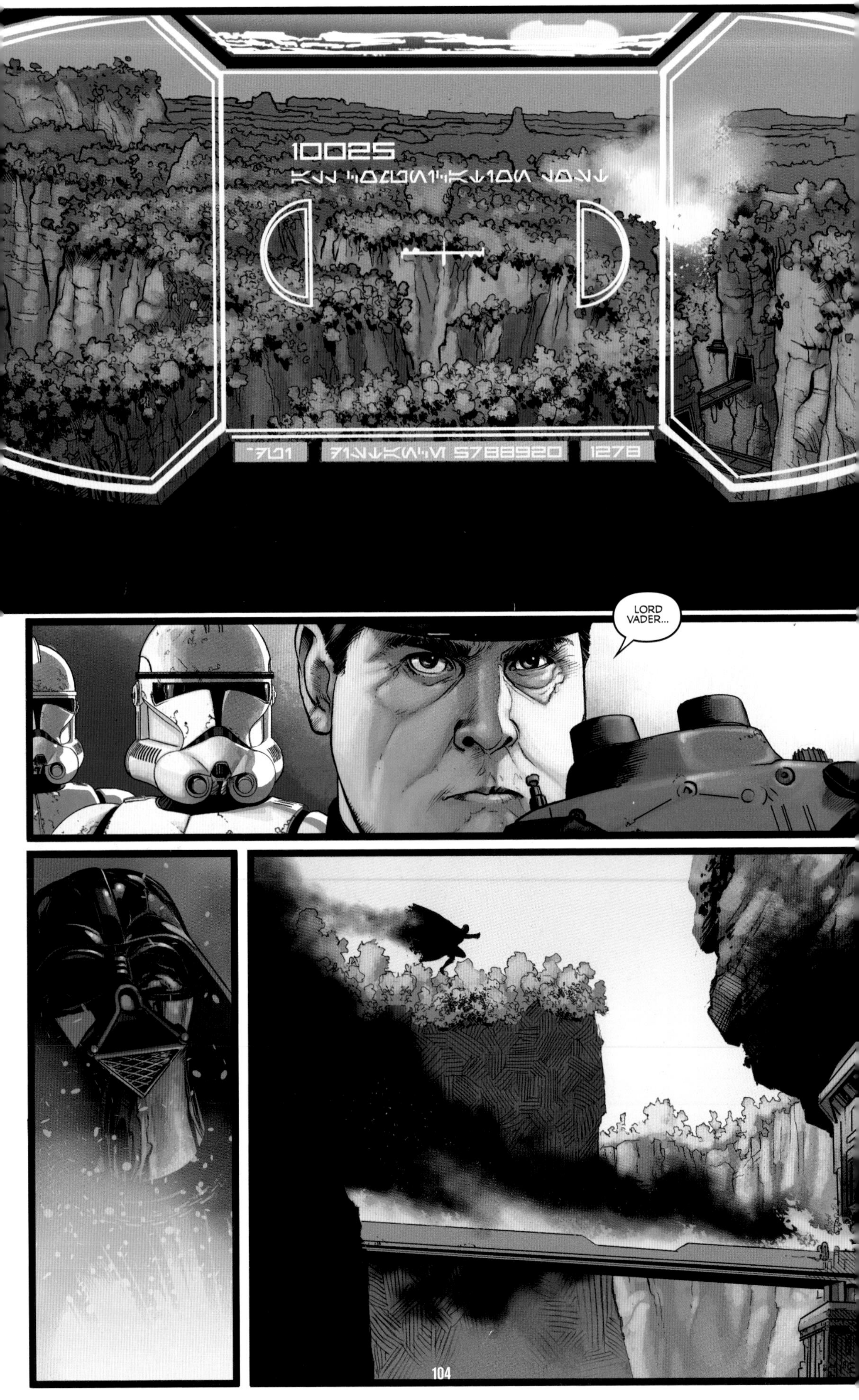
10025
5788920
1278
LORD VADER...

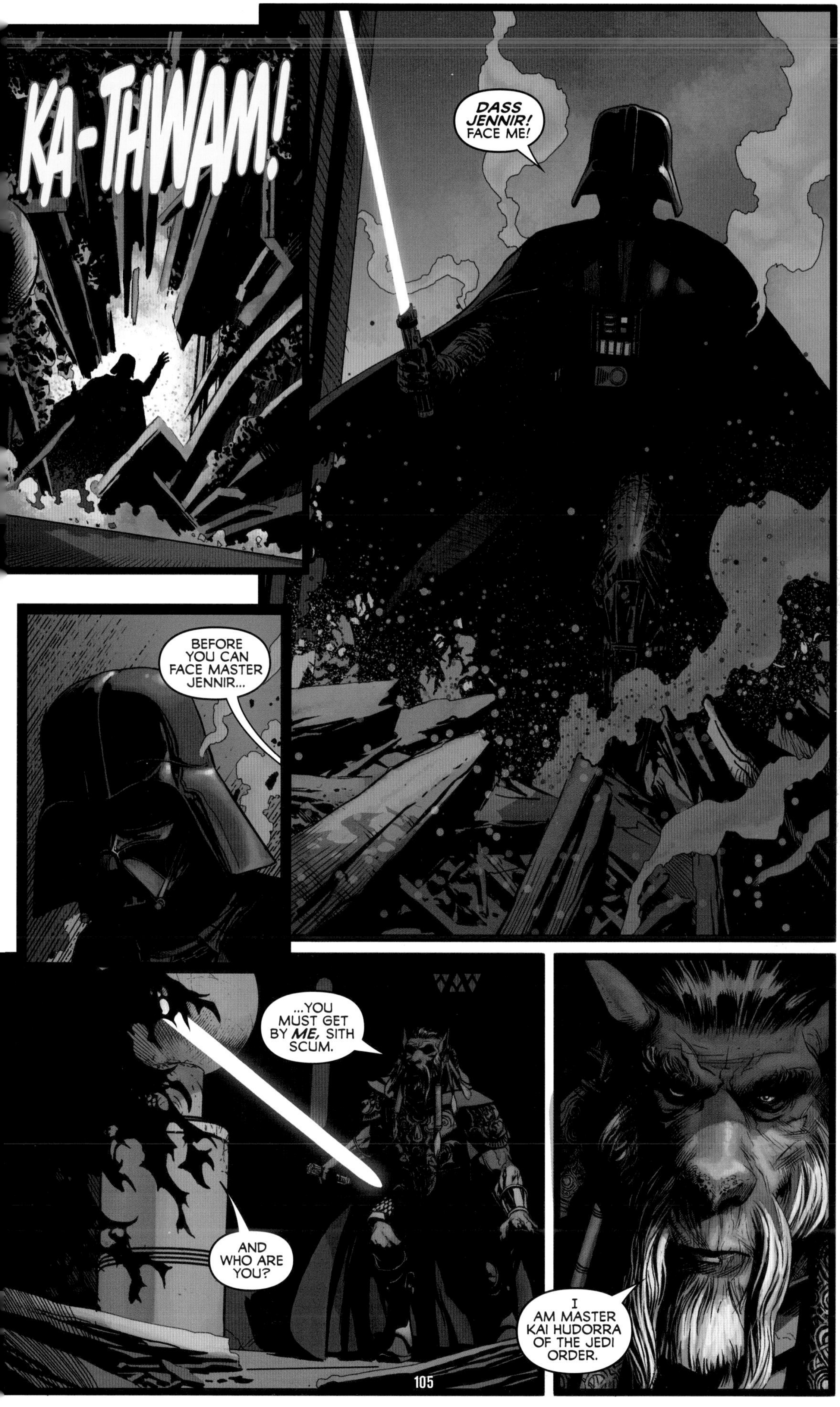
KA-THWAM!
DASS JENNIR! FACE ME!
BEFORE YOU CAN FACE MASTER JENNIR...
...YOU MUST GET BY ME, SITH SCUM.
AND WHO ARE YOU?
I AM MASTER KAI HUDORRA OF THE JEDI ORDER.

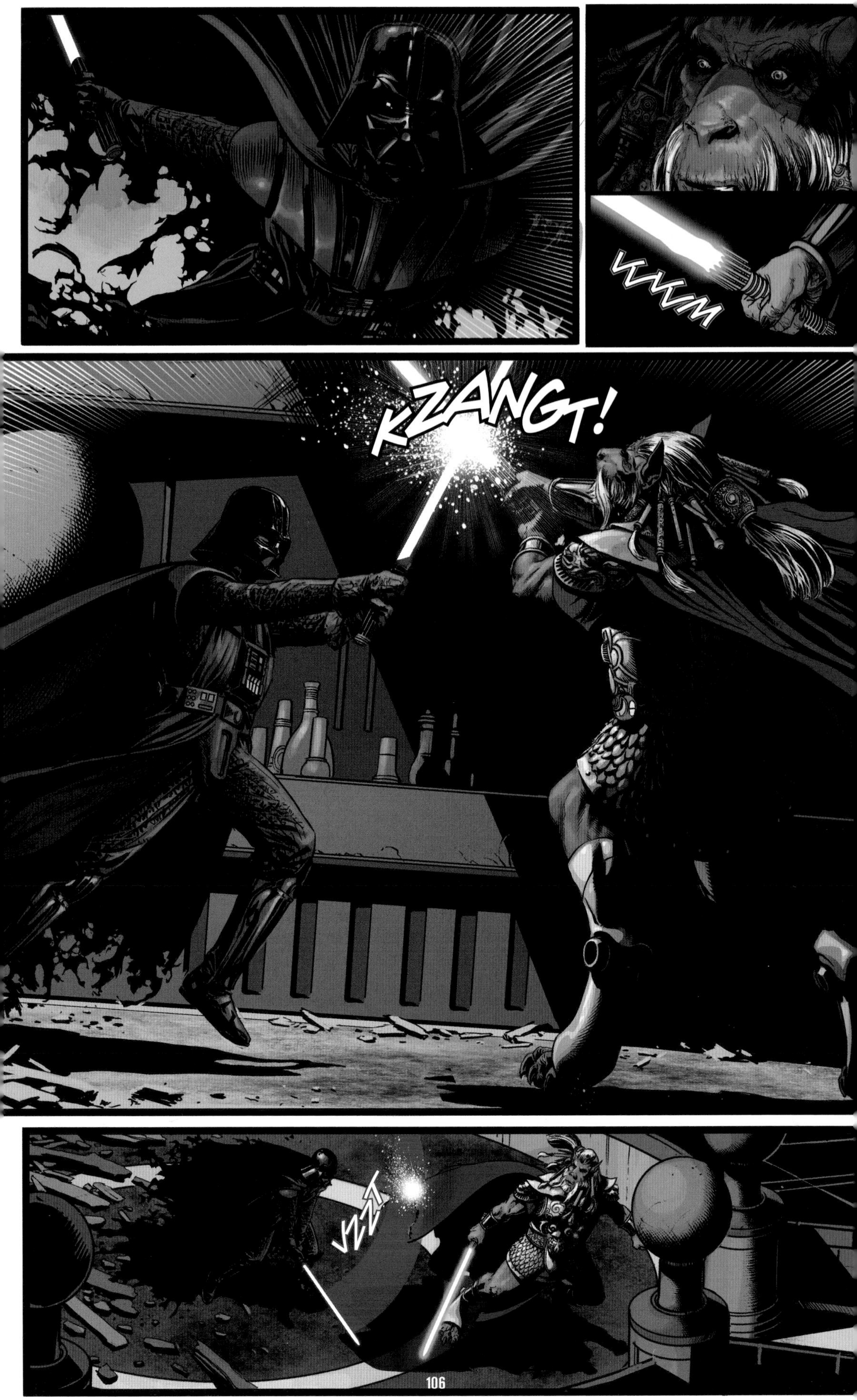
VVVM
KZANGT!
VZZT

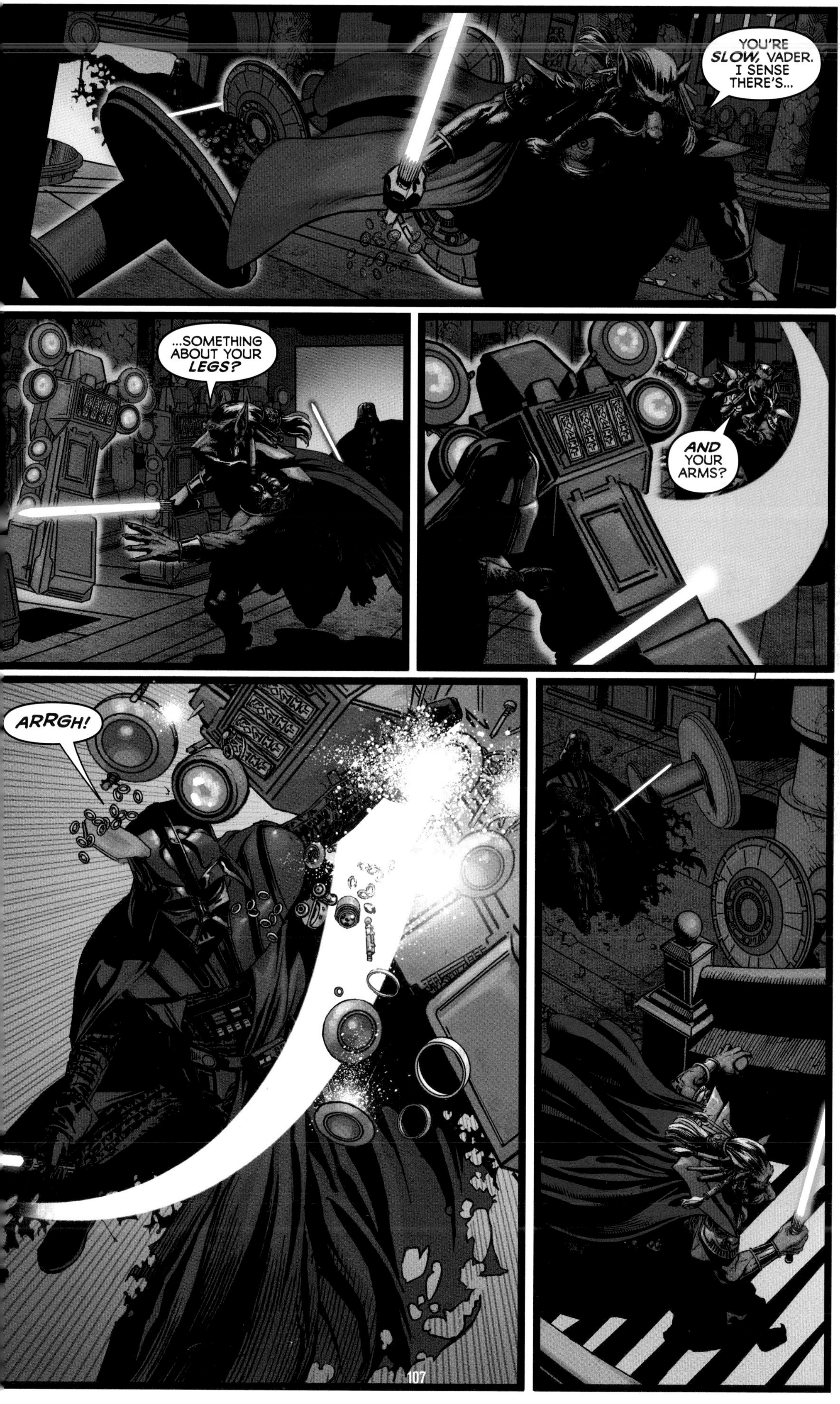
YOU'RE SLOW, VADER. I SENSE THERE'S...
...SOMETHING ABOUT YOUR LEGS?
AND YOUR ARMS?
ARRGH!

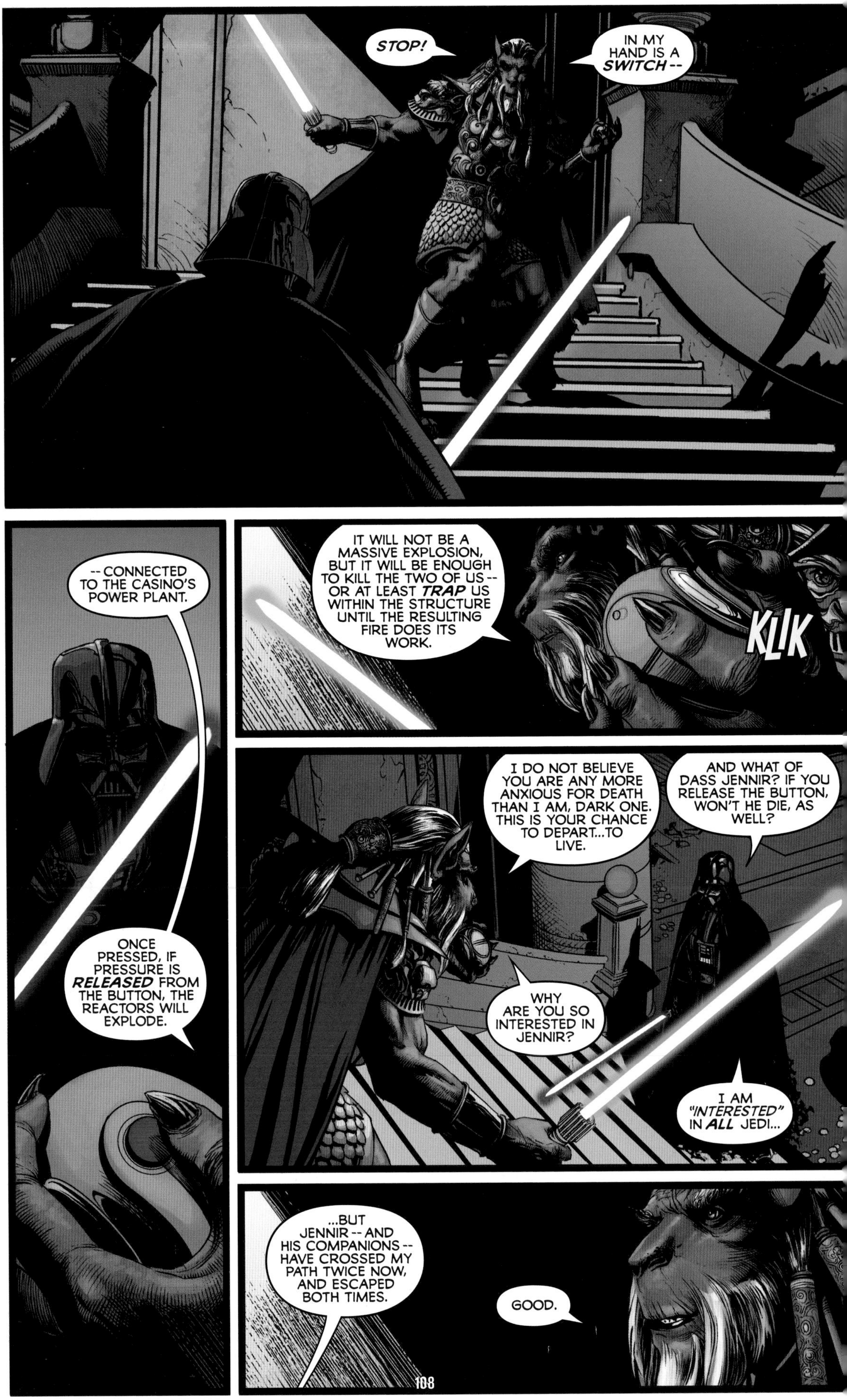
STOP!
IN MY HAND IS A SWITCH --
-- CONNECTED TO THE CASINO'S POWER PLANT.
ONCE PRESSED, IF PRESSURE IS RELEASED FROM THE BUTTON, THE REACTORS WILL EXPLODE.
IT WILL NOT BE A MASSIVE EXPLOSION, BUT IT WILL BE ENOUGH TO KILL THE TWO OF US -- OR AT LEAST TRAP US WITHIN THE STRUCTURE UNTIL THE RESULTING FIRE DOES ITS WORK.
KLIK
I DO NOT BELIEVE YOU ARE ANY MORE ANXIOUS FOR DEATH THAN I AM, DARK ONE. THIS IS YOUR CHANCE TO DEPART...TO LIVE.
AND WHAT OF DASS JENNIR? IF YOU RELEASE THE BUTTON, WON'T HE DIE, AS WELL?
WHY ARE YOU SO INTERESTED IN JENNIR?
I AM "INTERESTED" IN ALL JEDI...
...BUT JENNIR -- AND HIS COMPANIONS -- HAVE CROSSED MY PATH TWICE NOW, AND ESCAPED BOTH TIMES.
GOOD.

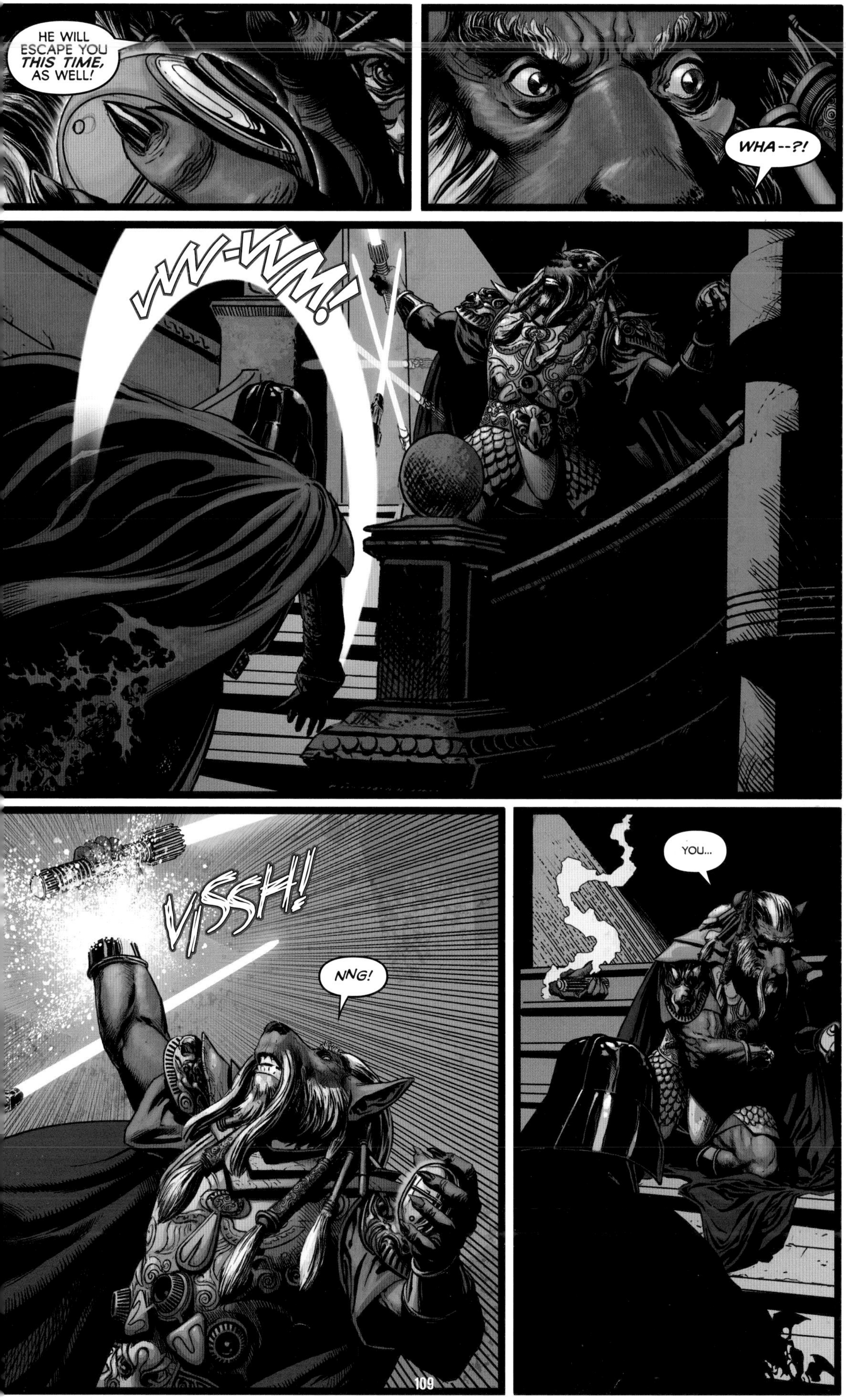
HE WILL ESCAPE YOU THIS TIME, AS WELL!
WHA--?!
VVV-VVM!
VISSH!
NNG!
YOU...

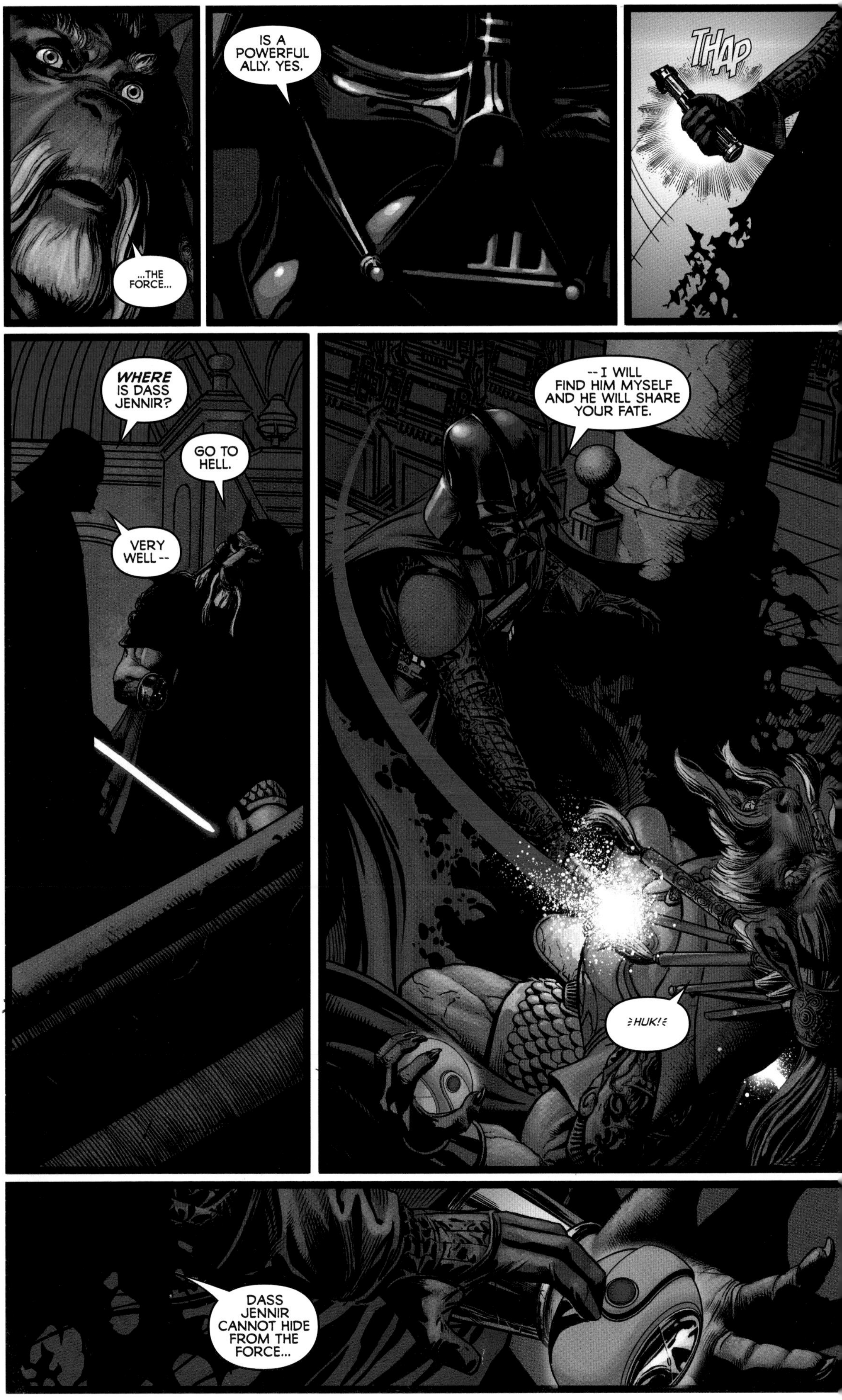
...THE FORCE...
IS A POWERFUL ALLY. YES.
THAP
WHERE IS DASS JENNIR?
GO TO HELL.
VERY WELL --
-- I WILL FIND HIM MYSELF AND HE WILL SHARE YOUR FATE.
HUK!
DASS JENNIR CANNOT HIDE FROM THE FORCE...

"...NOR FROM ME."

I CAN FEEL YOU, JENNIR... I CAN FEEL YOU STRUGGLING TO USE THE FORCE...

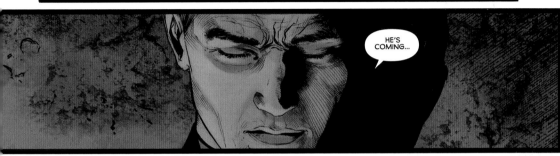

HE'S COMING...

...HERE!

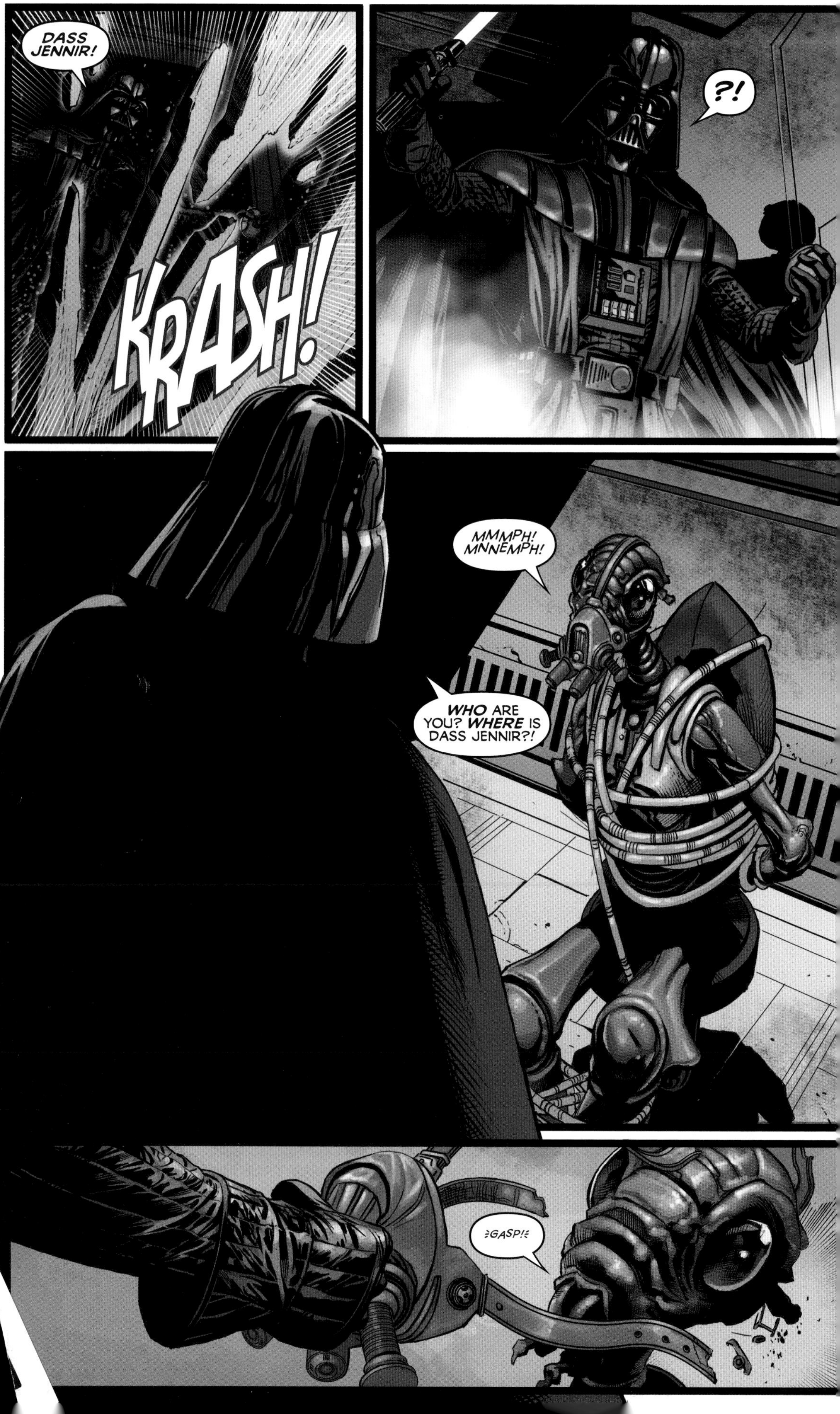
DASS JENNIR!
KRASH!
?!
MMMPH! MNNEMPH!
WHO ARE YOU? WHERE IS DASS JENNIR?!
GASP!

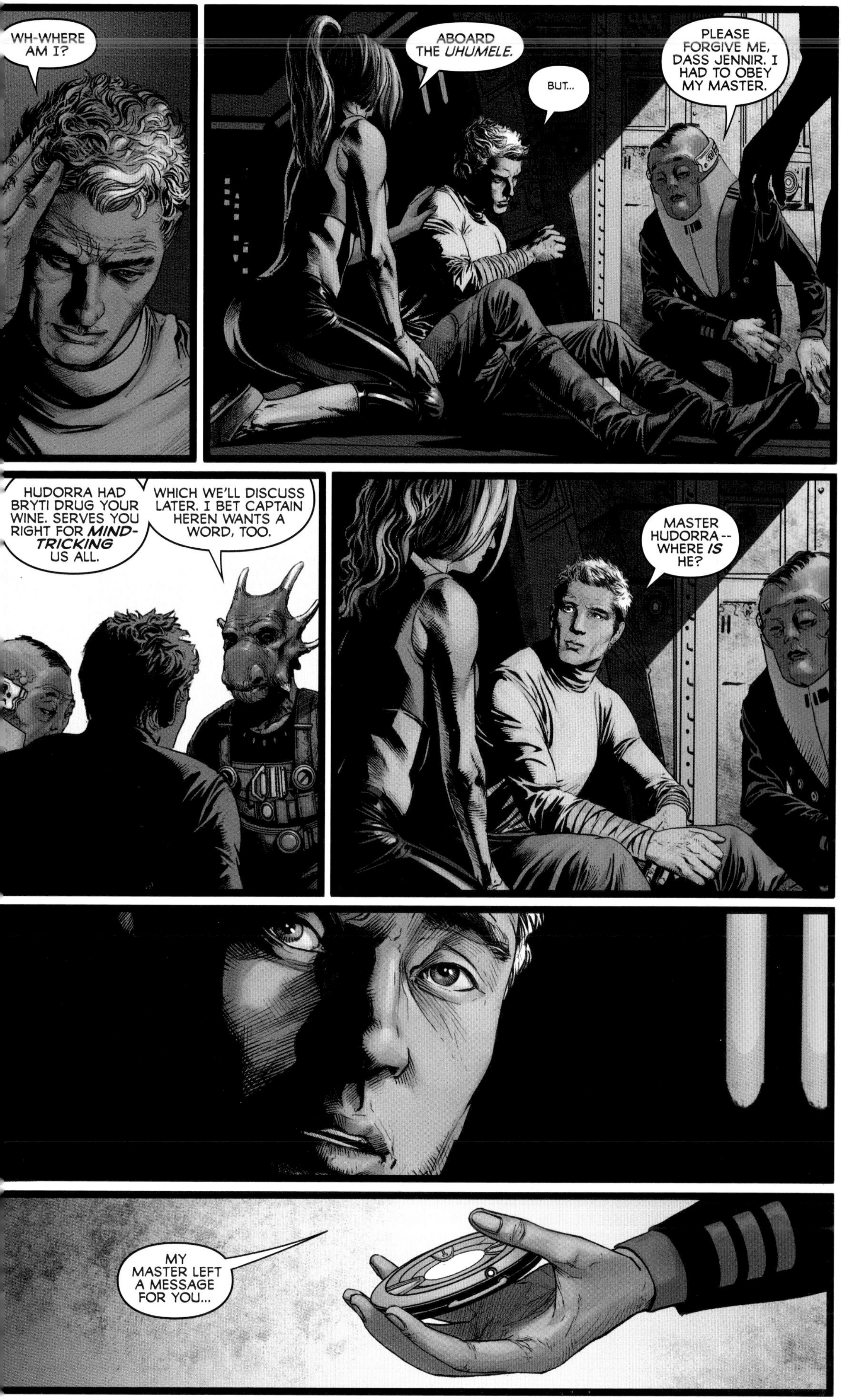
WH-WHERE AM I?
ABOARD THE *UHUMELE.*
BUT...
PLEASE FORGIVE ME, DASS JENNIR. I HAD TO OBEY MY MASTER.
HUDORRA HAD BRYTI DRUG YOUR WINE. SERVES YOU RIGHT FOR ***MIND-TRICKING*** US ALL.
WHICH WE'LL DISCUSS LATER. I BET CAPTAIN HEREN WANTS A WORD, TOO.
MASTER HUDORRA-- WHERE ***IS*** HE?
MY MASTER LEFT A MESSAGE FOR YOU...

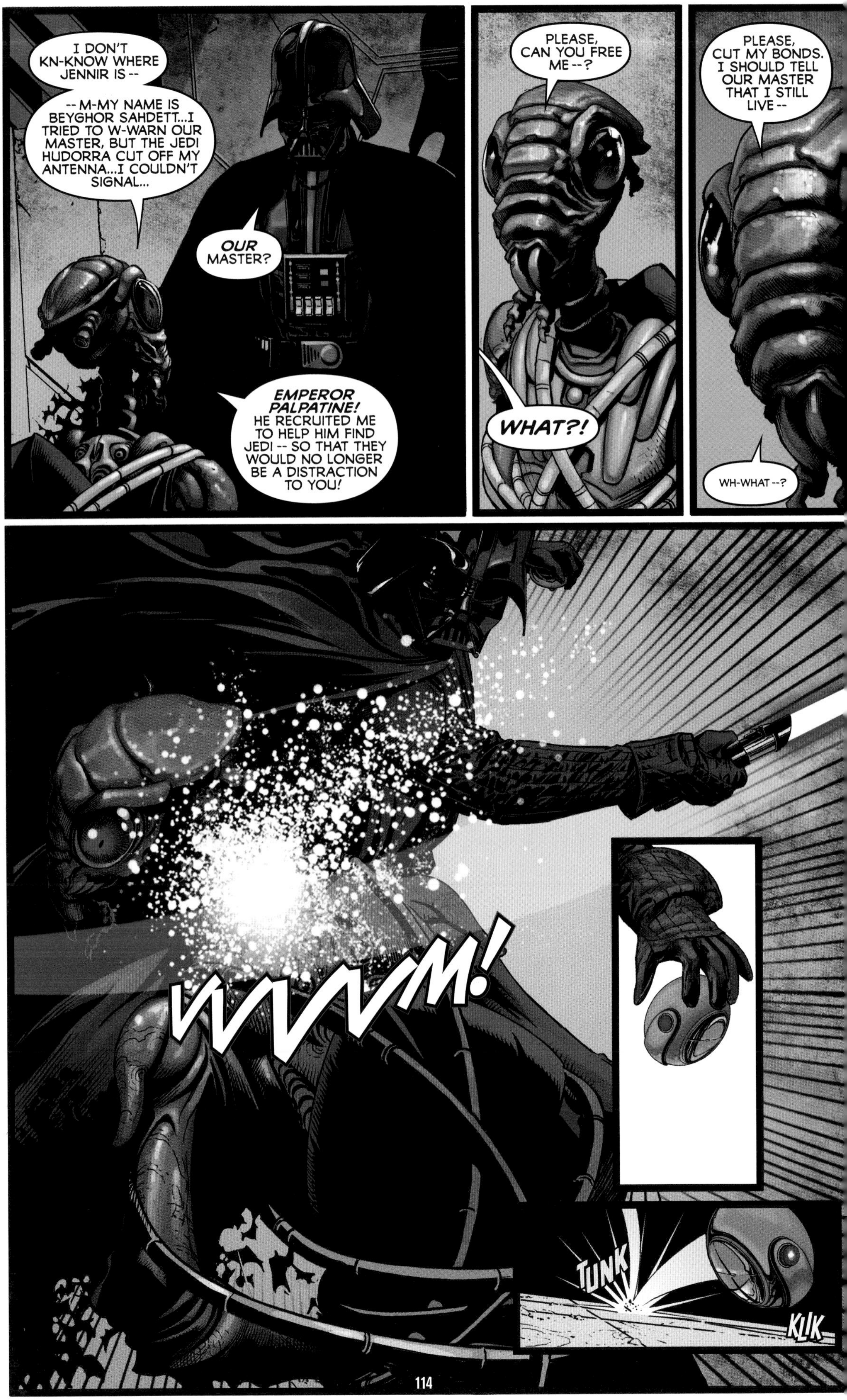
I DON'T KN-KNOW WHERE JENNIR IS --
-- M-MY NAME IS BEYGHOR SAHDETT...I TRIED TO W-WARN OUR MASTER, BUT THE JEDI HUDORRA CUT OFF MY ANTENNA...I COULDN'T SIGNAL...
OUR MASTER?
EMPEROR PALPATINE! HE RECRUITED ME TO HELP HIM FIND JEDI -- SO THAT THEY WOULD NO LONGER BE A DISTRACTION TO YOU!
PLEASE, CAN YOU FREE ME --?
WHAT?!
PLEASE, CUT MY BONDS. I SHOULD TELL OUR MASTER THAT I STILL LIVE --
WH-WHAT --?
VVVVM!
TUNK
KLIK

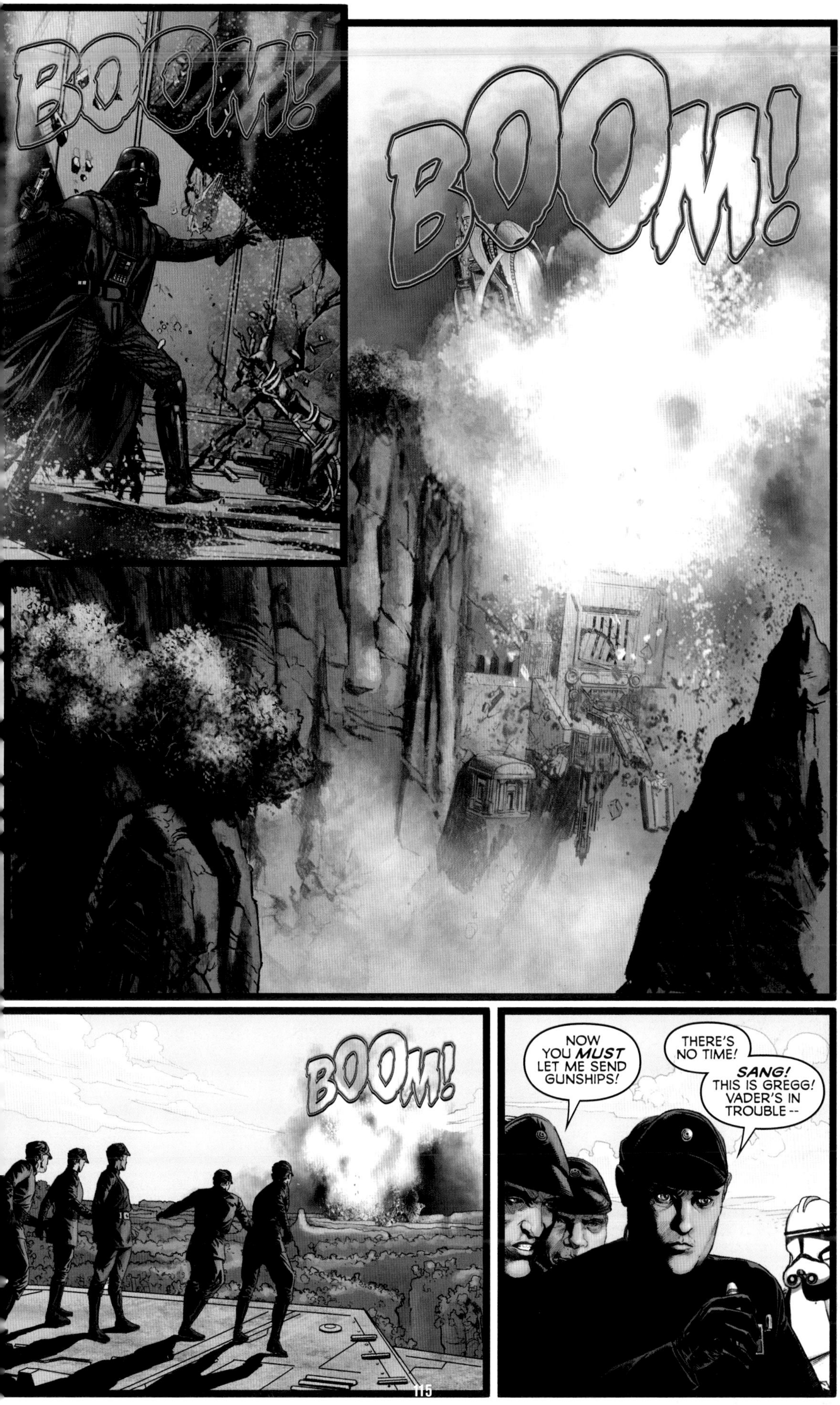
BOOM!
BOOM!
BOOM!
NOW YOU MUST LET ME SEND GUNSHIPS!
THERE'S NO TIME!
SANG! THIS IS GREGG! VADER'S IN TROUBLE --

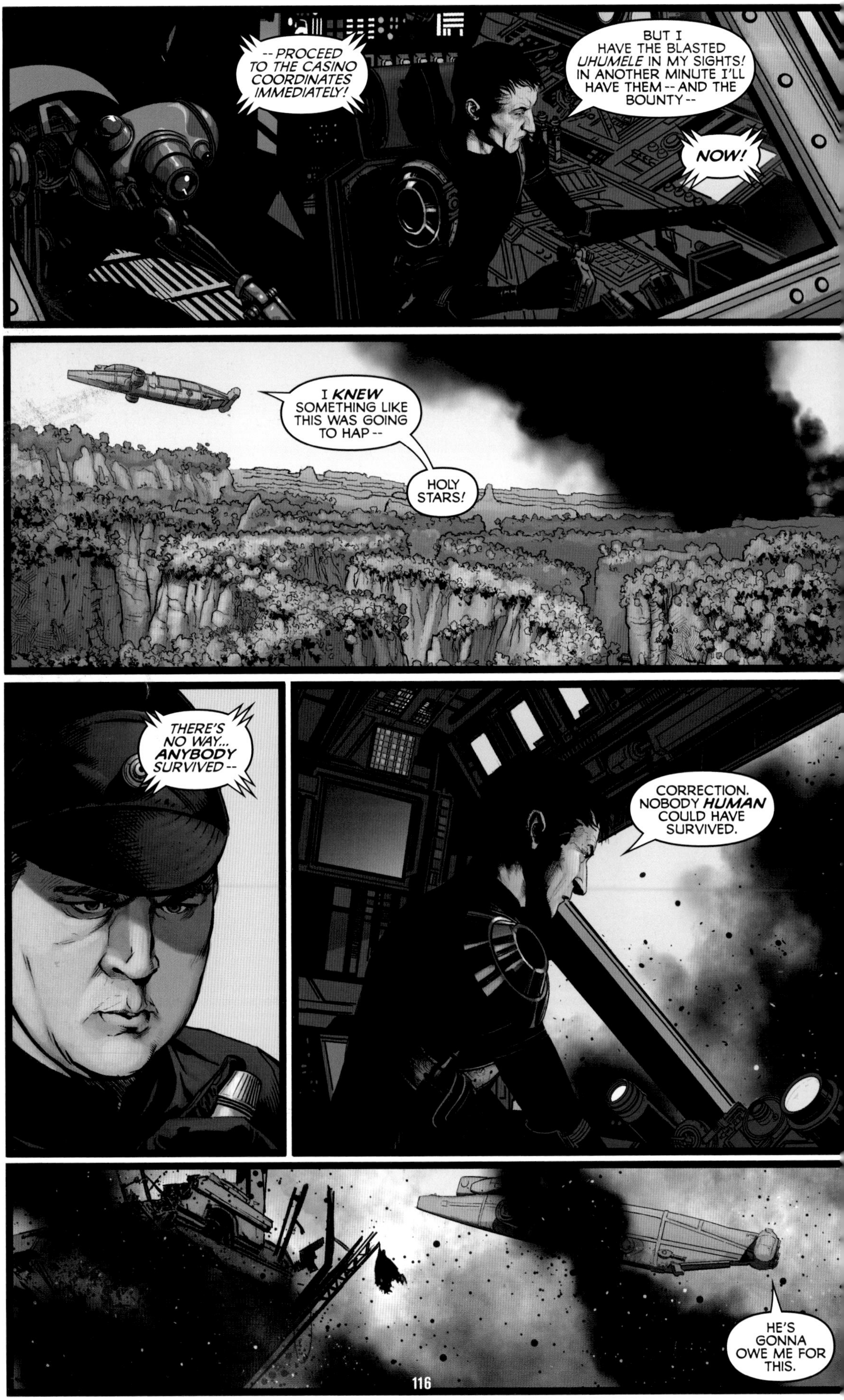
-- PROCEED TO THE CASINO COORDINATES IMMEDIATELY!
BUT I HAVE THE BLASTED UHUMELE IN MY SIGHTS! IN ANOTHER MINUTE I'LL HAVE THEM -- AND THE BOUNTY --
NOW!
I KNEW SOMETHING LIKE THIS WAS GOING TO HAP --
HOLY STARS!
THERE'S NO WAY... ANYBODY SURVIVED --
CORRECTION. NOBODY HUMAN COULD HAVE SURVIVED.
HE'S GONNA OWE ME FOR THIS.

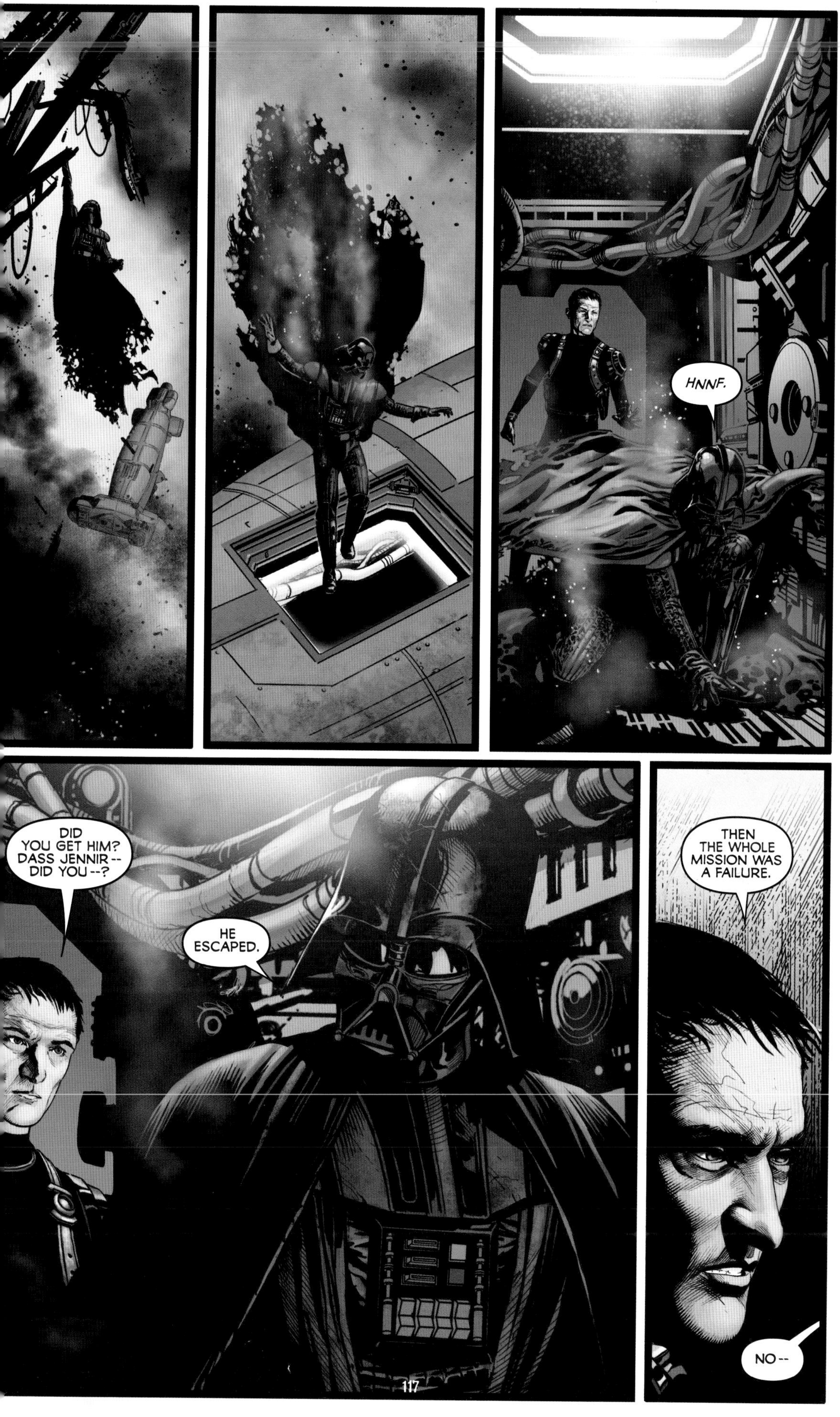
HNNF.
DID YOU GET HIM? DASS JENNIR -- DID YOU --?
HE ESCAPED.
THEN THE WHOLE MISSION WAS A FAILURE.
NO --

"--TWO JEDI DIED."

...BUT TODAY THE JEDI ORDER SURVIVED...

...EVEN IF YOU, DASS JENNIR, ARE THE **LAST** OF THAT ORDER. THOUGH I BELIEVE -- I **SENSE** -- THAT YOU ARE NOT. I HAVE HOPE.

I KNEW THAT WE COULD NOT BOTH RUN FROM THIS FIGHT. AT FIRST I RESENTED YOU FOR BRINGING THIS BATTLE TO MY DOORSTEP. BUT AFTER HEARING OF YOUR EXPLOITS -- AND YOUR SACRIFICES --

-- FROM EMBER CHANKELI AND THAT DROID OF YOURS, I KNEW THAT I COULD NOT ALLOW YOU TO THROW YOUR LIFE AWAY ON A FIGHT WE HAD SO LITTLE CHANCE OF WINNING.

IF YOU ARE VIEWING THIS, I AM DEAD.

BUT PLEASE, LET THERE BE NO SADNESS AT MY PASSING...

...FOR I CAN GO TO MY FATE SECURE IN THE KNOWLEDGE THAT IN THE GALAXY A VITAL SPARK OF THE JEDI REMAINS.

MAY THE FORCE BE WITH YOU ALL.

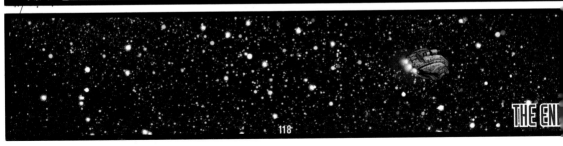

THE END

STAR WARS GRAPHIC NOVEL TIMELINE (IN YEARS)

Dawn of the Jedi—36,000 BSW4

Omnibus: Tales of the Jedi—5,000–3,986 BSW4

Knights of the Old Republic—3,964–3,963 BSW4

The Old Republic—3678, 3653, 3600 BSW4

Lost Tribe of the Sith—2974 BSW4

Knight Errant—1,032 BSW4

Jedi vs. Sith—1,000 BSW4

Jedi: The Dark Side—53 BSW4

Omnibus: Rise of the Sith—33 BSW4

Episode I: The Phantom Menace—32 BSW4

Omnibus: Emissaries and Assassins—32 BSW4

Omnibus: Quinlan Vos—Jedi in Darkness—31–30 BSW4

Omnibus: Menace Revealed—31–22 BSW4

Honor and Duty—22 BSW4

Blood Ties—22 BSW4

Episode II: Attack of the Clones—22 BSW4

Clone Wars—22–19 BSW4

Omnibus: Clone Wars—22–19 BSW4

Clone Wars Adventures—22–19 BSW4

Darth Maul: Death Sentence—20 BSW4

Episode III: Revenge of the Sith—19 BSW4

Purge—19 BSW4

Dark Times—19 BSW4

Omnibus: Droids—5.5 BSW4

Omnibus: Boba Fett—3 BSW4–10 ASW4

Agent of the Empire—3 BSW4

The Force Unleashed—2 BSW4

Omnibus: At War with the Empire—1 BSW4

Episode IV: A New Hope—SW4

Star Wars—0 ASW4

Classic Star Wars—0–3 ASW4

Omnibus: A Long Time Ago. . . .—0–4 ASW4

Empire—0 ASW4

Omnibus: The Other Sons of Tatooine—0 ASW4

Omnibus: Early Victories—0–3 ASW4

Jabba the Hutt: The Art of the Deal—1 ASW4

Episode V: The Empire Strikes Back—3 ASW4

Omnibus: Shadows of the Empire—3.5–4.5 ASW4

Episode VI: Return of the Jedi—4 ASW4

Omnibus: X-Wing Rogue Squadron—4–5 ASW4

The Thrawn Trilogy—9 ASW4

Dark Empire—10 ASW4

Crimson Empire—11 ASW4

Jedi Academy: Leviathan—12 ASW4

Union—19 ASW4

Chewbacca—25 ASW4

Invasion—25 ASW4

Legacy—130–138 ASW4

Dawn of the Jedi
36,000 years before
Star Wars: A New Hope

Old Republic Era
25,000–1000 years before
Star Wars: A New Hope

Rise of the Empire Era
1000–0 years before Star
Wars: A New Hope

Rebellion Era
0–5 years after
Star Wars: A New Hope

New Republic Era
5–25 years after
Star Wars: A New Hope

New Jedi Order Era
25+ years after
Star Wars: A New Hope

Legacy Era
130+ years after
Star Wars: A New Hope

Vector
Crosses four eras in timeline

Volume 1 contains:
Knights of the Old Republic Volume 5
Dark Times Volume 3
Volume 2 contains:
Rebellion Volume 4
Legacy Volume 6

Infinities
Does not apply to timeline

Sergio Aragones Stomps Star Wars
Star Wars Tales
Omnibus: Infinities
Tag and Bink
Star Wars Visionaries

SW4 = before *Episode IV: A New Hope*. ASW4 = after *Episode IV: A New Hope*.

STAR WARS OMNIBUS COLLECTIONS

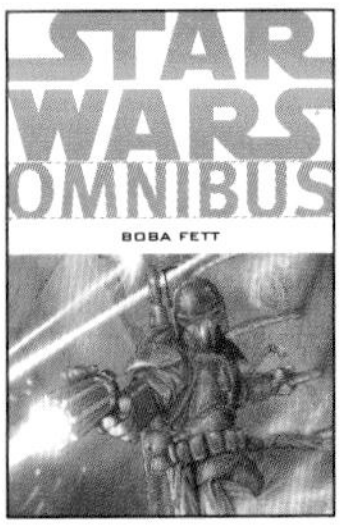
STAR WARS
OMNIBUS
BOBA FETT

STAR WARS: BOBA FETT

Boba Fett, the most feared, most respected, and most loved bounty hunter in the galaxy, now has all of his comics stories collected into one massive volume!

ISBN 978-1-59582-418-9 | $24.99

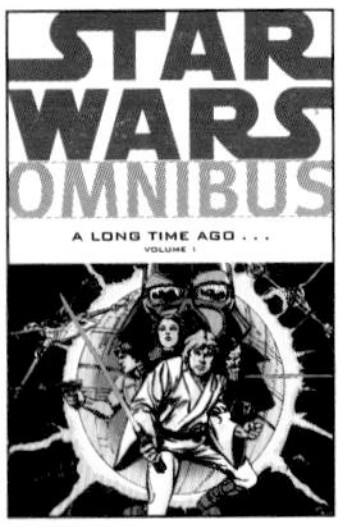
STAR WARS
OMNIBUS
A LONG TIME AGO . . .

STAR WARS: INFINITIES

Three different tales where *one thing* happens differently than it did in the original trilogy of *Star Wars* films. Luke Skywalker, Princess Leia, Han Solo, and Darth Vader are launched onto new trajectories!

ISBN 978-1-61655-078-3 | $24.99

STAR WARS: A LONG TIME AGO. . . .

Star Wars: A Long Time Ago. . . . omnibus volumes feature classic *Star Wars* stories not seen in over twenty years! Originally printed by Marvel Comics, these recolored stories are sure to please Star Wars fans both new and old.

Volume 1: ISBN 978-1-59582-486-8 | $24.99
Volume 2: ISBN 978-1-59582-554-4 | $24.99
Volume 3: ISBN 978-1-59582-639-8 | $24.99
Volume 4: ISBN 978-1-59582-640-4 | $24.99
Volume 5: ISBN 978-1-59582-801-9 | $24.99

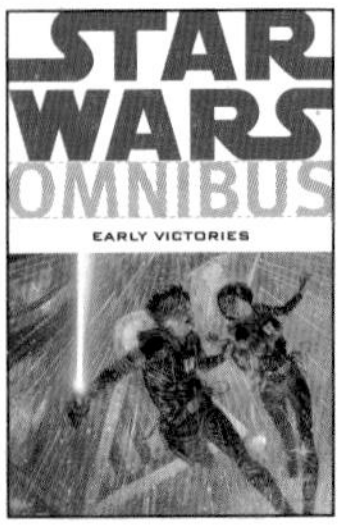
STAR WARS
OMNIBUS
EARLY VICTORIES

STAR WARS: WILD SPACE

Rare and previously uncollected stories! Contains work from some of comics' most famous writers and artists (including Alan Moore, Chris Claremont, Archie Goodwin, Walt Simonson, and Alan Davis), plus stories featuring the greatest heroes and villains of *Star Wars*!

Volume 1: ISBN 978-1-61655-146-9 | $24.99
Volume 2: ISBN 978-1-61655-147-6 | $24.99

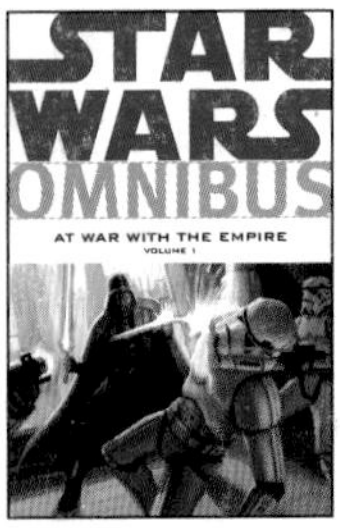
STAR WARS
OMNIBUS
AT WAR WITH THE EMPIRE

STAR WARS: EARLY VICTORIES

Following the destruction of the first Death Star, Luke Skywalker and Princess Leia find there are many more battles to be fought against the Empire and Darth Vader!

ISBN 978-1-59582-172-0 | $24.99

STAR WARS: AT WAR WITH THE EMPIRE

Stories of the early days of the Rebel Alliance and the beginnings of its war with the Empire—tales of the *Star Wars* galaxy set before, during, and after the events in *Star Wars: A New Hope!*

Volume 1: ISBN 978-1-59582-699-2 | $24.99
Volume 2: ISBN 978-1-59582-777-7 | $24.99

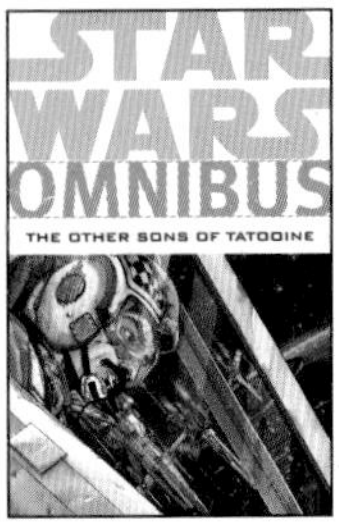
STAR WARS
OMNIBUS
THE OTHER SONS OF TATOOINE

STAR WARS: THE OTHER SONS OF TATOOINE

Luke's story has been told time and again, but what about the journeys of his boyhood friends, Biggs Darklighter and Janek "Tank" Sunber? Both are led to be heroes in their own right: one of the Rebellion, the other of the Empire . . .

ISBN 978-1-59582-866-8 | $24.99

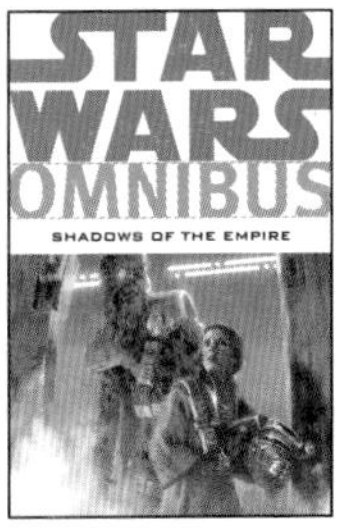
STAR WARS
OMNIBUS
SHADOWS OF THE EMPIRE

STAR WARS: SHADOWS OF THE EMPIRE

Featuring all your favorite characters from the *Star Wars* trilogy—Luke Skywalker, Princess Leia, and Han Solo—this volume includes stories written by acclaimed novelists Timothy Zahn and Steve Perry!

ISBN 978-1-59582-434-9 | $24.99

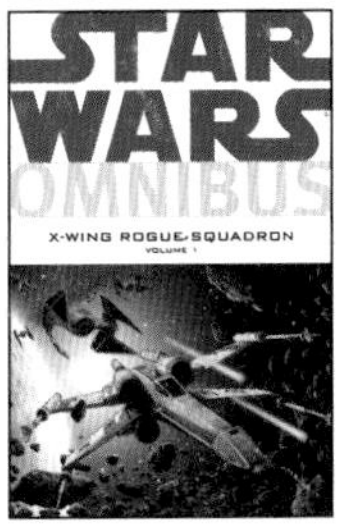
STAR WARS
OMNIBUS
X-WING ROGUE SQUADRON

STAR WARS: X-WING ROGUE SQUADRON

The starfighters of the Rebel Alliance become the defenders of a new Republic in these stories featuring Wedge Antilles and his team of ace pilots known throughout the galaxy as Rogue Squadron.

Volume 1: ISBN 978-1-59307-572-9 | $24.99
Volume 2: ISBN 978-1-59307-619-1 | $24.99
Volume 3: ISBN 978-1-59307-776-1 | $24.99

AVAILABLE AT YOUR LOCAL COMICS SHOP OR BOOKSTORE!

To find a comics shop in your area, call 1-888-266-4226

For more information or to order direct: • On the web: DarkHorse.com • E-mail: mailorder@darkhorse.com • Phone: 1-800-862-0052 Mon.–Fri. 9 AM to 5 PM Pacific Time •